D1392674

Co-operative Inquiry

Co-operative Inquiry

Research into the Human Condition

John Heron

SAGE Publications

London • Thousand Oaks • New Delhi

© John Heron 1996

First published 1996

All rights reserved. No part of this publication may be
reproduced, stored in a retrieval system, transmitted or utilized
in any form or by any means, electronic, mechanical,
photocopying, recording or otherwise, without permission in
writing from the Publishers.

 SAGE Publications Ltd
6 Bonhill Street
London EC2A 4PU

SAGE Publications Inc
2455 Teller Road
Thousand Oaks, California 91320

SAGE Publications India Pvt Ltd
32, M-Block Market
Greater Kailash – I
New Delhi 110 048

British Library Cataloguing in Publication data

A catalogue record for this book is
available from the British Library

ISBN 0 8039 7683 6
ISBN 0 8039 7684 4 (pbk)

Library of Congress catalog record available

11578262

Learning Resources
Centre

Typeset by Mayhew Typesetting, Rhayader, Powys
Printed in Great Britain by Redwood Books,
Trowbridge, Wiltshire

Contents

Preface   x

1   Introduction   1
A brief history of co-operative inquiry   1
The problem of a new orthodoxy   6
The overlap with other forms of participative research   7
The relation with qualitative research   9
The fifth paradigm   10
The poststructural antiparadigm paradigm   12
Truth, validity and beyond   13
Precursors of the participative paradigm   13
The question of data   18

2   Research Method and Participation   19
Participative research *with* people   19
Epistemic and political participation   20
   Full form co-operative inquiry   22
   Partial form co-operative inquiry   23
   Supported action inquiry   24
Quantitative research *on* people   25
   Problems for traditional quantitative research   26
Qualitative research *about* people   26
   Problems for traditional qualitative research   28
Research *for* people   30
   The academic status quo   31
   Authoritarian collusion between teaching and research   31
   Extension of human rights   32
   Propositional bias   32
   Holistic knowledge and systemic logic   33
   Primacy of the practical   34

3   Overview of Co-operative Inquiry   36
Inquiry outcomes   36
The range of inquiry topics   37
Launching an inquiry group   38
   Initiators' call   38
   Call for initiators   40
   Group bootstrap   40

Types of inquiry   40
  Internally or externally initiated   40
  Full or partial form   41
  Same, reciprocal, counterpartal or mixed role   42
  Inside or outside   42
  Closed or open boundary   44
  Apollonian or Dionysian   45
  Informative or transformative   48
An outline of inquiry stages   49
Extended epistemology and the inquiry cycle   52
  The pyramid and circuit models   52
  Four kinds of belief   52
  Four cognitive modes and stages of the inquiry cycle   54
Validity, special inquiry skills and validity procedures   57
  Special inquiry skills   58
  Validity procedures   59

4 Initiating an Inquiry Group   62
Three-stranded initiation   62
The inquiry strand   65
The collaboration strand   67
The emotional and interpersonal strand   69
Initiators, academia and reports   72

5 Stages of the Inquiry Cycle   73
Stage 1 (1) Focus and type of inquiry   74
Stage 1 (2) A launching statement   75
Stage 1 (3) The first action plan   75
  Divergent and convergent   76
  Part and whole   78
  Length of the action phase   79
Stage 1 (4) Data generation methods   80
  Standard methods   80
  Presentational methods   81
  Radical memory   81
Stage 1 Inquiry culture   82
Stage 2 The first action phase   82
  Issues of recording data   82
Stage 3 Experiential immersion   84
  Falling asleep   84
  Threshold oscillation   84
  Celebration, inquiry and creativity   85
Stage 4 (1) The second reflection phase: making sense   86
  Reporting, collating and reviewing   86
  Making sense and reaching agreement   87
  Presentational and propositional meaning   88

Informative meaning in propositional form   91
Transformative meaning: portrayals and propositions   92
Stage 4 (2)   Planning the second action phase   93
Imagination, motivation and the logic of method   94
Stage 4 (3)   Review of inquiry procedures   95
Subsequent stages   95
Dionysian and Apollonian cultures   95
Reflection meeting format   96
Validity: procedures and skills   97
Final reflection   98
Endings, outcomes and reports   100

6 Inquiry Outcomes   104
Holistic epistemology and the primacy of the practical   104
Four kinds of outcome   105
Inseparable and separable outcomes   107
Transformative, illuminative and informative outcomes   107
The range of propositional outcomes   109
Outcomes and meta-outcomes   110
Transcendent practice   111
The ineffability of knacks   111
A culture of competence   111
The action paradox   113

7 Radical Memory and Inquiry Skills   115
Informative memory and paying heed   115
The routinization of perception   116
Extraordinary perceptual heed   116
Transformative memory and paying heed   118
Extraordinary practical heed   118
Informative inquiry skills   118
Radical perception: being present and imaginally open   119
Varieties of bracketing   120
Reframing   121
The relevance of Buddhist practices   122
Transformative inquiry skills   122
Radical practice: dynamic congruence   122
Emotional competence   124
Non-attachment   125
Self-transcending intentionality   126
Skill in articulating values   126
Values and principles   127
Inquiry skills and critical subjectivity   127
Extraordinary consciousness and multi-level mind   128
Training for inquiry   129

8 Validity Procedures 131
Research cycling 131
Individual research cycling 132
Collective research cycling 132
Combined research cycling 133
Fourfold interaction 134
The balance of divergence and convergence 134
Within and between phases 134
Total divergence 135
Total convergence 135
Intermediate model 136
Polarities of method 138
The reflection phase 139
The balance between reflection and action 140
Aspects of reflection 142
Description 142
Evaluation 142
Explanation 143
Application 144
Challenging uncritical subjectivity 145
Chaos and order 148
The management of unaware projections 149
Sustaining authentic collaboration 152
Open and closed boundaries 156
Variegated replication 156
Concerted action 157

9 Validity and Beyond 158
Validity in quantitative research 159
Validity in qualitative inquiry 160
Participative reality 162
Truth as the congruent articulation of reality 163
The primacy of the practical 164
Practice as consummation 165
Grounding and consummation 166
More on the congruence theory of truth 168
Beyond pragmatism 168
Autonomous forms of validity 169
The validation of practice 170
Executive criteria 170
Technical criteria 171
Psychosocial criteria 171
Intentionality criteria 171
Value criteria 171
The validation of propositions 172
Participative knowing 173

Agreements about findings 174
Reality-making social contracts 175

10 A Postconceptual Worldview 178
Primary and secondary meaning 178
Linguistic forms of secondary meaning 180
Preconceptual, conceptual and postconceptual worlds 181
The classic problem of phenomenology 184
A sketch of a postconceptual world 185
Participation 186
Communion 186
Seamlessness 186
Imagination is reality 187
Centre and circumference 187
Figure and ground 189
The body as imaginal artefact 190
Presences and objects 191
Consciousness is spatial 192
Conclusion 196

11 Arguments for Co-operative Inquiry 197
The problems of positivism 197
Positivist research in trouble: the medical case 198
Arguments for co-operative inquiry 200
The human condition 200
Persons in relation 201
Research behaviour and self-determination 202
Research behaviour and intentionality 203
An extended epistemology 204
The use of language 205
The rights and duties of subjects and researchers 206

References 209

Index 217

Preface

While busy with this book in the northern summer of 1995, I broke off from the writing to join in two co-operative inquiries at my research centre in Tuscany. This timely immersion in the method was a valuable source of inspiration. I am grateful to my colleagues in these events, and indeed to everyone in the co-operative inquiry groups of which I have been a member over the years, for their creative commitment to our shared experience and reflection, which constitute the foundation of this book.

My thanks go also to all those in other co-operative inquiry groups of which I have not been a member. I have learnt a great deal from their reports, many of which are cited in the pages that follow.

Since we first met in 1976, Peter Reason has made a very large contribution to the theoretical and practical development of co-operative inquiry. I gratefully acknowledge that every chapter in the book reflects this. He has read and made detailed, insightful comments on the manuscript. In taking account of these, I have been able to improve the presentation of several key issues.

I am grateful to Yvonna Lincoln for helpful comments on an early draft of parts of Chapter 9.

In writing this book, I have sought to keep a balance between practical guidance and theoretical depth. The first two chapters provide background and foundation themes. Chapters 3, 4 and 5 take the reader into the heart of the method. Chapters 6, 7 and 8 go in more depth into outcomes, skills and procedures, respectively. Chapters 9, 10 and 11 develop theoretical foundations. Chapter 3 provides a comprehensive overview of co-operative inquiry, and some readers may find this a convenient starting point to get a sense of what it is all about.

John Heron
San Cipriano

1

Introduction

A brief history of co-operative inquiry

Co-operative inquiry involves two or more people researching a topic through their own experience of it, using a series of cycles in which they move between this experience and reflecting together on it. Each person is co-subject in the experience phases and co-researcher in the reflection phases. While this model has affinities with the account of action research and experiential learning arising from the work of Kurt Lewin (1952), its source, range of application and epistemology – as I have conceived these – are quite distinct, and take it on to a different plane. It is a vision of persons in reciprocal relation using the full range of their sensibilities to inquire together into any aspect of the human condition with which the transparent body-mind can engage.

The co-operative inquiry model was born, in my world, in 1968–69 when I started to reflect on the experience of mutual gazing in interpersonal encounters. Out of this experience I wrote a paper called 'The phenomenology of social encounter: the gaze' which was published in *Philosophy and Phenomenological Research* (Heron, 1970). To cut a long paper short, I made several points about the gaze:

- It is a distinct phenomenal category which cannot be reduced to any set of statements about the eyes as physical objects.
- Its combination of both spatial and mental properties involves a non-Cartesian account of mind.
- It provides participative noninferential but partial knowledge of the state of mind of the other.
- Its inherent mutuality of meaning is presupposed by, and the ground of, the use of speech.

I also made the point that the conventional social scientist cannot properly inquire into the nature of the gaze by doing experiments on and gathering data from other people. The status and significance of the gaze can only be explored fully from within, by full engagement with the human condition. This means the researcher is also the socially sensitive subject involved in mutual gazing with another. There was the unstated implication that any such research, in which experimenter and subject are one and the same person, would also be co-operative, involving a reciprocal relation with another person with the same double role.

From March 1970 there was an influx of experiential groups of many kinds in London. Various verbal and nonverbal one-to-one exercises, followed by shared feedback, were in vogue. Exploring these convinced me that only shared experience and shared reflection on it could yield a social science that did justice to the human condition. I thought that the researcher who wants to do research on or about other people's experience of the human condition is not only likely to misrepresent it, but is open to the charge of being in flight from a full openness to his or her own experience. Moreover, the misrepresentation and the flight are likely to reinforce each other.

Also in 1970 I felt that the human condition within myself, in relating with others, and on the wider canvas, was about increasing self-direction in living, in co-operation with other persons similarly engaged. And that this quest for personal and social transformation, for the interacting values of autonomy and co-operation, was at the heart of any truly human social science.

Many cultural strands of the postwar decades fed into this view: the focus on freedom, and on the person as self-creating, in European personalism and existentialism; Macmurray's account (1957) of the self as agent in reciprocal relation with other agents; the reaffirmation among many English-speaking academic philosophers of Kantian views of human freedom, autonomy and rational agency as transcending 'determination by alien causes' (Peters, 1958; Kenny, 1963; Taylor, 1966); the affirmation of self-directed and whole person learning by Rogers (1969), and of self-esteem and self-actualization by both Rogers (1961) and Maslow (1962); the humanistic, participative, democratic values and technologies of experiential learning and action research emerging from T-groups and laboratory method and the work of Kurt Lewin (Bradford et al., 1964); the Leicester–Tavistock conferences on group dynamics; a paper by Sid Jourard (1967) on experimenter–subject dialogue; the values of the civil rights and anti-war student struggles of the sixties in the USA and of the students' mentor Marcuse (1964); the women's liberation movement of the sixties and the feminist texts of Friedan (1963), Millett (1977) and Greer (1970); the emergence of radical action and body-oriented therapies from the pioneer work of Moreno and Reich; the appearance of peer self-help groups of diverse kinds as a major social phenomenon; the occurrence of holistic and systemic models of explanation for organic and psychosocial life, as in Koestler (1964), von Bertalanffy (1968); and so on.

In November 1970 I founded the Human Potential Research Project at the University of Surrey to explore what a person-centred science might be like, and presented a paper about it at the annual conference of the British Psychological Society in 1971. About seventy psychologists attended the session and seemed to find it an entertaining distraction from the mainline offerings of the day. This paper, 'Experience and method', was published in 1971 as a monograph by the University of Surrey, and was my first formal account of co-operative inquiry. In those days I called it experiential research.

In my paper I argued that the basic explanatory model for creative, original research behaviour is that of intelligent self-direction. Original researchers in any field, because they generate new ideas that are in principle unpredictable, are the free, autonomous cause of their own behaviour, which thus transcends any sufficient explanation in terms of causal laws of physical or psychic determinism. Such researchers *in psychology* cannot with any consistency exhibit this autonomous explanatory model in their own behaviour and at the same time deny its relevance to the behaviour of their subjects, for example by explaining their subjects' behaviour in terms of strict causal determinism.

I then suggested that the central research question for psychology is 'How can self-directing capacity be developed?', and that this question can only properly be answered, logically and morally, from the standpoint of the agent, that is, of the person who is developing their self-directing capacity. Thus the researcher is necessarily also the inquiring agent, who is both experimenter and subject combined.

I took it as a fundamental assumption of the method that self-directing persons develop most fully through fully reciprocal relations with other self-directing persons. Autonomy and co-operation are necessary and mutually enhancing values of human life. Hence experiential research involved a co-equal relation between two people, reversing the roles of facilitator and agent, or combining them at the same time. They would support each other in applying to themselves, on a peer basis, some theory of personal development, where any such theory would involve relations between the potential self, the socially conditioned self, the directing self and the transformed self. The examples I suggested were co-counselling (Jackins, 1965; Scheff, 1971), transactional analysis (Berne, 1961), bio-energetic analysis (Lowen, 1970). They would also give each other feedback, and together evaluate the theory in the light of their experience of it.

As well as, or instead of, this personal development approach, they could explore the ongoing dyadic relation itself and its potential. And both approaches could be developed by a larger number of people using group interaction methods. The paper also looked at issues of validity, compared and contrasted the experiential method with the traditional experimental method in psychology, and considered their relative advantages and disadvantages, especially the problem of consensus collusion in experiential research.

In October 1971 I applied the method, through the Human Potential Research Project at the University of Surrey, in an adult education 20-week training course in co-counselling. The training was at the same time an experiential peer inquiry, including myself, into the theory and practice of co-counselling. An account of this rudimentary endeavour was published in the *British Journal of Guidance and Counselling* (Heron, 1972).

Looking back now on the original paper and this early application of it, some obvious limitations stand out. While the paper was clear about the danger of consensus collusion, it had no suggestions about how to counter this; nor did it consider any other validity procedures, as they were called later. It said nothing about research cycling, moving to and fro between experience and reflection. It considered as topics for inquiry only personal and interpersonal growth through mutual aid; it did not address social and political issues such as disempowerment and oppression; nor did it consider the wider reaches of research that embrace any aspect of the human condition.

During the seventies I continued to apply the method in rudimentary form in workshops on a wide range of topics, and as facilitator I was also the initiating researcher inviting participants to be co-inquirers. These workshops were run informally in the spirit of co-operative inquiry, certainly not with any rigour: the participative method was improvisatory, not highly formalized. As well as personal growth through mutual aid, the topics included: the elements of human communication and encounter; intrapsychic states and processes; interpersonal and professional skills; group dynamic phenomena; altered states of consciousness; peer self-help networks; peer learning communities; peer review audits of professional practice (Heron, 1973a, 1973b, 1974a, 1974b, 1974c, 1974d, 1974e, 1975a, 1975b, 1975c, 1977a, 1977b, 1977c, 1977d, 1978a, 1978b, 1978c, 1979).

During this period three developments occurred. The first was an interim account of experiential research method (Heron, 1977a), which affirmed the interdependence between phenomenological mapping and intentional action: between noticing phenomena and trying out new behaviours. The second was the importance of applying peer experiential research in the burgeoning field of transpersonal psychology (Heron, 1975b) as a counter to the dogmatic intuitionism and traditional authoritarianism to which spiritual experience so readily falls prey. The third was to extend co-operative inquiry, as a project for the future, to include all aspects of social life in what I call a self-generating culture (Heron, 1978c), as a counter to prevailing forms of social oppression and disempowerment.

A self-generating culture, I should explain in passing, is a society whose members are in a continuous process of co-operative learning and development, and whose forms are consciously adopted, periodically reviewed and altered in the light of experience, reflection and deeper vision. Its participants continually recreate it through cycles of collaborative inquiry in living. It includes several strands: forms of decision-making and political participation; forms of association; forms of habitation; revisioning a wide range of social roles; forms of economic organization; forms of ecological management; forms of education for all ages; forms of intimacy and parenting; forms of conflict resolution; forms of aesthetic expression and celebration; forms of transpersonal association and ritual (Heron, 1993a).

In 1978 Peter Reason, John Rowan and I set up the New Paradigm Research Group in London. Peter had realized in his postgraduate work that it is impossible to conduct intimate inquiry into human relationships as an outsider (Reason, 1976). John had distributed in 1976 his seminal paper 'A dialectical paradigm for research' (Rowan, 1981). The New Paradigm

Research Group met every three weeks or so for three years and provided a major forum for the development of creative thinking and of practical projects in the field, including my own. It also set the scene for Peter and John editing their breakthrough work *Human Inquiry: A Sourcebook of New Paradigm Research* (Reason and Rowan, 1981a).

I contributed two chapters to this (Heron, 1981a, 1981b). The philosophical one expanded the case for co-operative inquiry in several directions beyond the 1971 paper, including a new argument from an extended epistemology, about the interdependence of propositional, practical and experiential knowledge. The methodological chapter introduced the snowperson diagram (see Figure 3.1, Chapter 3) and gave a more coherent account of the stages of the co-operative inquiry cycle, in terms of this extended epistemology.

Peter and John wrote an important chapter (Reason and Rowan, 1981c) on issues of validity in new paradigm research, which was influential in my own thinking. Peter and I then began an active phase of collaboration in developing together the methodology of co-operative inquiry. We initiated two inquiries with co-counselling colleagues (Heron and Reason, 1981, 1982). These together with an inquiry I launched in 1981 on altered states of consciousness (Heron, 1988c), led to a paper of mine on validity in co-operative inquiry which set out a whole range of validity procedures and associated skills (Heron, 1982b; revised and restated in Heron, 1988b). After over a decade of preliminaries, and with the strong creative input of Peter Reason, co-operative inquiry had acquired an innovative, rigorous and coherent form.

The next step was to apply the method in a more substantial setting. This proved to be at the British Postgraduate Medical Federation, University of London, where I was then Assistant Director. I invited Peter Reason to join me in initiating with a group of general practitioners a co-operative inquiry into whole person medicine, which ran from the summer of 1982 to the summer of 1983 (Heron and Reason, 1985; Reason, 1988c). Peter and I then started to share the fruits of four years of collaborative thinking and action, authoring a series of papers presenting co-operative inquiry to a wider audience (Heron and Reason, 1984, 1986a, 1986b; Heron, 1985; Reason, 1986, 1988d; Reason and Heron, 1995).

Since the mid-eighties, the academic centre for co-operative inquiry and related forms of participative research in the UK has been sustained by Peter Reason and colleagues, and their Postgraduate Research Group, in the School of Management at the University of Bath. This centre hosts the newsletter *Collaborative Inquiry*, edited by Peter Reason, and annual conferences on participative approaches to inquiry. It has generated a diversity of research projects, many in the field of professional practice, and two important books edited by Peter Reason (1988a, 1994a).

The first of these, *Human Inquiry in Action*, in its introduction and first two chapters, gives a well-grounded, accessible account of co-operative inquiry in its developed form. The second, *Participation in Human Inquiry*, includes Peter's important perspective on participative knowing. Both include a wide range of research reports by a number of different inquiry groups. This work, including other approaches to participative inquiry, became formally constituted in 1994 as the Centre for Action Research in Professional Practice, directed by Peter Reason. CARPP hosted an international conference on Quality in Human Inquiry in March 1995.

I left the British Postgraduate Medical Federation at the end of 1985 to pursue an independent career as consultant, educator, researcher and writer. In 1989–90 I established a centre in Tuscany, Italy, where I have initiated three co-operative inquiries in the transpersonal field, and explored twice in micro-format the shared experience of a self-generating culture. I have also initiated three transpersonal co-operative inquiries in New Zealand, where I have been commuting for several months each year. This work (Heron, 1993b, 1995) will be the subject of a separate volume.

Writing this book gives me an opportunity to bring my version of the theory and practice of co-operative inquiry into much sharper focus than hitherto. In doing so, I am conscious at the outset of four main issues, which I address in the remainder of this chapter:

- The problem of a new orthodoxy.
- The overlap with other forms of participative research.
- The relation between co-operative inquiry and the very broad field of qualitative research in the social sciences.
- The nature of the inquiry paradigm underlying the method and its relation with other paradigms.

The problem of a new orthodoxy

It follows from the model of reality as subjective–objective, which I elaborate in this book, that there is no such thing as *the* account of co-operative inquiry, only *an* account, including varying degrees of inter-subjective agreement and disagreement with others who use the method. However, the more I elaborate and articulate *an* account, the greater the danger that it will be construed by the beginner in the field as *the* account, which prescribes how to do a co-operative inquiry properly and correctly.

So I here and now disavow that this book is laying down an objective canon of valid inquiry. I am exploring a *subjective*–objective canon and this is a very different matter. The discussion of validity and validity procedures in this book does not hark back to the outmoded objective stance of positivism. It is not a masked attempt, as the poststructural critic might insist, to exert power and authority over the reader and potential inquirer. It is an attempt to discover, in dialogue with my peers, how I can engage in co-operative inquiry with integrity. It develops a personal canon which legitimates, for me, my participation in continuing dialogue. That canon will and must change as the dialogue proceeds.

I have waited for over a quarter of a century before writing a comprehesive book on my view of co-operative inquiry. One main reason has been that the method is in such a rudimentary phase of development, and the challenges it poses to the expansion of human consciousness are so considerable, that it has seemed wiser to explore the lower slopes and issue only interim short reports. Another reason is the very small number of reported and published studies using the method; and I am thinking here only of studies consciously generated from within the ethos of co-operative inquiry. Even today it is only a score or so; and this is a small database for winnowing out issues that arise in practice. However, despite the problem of orthodoxy and the small database, the time has come to issue an extended report, still from the lower slopes.

The overlap with other forms of participative research

The most obvious overlap is with action research, stemming from the work of Kurt Lewin. It had its apogee in the 1960s and 1970s, but has been continuously applied in several fields ever since, especially in higher education. It involves repeated cycles of planning, acting, observing, reflecting, replanning, and so on. It requires in its advanced forms, such as emancipatory action research (Carr and Kemmis, 1986), a full degree of participation and collaboration.

> In action research, all actors involved in the research process are equal participants, and must be involved in every stage of the research process . . . Collaborative participation in theoretical, practical and political discourse is a hallmark of action research and the action researcher. (Grundy and Kemmis, 1982: 87)

Nevertheless there are very clear differences, of a friendly and non-competitive kind. Action research is research into current, ongoing practice by practitioners for practitioners (Zuber-Skerritt, 1992: 11–17). Its focus is on problem-solving in existing professional performance and related organizational structures. It disregards theory-building and the generative power of theory (Cooperrider and Srivastva, 1987). It is not a wide-ranging research method for inquiring into any aspect or any theory of the human condition. It has not developed an extended epistemology which enables it to do this. Nor does it view the full range of human sensibilities as an instrument of research. And it has not articulated a set of validity procedures and special skills required for radical, comprehensive experiential inquiry. It does not work with the complementarity of informative and transformative engagement with the inquiry domain. In all these fundamental respects, co-operative inquiry goes beyond the area of overlap.

A related kind of action-oriented research, subject to the same qualifications, is in one wing of feminist qualitative research, where some feminists do not want to exploit women as research subjects, but prefer to empower them to do their own research on what interests them (Olesen, 1994). In the most developed form of this approach, women participants become full co-researchers working together with the initiating researchers on all phases of the project (Light and Kleiber, 1981; Cancian, 1992; Craddock and Reid, 1993). This openness to explore women's reality through co-research, to deal with issues of honouring the diversity of women's views about women (Hess, 1990), and of giving participants full voice in any account (Fine, 1992), makes for a unique approach to participative inquiry.

Appreciative inquiry (Cooperrider and Srivastva, 1987) proposes re-awakening collaborative action research so that it is grounded on a deep kind of participative, intuitive and appreciative way of knowing, and so that it includes generative theory as a prime mover in organizational innovation. This certainly brings it closer to co-operative inquiry. Yet its epistemology, though extended, is still relatively underdeveloped. It is restricted to research into organizational life. And it lacks the several features I have mentioned as requisite for wide-ranging human condition inquiry.

Participative action research is also an area of overlap. This phrase is used for liberationist inquiry in underprivileged parts of the third world and of the developed world. Its task is the 'enlightenment and awakening of common people' (Fals-Borda and Rahman, 1991: vi). It wants to help people grasp the role of knowledge as an instrument of power and control: it provides people with knowledge useful for the immediate empowering of their own action, and raises their consciousness about the way established authority uses its knowledge for purposes of oppression.

Co-operative inquiry differs from participative action research (PAR) in the same respects as it does from ordinary action research. Also PAR uses improvisatory processes of developmental dialogue and collaboration, rather than any formal cycles of reflection and action. The animator or initiating researcher is highly educated and motivated, the participants are relatively uneducated and unmotivated and this affects the whole nature of their collaboration.

A further difference is that co-operative inquiry is complementary to PAR on the issue of social oppression and disempowerment. The initiating researcher in PAR goes out from a privileged setting to co-operate with and help to liberate people in an underprivileged setting, and leaves his or her own privileged setting unchanged. Co-operative inquirers who are exploring the first steps in living in a self-generating culture see their privileged setting as deformed and seek a transformation of it.

Co-operative inquiry overlaps with action science (Argyris and Schön, 1974; Schön, 1983; Argyris et al., 1985), developed as action inquiry by Torbert (1991). Action inquiry, which I describe in Chapter 2, is concerned with increased intentionality, cognitive reframing and holistic awareness in the midst of individual action. As such, it is precisely what is needed in the action phase of a co-operative inquiry, when each person is busy implementing some action-plan decided on in the prior reflection phase. The skills of action inquiry are thus a fundamental component of co-operative inquiry, but they also reach far beyond it, and have a challenging claim on any one at any time whether they are part of a co-operative inquiry or not.

My colleague Peter Reason has written a lucid account of co-operative inquiry, PAR and action inquiry, and of the relations between them. It concludes with an account of their possible integration, in which a group of PAR animators constitute a co-operative group inquiring into their PAR practices, each member of the group engaged in their own local PAR, and each scrutinizing their individual practice through action inquiry, the data from which would be shared with, and reflected upon in, the co-operative inquiry group (Reason, 1994b).

Participants' involvement in the research process may also be found in varying degrees in empowering evaluation (Guba and Lincoln, 1989; Fetterman, 1993), intervention research (Fryer and Feather, 1994), critical worker research (Kincheloe and McLaren, 1994), some phenomenological studies (Moustakas, 1994), and some forms of clinical research (Miller and Crabtree, 1994).

It is essential, in discussing the overlap between co-operative inquiry and other forms of participative research, to distinguish between the democratization of content, which involves all informants in decisions about what the research is seeking to find out and achieve; and the democratization of method, which involves participants in decisions about what operational methods are being used, including those being used to democratize the content. The overlap is usually restricted to democratization of research content. It is rare to find any full-blown commitment to collaboration about research method, although Guba and Lincoln strongly commend it (1989: 260). In practice, it may be reduced to no more than seeking fully informed consent of all informants to the researcher's pre-existent or emerging operational plan, and to modifying the plan in order to obtain such consent.

The relation with qualitative research

Qualitative research, using multiple methodologies, is about other people studied in their own social setting and understood in terms of the meanings those people themselves bring to their situation (Denzin and Lincoln, 1994: 2). To say that it is *about* other people in their own setting is to say one central thing: the researcher in *mainline* qualitative research does not involve informants in decisions about research methodology, about the design of operational procedures. He or she only seeks to negotiate, with the people being studied, (1) access to their setting, (2) issues involved in ongoing management of the research, and (3) the interpretations arrived at.

Co-operative inquiry by contrast does research *with* other people, who are invited to be full co-inquirers with the initiating researcher and become involved in operational decision-making, and is committed to this kind of participative research design in principle, both politically and epistemologically. The co-inquirers are also fully involved in decisions about research content, that is, about the focus of the inquiry, what it is seeking to find out and achieve.

Qualitative research is a *social* science, about other people in their own social setting; whereas co-operative inquiry is a wide-ranging science about any aspect of the human condition which a group of co-researchers choose to explore through the instrumentality of their own experience. It certainly deals with central social and political issues such as the liberatory trans-formation of conventional roles, of community life, of organizational process and structure, of professional practice and of related aspects of a culture. It also includes innumerable other topics such as: art as a mode of knowledge, intentional self-healing, participative knowledge of organic and inorganic forms, altered states of consciousness and many more.

✳   Finally, there is the matter of underlying paradigms. Guba and Lincoln (1994) propose four basic inquiry paradigms: positivism, postpositivism, critical theory and constructivism. They have espoused the last of these and have written widely about it (Lincoln and Guba, 1985; Guba and Lincoln 1989, 1994). Following their lead much qualitative research today is con-strued as interpretative science within a constructivist paradigm.

Their constructivist ontology is possibly idealist, certainly pluralist and relativist. The real is a mental construct of individuals and such constructs do not exist outside the minds that create and hold them (1989: 143); thus there can be many such constructed realities; and they may be conflicting and incompatible. Truth is a local consensus about the most sophisticated construction around and is relative to a given group of people at a given time and place.

There is an immediate difficulty with the idea that reality is a construction within an individual mind. It raises the problem of solipsism, which is an ironic problem for a science of the Other. For if reality is *nothing but* an internal mental construct, no warrant can be given for supposing that the other people being studied actually exist, let alone for supposing that the researcher's view of them adequately represents their own view of their situation. However, Guba and Lincoln are ambiguous in their account of constructivism. They also say that the mental constructions are related to 'tangible entities', which would thus appear to have some reality inde-pendent of the constructions (Schwandt, 1994: 134). So their explicit idealist stance seems to rest on an implicit realism, and leaves the paradigm in a state of wobble.

The fifth paradigm

✳   Co-operative inquiry rests on a related, but distinct, fifth inquiry paradigm, that of participative reality, which I discuss in Chapters 9 and 10. This holds that there is a given cosmos in which the mind creatively participates, and which it can only know in terms of its constructs, whether affective, imaginal, conceptual or practical. We know through this active *participation* of mind that we are in touch with what is other, but only as articulated by all our mental sensibilities. Reality is always subjective-objective: our own   NB. constructs clothe a felt participation in what is present. Worlds and people are what we *meet*, but the meeting is shaped by our own terms of reference   ✳ (Merleau-Ponty, 1962; Bateson, 1979; Reason and Rowan, 1981c; Spretnak, 1991; Heron, 1992; Varela et al., 1993; Skolimowski, 1994; Reason, 1994a).

In meeting people, there is the possibility of reciprocal participative knowing, and unless this is truly mutual, we don't properly know the other. The reality of the other is found in the fullness of our open relation (Buber, 1937), when we each engage in our mutual participation. Hence the importance of co-operative inquiry *with* other persons involving dialogue, parity and reciprocity in all its phases.

This participative paradigm has two wings, the epistemic introduced above, and the political. The epistemic wing, concerned with truth-values, is formed by:

- An ontology that affirms a mind-shaped reality which is subjective-objective: it is subjective because it is only known through the form the mind gives it; and it is objective because the mind interpenetrates the given cosmos which it shapes.
- An epistemology that asserts the participative relation between the knower and the known, and, where the known is also a knower, between knower and knower. Knower and known are not separate in this interactive relation. They also transcend it, the degree of participation being partial and open to change. Participative knowing is bipolar: empathic communion with the inward experience of a being; and enactment of its form of appearing through the imaging and shaping process of perceiving it.
- A methodology that commends the validation of outcomes through the congruence of practical, conceptual, imaginal and empathic forms of knowing among co-operative knowers, and the cultivation of skills that deepen these forms. It sees inquiry as an intersubjective space, a common culture, in which the use of language is grounded in a deep   ✳ context of nonlinguistic meanings, the lifeworld of shared experience, necessarily presupposed by agreement about the use of language itself.

The political wing of the participative paradigm, concerned with being-values, is formed by an axiology, a theory of value which holds that:

- Human flourishing is intrinsically worthwhile: it is valuable as an end in itself. It is construed as a process of social participation in which there is a mutually enabling balance, within and between people, of autonomy, co-operation and hierarchy. It is conceived as interdependent with the flourishing of the planetary ecosystem.
- What is valuable as a means to this end is participative decision-making, which enables people to be involved in the making of decisions, in every social context, which affect their flourishing in any way.

And through which people speak on behalf of the wider ecosystem of which they are part.

Co-operative inquiry seeks to integrate these two wings by using participative decision-making to implement the methodology. Also by acknowledging that the quest for validity in terms of well-grounded truth-values is interdependent with another process which transcends it. This is the celebration of being-values in terms of flourishing human practice. I develop this theme in Chapter 9.

The poststructural antiparadigm paradigm

Over against this and any other paradigm, there is to be considered the antiparadigm stance of extreme poststructuralism (Denzin, 1994; Lincoln and Denzin, 1994). From this position, any metaphysical paradigm, with the epistemology that follows from it, is an attempt to set up rules outside a piece of research, so that these rules can then be called up to validate it. And these rules are only a mask for the researcher's desire for political authority, a desire to assert power over the reader and the wider world. Poststructural thought, deriving from the deconstruction of Derrida (1976, 1981), rejects the view that any text can have any kind of claim to epistemological validity, on the grounds that 'any text can be undone in terms of its internal structural logic' (Lincoln and Denzin, 1994: 579).

This account is itself a paradigm, a sceptics' paradigm, a poststructural antiparadigm paradigm (PAP), which asserts that all claims to truth in a text can be undone and thus all claims to truth are disguised bids for power over the reader. The trouble is that this statement of PAP presumably applies to itself. Any truth that it claims to have can be undone and exposed as a hidden bid for power. Hence it is suicidal and nihilistic, reducing itself and all other forms of textual discourse to competing bids for raw, purposeless power. Kincheloe and McLaren point out that while all claims to truth are implicated in relations of power, truth cannot simply be equated with an effect of power:

> Otherwise, truth becomes meaningless and, if this is the case, liberatory praxis has no purpose other than to win for the sake of winning. (1994: 153)

And Culler (1982) has asserted that deconstruction does not reject propositional truth but just stresses its contextuality. Wilber, too, has recently had his say on the matter:

> The postmodern poststructuralists, for example, have gone from saying that no context, no perspective, is final, to saying that no perspective has any advantage over any other, at which point they careen uncontrollably in their own labyrinth of ever-receding holons, lost in aperspectival space. (1995: 188)

Poststructural social science seeks its 'external grounding . . . in a commitment to a post-Marxism and a feminism with hope' (Lincoln and Denzin, 1994: 579), in 'morally informed social criticism' (Denzin, 1994:

511). This presupposes moral principles which inform the commitment and the criticism. If moral principles constitute 'external grounding', this means they are somehow valid, justifiable, not arbitrary. So the issue of epistemological validity has simply moved over from scientific discourse, where it has been rejected, to moral discourse, where it is tacitly invoked.

Poststructural social science still has to answer the question of how it can justify, validate, find worthy of belief, the moral principles which inform its commitment to social justice and empowerment. The problem here is that any answer it gives will be subject to demolition by its adherence to PAP, and then morality as well as science will have been crushed in its nihilistic grip.

Truth, validity and beyond

Terms like 'truth' and 'validity' have an excellent and healthy standing in ordinary discourse, and I do not see why they should be abandoned and turned into bogeymen in social science, just because they have been given a limiting definition and application by positivism, and politically used for unacceptable purposes of social control. This is to confuse their meaning with the abuse of their meaning.

Truth and validity degenerate in meaning when they are defined in objectivist terms, and then used to rationalize the pursuit of power, to provide a mask for political propaganda. But they are not intrinsically to do either with objectivism or with power and rationalization. They are to do with human reason, and other ways of knowing. They provide the preconditions of intelligent inquiry in any domain. And they cannot be reduced without remainder to central terms within any one particular realm of discourse. Any attempt to do so has to presuppose they have a meaning outside the terms of the reduction. Then they creep back into the argument in tacit, unacknowledged form, causing all kinds of logical and political trouble.

The challenge after positivism is to redefine truth and validity in ways that honour the generative, creative role of the human mind in all forms of knowing. This also means, I believe, taking inquiry beyond justification, beyond the validation of truth-values, towards the celebration and bodying forth of being-values, as the transcendent and polar complement to the quest for validity. I explore this challenge in Chapter 9.

Precursors of the participative paradigm

The participative paradigm underlying co-operative inquiry, outlined above, has a wide range of precursors. The partial genealogy which follows does not justify, or provide exact accord with, my version of the paradigm. It presents the cultural ground out of which it has grown.

The epistemic wing of the paradigm is about participative knowing. This, as basic experiential knowing, is bipolar: participation through empathic communion with the mode of awareness or affectivity of a being; and participation through imaging, in sensory and extrasensory ways, its form of appearing.

The interpenetration of knower and known has been a long-standing thesis of mysticism, East and West: in Taoism, Vedanta, Zen, Mahayana Buddhism, in Neoplatonism and among Christian mystics. Less radical and more restricted affirmations of the same participative point are found in diverse forms in many modern thinkers: Ash, Barfield, Bateson, Bergson, Berman, Bohm, Bookchin, Buber, Dewey, Freire, Gebser, William James, Langer, Maslow, Merleau-Ponty, Polanyi, Scheler, Skolimowski, Wahl, Whitehead, to name but a few.

A first corollary of participative knowing is that knowers can only be knowers when known by other knowers. Knowing is mutual awakening, mutual participative awareness. Buber (1937) thought that people only exist in their fullness in direct, open mutual relation; and that their reality is found in their relating. In wider social terms, knowing presupposes participation, through meeting and dialogue, in a culture of shared language, values, norms and beliefs. There have been a thousand versions of this going back to Aristotle's assertion in his *Nicomachean Ethics* that socialization is a necessary condition of anyone becoming a rational agent. A modern variant is Habermas' notion of the 'organization of enlightenment' in critical communities (Habermas, 1978). Wilber (1995) stresses the point that the intersubjective 'worldspace' of shared values and meanings of a culture is essential to understanding the human condition.

A second corollary is the distinction between explicit and tacit knowledge. To participate in anything explicitly is to participate in everything tacitly. The whole is thus implicit in the part. This holonomic principle, found in Buddhist logic (Govinda, 1960; Stcherbatsky, 1962), and a truism in the mystical traditions cited above, also has its adherents among theoretical physicists and biophysicists such as Schroedinger (1964, 1969), von Bertalanffy (1968) and Bohm (1980) as a derivation from holographic logic and quantum logic (Zukav, 1979). Other thinkers assert that the very concept of the universe as a whole entails the notion of the mutual participation of the parts in each other and the whole (Teilhard de Chardin, 1961; Skolimowski, 1985). There is an echo also in the theology of Karl Rahner (Kelly, 1993) with his notion of 'unthematic experience', which is the inherent openness of the human mind, prior to all education, to the infinite divine.

A third corollary is the distinction between participative knowing and alienated nonparticipative knowing in which the knower conceptually splits subject from object. For the Taoist this is the distinction between natural knowing and conventional knowing; for the Buddhist between directly feeling or perceiving the universe and talking ourselves into seeing our universe, between *prajna* and *vijnana*; for Meister Eckhart between daybreak knowledge and twilight knowledge; for William James between immediate or intuitive knowing and conceptual or representative knowing; for Whitehead between prehension and abstraction; and so on.

A fourth corollary is the idea of three stages of integration. In *Feeling and Personhood* (Heron, 1992: 82), I equate these three stages with a progression from the prepersonal state of the child in its undifferentiated participative world where it is over-participative and under-individuated, through ego development where the person is over-individuated and under-participative, to the transpersonal state where there is a mature integration of individuating and participative ways of being.

Reason (1994a), following Barfield (1957), Kremer (1992), Wilber (1983) and others, fashions a broader myth of the historical development of human consciousness through these three stages. The first stage is that of 'original participation' in which people are embedded in their world with an awareness that is unitive but relatively undifferentiated and unreflective. The second stage, reaching a peak in Western industrial societies, is that of 'unconscious participation', when the differentiated ego emerges but becomes alienated and controlling because it not only transcends original participation but represses it. This leads to the dualistic separation of subject from object, and the fragmentation of positivist inquiry. The third stage is one of 'future participation' towards which we are now moving and which involves a dialectical interplay between a re-awakened unitive, and an enlightened differentiated, awareness. Reason underlines strongly the feminist account of this story:

> From a feminist perspective, this story of human development in the West is a story of a masculine path. It is clear that the evolution of the Western mind has been a masculine project (Tarnas, 1991) and has been founded on the repression of the feminine – not only the repression of the undifferentiated consciousness of original participation, but also of the feminine wisdom principle, personified in the figure of Sophia who, as Long shows (1992) originally stood alongside and ultimately contained the masculine deity. Feminist writers argue that women in industrial societies carry the muted voice of participative consciousness within patriarchal culture and are aware of the violence done to human and planetary relationships by loss of participation, hierarchy and alienation. Modern feminist scholarship points to potential differences between women and men in styles of thinking and valuing (Marshall, 1993). Thus Gilligan (1982) writes of the importance of relationship and Miller (1976) of affiliation as central to women's identity. Belenky and her colleagues (Belenky et al., 1986; Goldberger et al., 1987) have explored women's ways of knowing and emphasize the importance of dialogue, reciprocity and co-operation. Eco-feminists have asserted the parallels between the oppression of women and the destruction of the planet (Plant, 1989). While this work is important for women in developing their authentic identity in Western society, it is also crucial for humanity as a whole in showing that alienation from participation is not necessarily at the foundation of human consciousness. (Reason, 1994a: 23–4)

The historical precursor of the three-stage model is nineteenth century German idealism in the work of Schelling and Hegel, who saw spirit manifesting first as objective nature, then as subjective mind and finally in the unification of the two. Wilber (1995) makes much of this in his distinction between the eco camp and the ego camp and the call for their transpersonal integration.

A fifth corollary is holism of inquiry, in which the researchers' conclusions and applications are grounded in their own participative knowing. Holistic method, the interplay within the co-inquirers of thought and experience, has as its precursor the tradition of experiential learning where 'the learner is directly in touch with the realities being studied' (Keeton and Tate, 1978: 2). Key contributors here have been John Dewey (1938) in higher education, and Kurt Lewin (1952) in training and organizational development (Kolb, 1984). Lewin transformed the experiential learning cycle of Dewey into systematic action research, which, however, fell far short of a wide-ranging human condition inquiry model.

Participative knowing and its corollaries spring from the epistemic wing of the paradigm. There is also the political wing, based on an axiological theory about the intrinsic value of human flourishing, in individual and social life, in terms of an enabling balance of autonomy, co-operation and hierarchy; and about participative decision-making in every social context as a means to this end.

One corollary here is the asymmetrical interdependence between thought and action. Thought supports and validates action, in the sense that valid action presupposes a reflective grasp of standards and rules of practice. Action consummates and fulfils thought, completes it through manifestation. Action in the form of reshaping our worlds – economically, technologically, ecologically, aesthetically, politically, socially – is the end of thought, thought is not the end of action; this is the basic asymmetry.

In terms of cosmic philosophy, Plato is the classic progenitor: the transcendent archetypal realm of Forms, divine thought, is made more complete by its manifestation in the physical world; similarly with Plotinus (Wilber, 1995). Dewey (1929) is one modern precursor with his view that knowledge is an instrument for action rather than an object of disinterested contemplation. Macmurray (1957) expressed the asymmetry more cogently: a person can't exist as a thinking subject, but only as an agent in whom all human capacities are employed. A person as thinking subject exists in and for the person as agent; so action includes thought but not vice versa, and thought is for the action which consummates it. Pragmatism as a theory of truth is not a precursor: I reject any genealogy of pragmatism in this epistemological sense, and explain this in Chapter 9.

A second corollary is that of universal political rights. This is an advanced version of the more limited and widely accepted human right of any person to political membership of their community, that is, to participate in the framing and working of political institutions. The universal version comes to the fore when every social situation of decision-making is regarded as political. Then we have the all-pervasive right of persons to participate in any decision-making that affects the fulfilment of their needs and interests, the expression of their preferences and values.

This right to political participation in the universal sense is on an unidentified march throughout the world, claiming attention not only in political institutions, but, in piecemeal fashion, in the family, in education, in medicine, in industry, in other arenas, and now in research. To my knowledge it has nowhere been clearly stated and acknowledged in its all-inclusive, universal and uncompromising form.

The precursor here is the doctrine of human rights originating in Renaissance humanism with the idea of the free and self-determining human person. Locke and Kant translated this into the political terms of the liberal state whose task is to protect its citizens' rights. Classical human rights include freedom of religion, conscience, expression of opinion, press, association, disposal of property, equality before the law, security of the person, and political membership of the community. The doctrine has been expanded in this century to include new social, economic and cultural rights, and versions of the doctrine occur in international documents such as the United Nations' Universal Declaration of Human Rights of 1948, and the European Convention on Human Rights of 1953, as well as in several national constitutions. All of this, admirable as it is, still falls far short of acknowledging the human right to political participation in the universal sense, which in principle subsumes practically all other rights.

A third corollary is that action manifests personal value or the suppression of it. Every choice, every decision to do something, stems from a personal preference, or from a pseudo-preference when a personal preference is suppressed or unidentified. Every authentic preference involves an explicit or implicit vision of a valued way of life or of some aspect of it. In this sense, action, as the expression of preference, manifests personal values.

Action relates to the doings of purposive agents. Aristotle distinguished *poiesis*, what a person does, from *pathos*, what merely happens to him or her. Parsons (1957) suggested that the concept of an action includes an agent with goals and alternative means who is in partial control of a situation, who is governed by values for the goals, by norms for the means and by beliefs about the situation. What is overriding here are the values for the goals of action. Thus Macmurray (1957) said values were constitutive of action, inherent in its nature. Recent work on emotional intelligence (Goleman, 1995) shows that effective choice is rooted in emotional values.

A fourth corollary is that autonomous preference precedes authentic co-operative choice. In any negotiation preceding a co-operative choice, each agent needs to identify and state his or her preferences, and where relevant their underlying values, otherwise real co-operation is not possible.

A fifth corollary is about research subjects' political rights. Every human subject in a piece of social science research has a right to participate actively, directly or through representation, in decisions about the research design. This is so that each subject can have the opportunity to identify, own and manifest his or her personal values in and through the design; can therefore be present as a fully human person in the study; and can avoid being misrepresented by the researcher's implicit value system.

Every unilateral design decision of a social researcher imposes personal preferences and values on those being studied and is thus oppressive and disempowering, however enlightened the values. Nor is it sufficient only to seek the *passive* assent of those being studied to the unilateral design: this is simply to ask them to collude with their oppressors. The subjects studied then settle for their own pseudo-preferences, while their own authentic preferences remain unasked for and unidentified.

The unilateral controlling relationship between researcher and researched has been questioned on and off over the years (Jourard, 1967; Miller, 1969; Argyris, 1970; Haney et al., 1973; Rowan, 1974; Warr, 1977). And feminist researchers have confronted the gender aspect of unilateral control (Eagley, 1987; Leonard, 1984). Earlier in this chapter, I cited action science, forms of action research and of feminist research, which, as well as co-operative inquiry, seek to abandon this kind of dominion; and I referred to some other forms of participative research moving in this direction.

The question of data

In the chapters that follow, when I use the term 'data' in the context of discussing various features of co-operative inquiry, I shall invariably use it with the verb 'to generate'. Thus I shall speak of the inquirers 'generating data'. What I mean to imply by this is that the inquirers are shaping their experience of the given cosmos. The data does not lie about in ready-made form: it is the fruit of active construing by the mind, of its creative trans-action with the 'primordial ontological datum' of the universe (Skolimowski, 1994: 177).

2

Research Method and Participation

This chapter defines, and gives simple reasons for using, the research method of co-operative inquiry in terms of the two basic kinds of participation, epistemic and political, introduced in the previous chapter. These are also used to identify the other principal research methods in the human sciences, with some of the problematic issues that arise for each. In ordinary language, I take an overview of research *with* people, research *on* people, research *about* people, with some concluding thoughts relating to research *for* people.

Participative research *with* people

Co-operative inquiry is a form of participative, person-centred inquiry which does research *with* people not *on* them or *about* them. It breaks down the old paradigm separation between the roles of researcher and subject. In traditional research in the human sciences these roles are mutually exclusive: the researcher only contributes the thinking that goes into the project – conceiving it, designing it, managing it and drawing knowledge from it – and the subjects only contribute the action to be studied.

In co-operative inquiry this division is replaced by a participative relationship among all those involved. This participation can be of different kinds and degrees. In its most complete form, the inquirers engage fully in both roles, moving in cyclic fashion between phases of reflection as co-researchers and of action as co-subjects. In this way they use reflection and action to refine and deepen each other. They also adopt various other procedures to enhance the validity of the process and its outcomes.

The defining features of co-operative inquiry, I believe, are:

- *All* the subjects are as fully involved as possible as co-researchers in *all* research decisions – about both content and method – taken in the reflection phases.
- There is intentional interplay between reflection and making sense on the one hand, and experience and action on the other.
- There is explicit attention through appropriate procedures to the validity of the inquiry and its findings.
- There is a radical epistemology for a wide-ranging inquiry method that can be both informative about and transformative of any aspect of the

human condition accessible to a transparent body-mind, that is, one that has an open, unbound awareness.

- There are as well as validity procedures a range of special skills suited to such all-purpose experiential inquiry.
- The full range of human sensibilities is available as an instrument of inquiry.

Wilber (1995), in a work which is anomalous in its upper reaches, proposes in its lower reaches a useful though oversimplified model for understanding the human condition. It has four essential ingredients: cultural intersubjectivity, social structure and function, individual subjectivity, and individual behaviour. The first and second are social; the third and fourth are individual. The first and third involve interior experience; the second and fourth involve exterior observation. Co-operative inquiry integrates these four components within the inquiry process. It also grounds them in a fifth domain which Wilber does not fully articulate in his model, but bunches together with the intersubjective space of culture and language.

This is the realm of integral, lived experience which is both prelinguistic and continuously extralinguistic. It is, through empathic communion, a world of shared primary meaning. This tacit, intersubjective, participative pre-understanding of our world is presupposed by our agreement about the use of language, and is continuously transformed into secondary, conceptual meaning by our use of language. It is a fifth domain underpinning all the other four, because these four are constructs which arise out of it, with the emergence of language and its principal pronouns: we, our, I, it.

Epistemic and political participation

There are two complementary kinds of participation involved in co-operative inquiry. There is *epistemic* participation to do with the relation between the knower and the known. The researchers as knowers participate and get involved as subjects in the experiences that are to be known and that are the focus of the inquiry. Furthermore, the subjects' experiences involve forms of knowing that participate in that to which these forms relate.

And there is *political* participation to do with the relation between people in the inquiry and the decisions that affect them. The subjects, those who provide information about themselves, also participate as researchers in the thinking and decision-making that generates, manages and draws knowledge from the whole research process.

The reasons for epistemic participation are:

- Propositions about human experience that are the outcome of the research are of questionable validity if they are not grounded in the researchers' experience.
- The most *rigorous* way to do this is for the researchers to ground the

statements directly in their own experience as co-subjects, where this experience itself involves a deep kind of participative knowing. They can, of course, also use data of a more traditional nature.

- This rigour is called for by the human condition, which is one of shared and dialogic embodiment. The researchers can't get outside, or try to get outside, the human condition in order to study it. They can only study it through their own embodiment, through the full range of their human sensibilities, in a relation of reciprocal participation and dialogue with others similarly engaged. Such an inquiry is an experiential, intersubjective culture, using language. This means, as a context for agreeing about the use of language, that the researchers share a nonlinguistic understanding of their being in a world, generated through empathic resonance with each other's lived experience.

> *The notion of knowing through participation lies at the core of the co-operative inquiry paradigm: I have that quality of attention so that I may be with you, alongside you, empathizing with you; and yet not losing myself in confluence with you because the dialogue between us both bridges and preserves our differences. (Reason, 1988d: 219)*

- This enables the researchers to come to know not just the external forms, individual and collective, of worlds and people, but also the inner prehension, affect, modes of awareness of these forms.

If the researchers are not subjects of their own research, they generate conclusions that are not properly grounded either in their own or in their subjects' personal experience, as in traditional quantitative research; or they try to ground them exclusively in their subjects' embodied experience, as in traditional qualitative research. I discuss the problematic nature of these two alternatives below.

The reasons for political participation are:

- Persons have a human right to participate in decisions about research design (including its management and the conclusions drawn from it), the purpose of which is to formulate knowledge about them.
- This gives them the opportunity to identify and express their own preferences and values in the design.
- It empowers them to flourish as fully human persons (Heron, 1992) in the study and to be represented as such in the conclusions.
- It avoids their being disempowered, oppressed and misrepresented by the researcher's values implicit in any unilateral research design.

This right is a particular application of the fundamental human right of people to participate in decisions that concern and affect them. The democratization of research management is as much a human rights issue as the democratization of government at national and local levels. This right of research subjects to participate in research decision-making has, as its correlate, the matching duty of researchers to encourage, educate and empower their subjects to exercise it. To generate knowledge about persons

Table 2.1   *Kinds and degrees of participation*

		Researcher	Subject
Political participation:	A	Full	Full
involvement in research	B	Full	Partial
thinking and decision-making	C	Full	Nil
Epistemic participation:	D	Full	Full
involvement in experience and	E	Partial	Full
action being researched	F	Nil	Full

without their full participation in deciding how to generate it, is to misrepresent their personhood and to abuse by neglect their capacity for autonomous intentionality. It is fundamentally unethical.

If research subjects do not exercise their right to self-determination with respect to research decision-making, and if they are required to produce behaviour according to a research protocol in which they have had no say, then they are not present in that behaviour as fully functioning, self-directed persons, but as conformist, other-directed subpersons. They are asked to acquiesce in being oppressed and disempowered by imposed values and norms. The research is thus not telling us anything at all about real human personhood. This is the case with traditional quantitative research. And while traditional qualitative research does seek to study people's own behaviour in their own settings, the authenticity of their acquiescence and of their behaviour in the study is compromised by the researchers' unilateral design of it.

Though epistemic and political participation are quite distinct and cannot be reduced to each other, they are also closely interlinked. The political participation by subjects in research decision-making empowers their epistemic integration. And epistemic participation by researchers in the experiences that are the focus of the inquiry involves political engagement with the subjects. There can be different degrees of these two kinds of participation, and mapping them out, as in Table 2.1, provides a basis for classifying a whole range of research methods in the human sciences. A particular method is defined by taking any one of the three political rows, A, B or C, and combining it with any one of the three epistemic rows, D, E or F.

Full form co-operative inquiry

Combining rows A and D in Table 2.1 provides the complete form of co-operative inquiry in which all those involved are both co-researchers and co-subjects in full measure, as shown in Table 2.2. In this form, as I have described above, the separation, both epistemic and political, between researcher and subject breaks down, everyone alternating between the roles of co-researcher and co-subject, between making sense of data and generating it through action.

Table 2.2   *Full form co-operative inquiry*

	Researcher	Subject
Participation in decisions	Full	Full
Participation in experience	Full	Full

Table 2.3   *Partial form co-operative inquiry*

	Researcher	Subject
Participation in decisions	Full	Full
Participation in experience	Partial	Full

What does not, however, break down is the difference, at the outset of the inquiry, in methodological know-how and facilitative guidance, between the initiating researcher and the other co-researchers. Working to break down this difference in the interests of both authentic participation and good-quality inquiry is one of the major challenges of co-operative inquiry, and its highly vulnerable Achilles' heel. I will return to this issue several times in the chapters ahead.

Partial form co-operative inquiry

As well as this full form, there is a partial form of co-operative inquiry. It is, more precisely, a form that is not quite full. In this everyone is involved as co-researchers in the research reflection, and almost all are fully involved as co-subjects in the experience that is being researched. But the one or two initiating researchers are only partially involved as co-subjects, because, as external consultants to the inquiry group, they are not members of the profession or organization in which the research action is focused. This is shown in Table 2.3, which combines rows A and E from Table 2.1.

In a partial form co-operative inquiry, the initiating researchers, as external consultants, introduce co-operative inquiry to a group of professionals, or a group of staff in some organization, who want to focus the inquiry on some aspect of their professional or organizational work. The initiating researchers educate group members to become full co-researchers, and continue to participate in research reflection with the group on a peer basis throughout the inquiry. However, since the initiating researchers are not members of the same profession or organization as the inquiry group, they get involved only partially in the action phases.

This partial involvement as co-subjects can have at least two different forms, of which I give examples in the next chapter. The initiators may become analogous co-subjects, that is, they research something similar in their own professional work or organizational setting. Or they may make occasional visits to the workplace of inquiry group members for participant observation or unstructured interviews and dialogue. In this case their generation of data is secondary to that of the co-subjects who are fully immersed in the action focus of the inquiry. Or they could do both of these things.

There are a range of qualitative research methods which are relatives of this partial form of co-operative inquiry, and I mentioned them in the previous chapter in the section on overlap. In these methods, the initiating researchers and participants collaborate, more or less, on some aspects of research thinking and planning. The participants are fully involved in the research action, but the initiating researchers will only marginally be engaged as ethnographers, unless they are active members of the participant culture or organization within which they are conducting the research.

These methods differ from co-operative inquiry in that the participants are involved mainly in decisions about research content, rather than research method. The methods are also more limited in their range of application, and in the scope of the paradigm that underlies them.

Supported action inquiry

A restricted but valuable kind of co-operative inquiry is one in which person A supports, facilitates and supervises the development of self-determination of person B, usually within some specified social role; and in which this development of self-determination is for B an intentional action inquiry. Thus person B is a researcher of his own experience and action, what Cunningham calls experiential research (Cunningham, 1988), and what Torbert calls action science or action inquiry (Torbert, 1991).

Person A is the initiating researcher who proposes the action inquiry to B and educates B in the use of it. Once B has got the hang of it, B is the primary researcher of his or her own behaviour and A is only a partial co-researcher. A has a secondary, supportive role, participating with B in regular reflection phases, discussing and facilitating ways in which B can make sense of past action and prepare for future ones, and make more congruent the interaction of B's goals, strategies, actions, outcomes and context. And person A is not involved as co-subject at all, except in the sense that the support situation will in some respects mirror the inquiry situation as in all supervision arrangements. This restricted form, which I call supported action inquiry, is shown in Table 2.4, the first row of which is not included in Table 2.1.

This is stretching the use of the Researcher and Subject headings in the table, since the 'Subject' becomes the full researcher and the 'Researcher', having launched the 'Subject', supports and facilitates him or her and is a very secondary researcher.

A good example of this approach is Robert Krim doing action inquiry on his own management style, having been initiated into action inquiry by Bill Torbert and having regular supervision sessions with Torbert (Krim, 1988).

Table 2.4   *Supported action inquiry*

	Researcher	Subject
Participation in decisions	Partial	Full
Participation in experience	Nil	Full

Table 2.5   *Traditional quantitative research*

	Researcher	Subject
Participation in decisions	Full	Nil
Participation in experience	Nil	Full

Supported action inquiry can be used by tutors supporting student autonomy in learning, doctors supporting intentional self-healing and self-help in patients, managers supporting employee self-determination at the site of work, parents supporting teenager autonomy, and so on. It has a great future. However, since it is tangential to co-operative inquiry, I don't explore it further in this book.

In the next three chapters, I go into the various types, features and stages of co-operative inquiry in more detail. Here I will review other research methods used in the human sciences, in terms of the different degrees of epistemic and political participation which are involved in them, together with some of the problematic issues which arise.

Quantitative research *on* people

The combination of rows C and F in Table 2.1 yields classic old paradigm research, in which the researcher does all the research thinking and decision-making and the subject does none of it; and in which the subject undertakes all the experience relevant to the inquiry, and the researcher is involved in none of it. This is shown in Table 2.5.

This is doing research *on* people in the traditional, positivist and quantitative mould. The researcher designs the project unilaterally, manages it directively without consulting the subjects, and does not in any way engage in the behaviour that is being researched. The conclusions about the subjects' behaviour are drawn exclusively by the researcher in terms of his or her own categories and theoretical constructs; and they are never checked with the subjects. These categories and constructs precede the research, define it and are held constant throughout it.

Quantitative methods include: true experiments in which matched subjects are randomly assigned to experimental and control groups; quasi experiments that use nonrandomized designs such as non-equivalent control group designs and time series designs; single case experimental designs; surveys, including cross-sectional and longitudinal studies using questionnaires or structured interviews.

Problems for traditional quantitative research

This way of doing research on people is problematic on two main grounds. On the political front, it ignores the human right, elaborated earlier in this chapter, of persons to participate in decisions that seek to gather knowledge about them. It also ignores the correlative duty of researchers to encourage their subjects to do so. In the experimental format, subjects assent to being subjects for the given research topic, usually being unaware of the dis-empowering collusion involved in their acquiescence. Everything they do, the purpose for which they do it, and the conclusions drawn from their having done it, are all under the exclusive control of the researcher. Thus the research subjects are also political subjects of an authoritarian ruler, who may be benign but who has a blithe disregard for their human rights. The ethically suspect nature of this relationship was pointed out long ago by Argyris (1970).

This means, further, that the behaviour being researched is not that of fully self-determining persons, but of conformist subpersons. Persons have the capacity to be self-directing. This is evident, as I argued in the last chapter, from the behaviour of any kind of researcher who breaks new ground, and thus transcends the predictable with creative advance. But if a researcher is both in principle and practice self-directing, he must extend the same model to his subjects and study them when they are fully in their personhood as self-directing beings. And for subjects to be truly self-directing within the research means that they contribute to the thought and decision that designs it, manages it and shapes their behaviour as subjects.

On the epistemic front, traditional quantitative research on people pro-duces propositional knowledge in terms of theoretical constructs that are experientially ungrounded. They are not grounded in the experience of the researchers, who do not get involved in the experience which is the focus of the research. And they are not grounded in the experience of the subjects, since while this is the focus of the research, the subjects have never been consulted about, or involved in any way in the selection of, the constructs which are used to make sense of their experience. There is thus a yawning gap of untested relevance between the researchers' constructs and the subjects' experience which the constructs are supposed to illumine. The more the research focuses on matters of deep human concern and signifi-cance, the more grave these political and epistemic limitations become.

Qualitative research *about* people ✳

The combination of rows B and E in Table 2.1 yields a research method in which the researchers are fully but not exclusively involved in the research thinking: they invite the subjects to be partially involved in it. And while the subjects are fully engaged in the behaviour that is being researched, the researchers are also partially involved with it. This is classic qualitative

Table 2.6 *Traditional qualitative research*

	Researcher	Subject
Participation in decisions	Full	Partial
Participation in experience	Partial	Full

research, shown in Table 2.6, which includes ethnography and participant observation, grounded theory methodology, case studies, phenomenological studies, ethnomethodology, symbolic interactionism, interpretative practice, biographical method and related strategies (Janesick, 1994). What these approaches have in common is the study of people *in situ* in their own social setting, and the understanding of them in terms of their own categories and constructs.

In terms of research thinking and decision-making, mainstream qualitative research projects are designed unilaterally by the researcher. Recent texts for graduate students on qualitative research design make no provision of any kind for the inclusion of subjects or informants in design decisions; nor is the issue of such participation anywhere discussed (Erlandson et al., 1993; Creswell, 1994; Marshall and Rossman, 1995).

The ongoing management of the research is also typically in the hands of the researcher, although this will involve negotiation with, and may invite feedback from, the subjects, since the research is conducted in the subjects' own natural setting. In drawing knowledge from the project, the researcher seeks to understand the subjects and their behaviour in terms of the subjects' own perspectives. These progressively emerge and become clarified as the research process unfolds. Above all, the researcher's account of the subjects' perspectives is validated and checked with the subjects themselves. This is the main part of the research thinking in which the subjects are involved; and it is regarded as the most important way of establishing the credibility of the research (Lincoln and Guba, 1985; Erlandson et al., 1993). But the basic interpretative models and operational methods used are not designed collaboratively with the subjects.

In qualitative studies, the researcher does not engage fully in the behaviour that is being studied, but does engage in fieldwork, that is, visits the natural setting where the behaviour occurs and is a participant observer and data gatherer of the subjects' perspectives and behaviour in that setting. A participant observer can get more or less involved in the activities of the social situation which he or she is observing, but is still only a partial participant in it.

Qualitative research *about* people is a half-way house between exclusive, controlling research *on* people and fully participatory research *with* people. The more it involves subjects in the full range of issues involved in research decision-making, not only about content issues but also about operational methods, and the more fully researchers participate in the cultures they are studying, the more it shifts in the direction of co-operative inquiry. Guba and Lincoln, in their account of fourth generation evaluation, point the way toward this shift:

> Fourth generation evaluation mandates that the evaluator move from the role of controller to that of collaborator. The evaluator must share control, however much that appears to threaten the 'technical adequacy' of the evaluation. That is, the evaluator must solicit and honor stakeholder inputs not only about the *substance* of constructions but also with respect to the *methodology* of the evaluation itself. (Guba and Lincoln, 1989: 260)

Problems for traditional qualitative research

Traditional qualitative research is problematic on the same two fronts as traditional quantitative research, although less so. On the political front, it has not grasped the right of informants to participate in formulating the research design, so that they can manifest fully their values in the way knowledge about them is generated. The great majority of its projects are still unilaterally shaped by the researchers, however emergent that shape may be. It is not aware that this approach, even at its most empathic and benign, subtly oppresses the informants, who are enmeshed in a discreet web of imported values implicit in every design thread the researcher spins.

Some qualitative research, of which I gave a few examples in Chapter 1, is concerned not just to understand, but also to empower, informants. But there are two levels at which such empowerment can occur. The first is when informants are liberated by a research design to voice their own views and values and to act in ways they judge to be productive. The second and higher-order level is when informants are empowered by being initiated in, and by collaborating in, the research design itself and the values embodied in it. The first without the second is something of a contradiction: it means informants are being empowered at level one through not being empowered at level two. They are liberated on the ground floor while being excluded from participating, on the upper floor, in shaping the methodology of liberation and the values it manifests. This is empowerment under the aegis of subtle benign oppression.

In general, whether the method is empowering or not, there is a dearth of any really full-blown, second level collaboration in qualitative research. This is why there is such an emphasis on gaining access to the research site. Part of this no doubt involves a genuine concern about the interpersonal and ethical issues of gathering knowledge about people in their natural setting. But part of it comes over as a rationalization of something more surreptitious, of which the researchers themselves are barely aware. This is to do with luring gatekeepers and informants into being studied by a design in which they are not invited to collaborate, and to which, at best, they are only invited to give informed consent.

Mainline qualitative research does seek to find out, by participant observation and data-gathering, about people who are being, to varying degrees, self-determining within their natural setting. And it does seek to make

credible its conclusions about all this by checking them with those concerned. But there are problems.

If I am simply the respondent to your unilateral research design, I may
tell you a great tale which could be a packet of conscious or unconscious
lies. Whereas if I were your active co-researcher, I would be challenged to
test my assertions in the crucible of aware action. Correlatively, if you, the
researcher, have got me, the informant, to agree to being other-directed by
you with respect to the methods by which (and often the purposes for
which) I am being researched, you have undermined my self-determination
as an informant. You have cajoled me into ignoring my right to have a
powerful say in how and why I will be researched. My authenticity as a
self-determining being in any of our interactions and interviews is subtly
compromised.

If you say, however, that you do not want to research my authentic self-
determination in action in my setting, but me as a person who is less than
self-determining, then your research is psychologically oppressive, socially
exploitative and ethically offensive.

It is clearly offensive to interpret a research subject's behaviour in terms
of methods, categories and information to which the subject doesn't have
access throughout the research, but which, if the subject did know about,
would empower him or her to be more self-determining. Intentionally to
keep people in ignorance of aids to their own betterment, for the purposes
of doing research about them, is exploitative. It is better to do research
with them, so that they can explore these aids from the outset in a self-
directed way. The alienated and unawakened nature of this stance in
qualitative research is well illustrated in the following passage from Denzin:

> In a certain sense, interpretive studies hope to understand the subject better than
> she understands herself. Often interpretations are formed that subjects would not
> give to their actions. This is so because the researcher is often in a position to see
> things the subject cannot see. The full range of factors that play on an indi-
> vidual's experience is seldom apparent to them. The interpreter has access to a
> picture of the subject's life that the subject often lacks. The interpreter also has a
> method of interpretation that the subject seldom has.

The only concession Denzin makes to the cognitive rights of the subject is
that:

> The interpretations that are developed about a subject's life, however, must be
> understandable to the subject. If they are not, they are unacceptable. (Denzin,
> 1989: 65)

In other words, the researcher's superior knowledge about the subject is
unacceptable if the subject can't understand it, but still acceptable if the
subject is denied access to co-operating with the researcher in its use. Of
course, this all assumes the researcher's interpretation is superior; and this
can always be doubted if the subjects have had no say in framing its
premises.

On the epistemic front, traditional qualitative research does strive to produce propositional knowledge in terms of theoretical constructs that are grounded in relevant experience. These constructs may marginally be grounded in the researchers' own experience of the subjects' culture, to the extent that the researchers participate in that culture. But because it is marginal, this kind of limited researcher grasp of the visited culture is very secondary to the subjects' indigenous grasp of it. So the researchers mainly seek – by observation, informal dialogue, structured interview, written records, visual evidence and member checks – to ground their constructs in their subjects' experience. But, once again, the adequacy and relevance of this grounding is suspect if the subjects are not invited to contribute to decisions about how, and for what purpose, data is gathered about their experience, and about what interpretative schema will be applied.

Furthermore, there is something odd about researchers wanting to ground their own interpretative models in other people's social experience, while ignoring ever present opportunities for more fully and reliably grounding theory either (1) in the researchers' own indigenous social conditions or (2) in others' conditions where the others have a full say, with the researchers, in framing *relevant* models and operational procedures.

The qualitative researcher may say that there must be a place for studying people just as they are in their own setting, so that we can learn about the extraordinary diversity of human social life. But inviting people to participate in designing a study about them doesn't put a stop to any of this. It just means you study people as they are in their own setting, only *more so* because of the extra dimension of their reflexivity and creative intentionality.

If the researcher then says that many people are just too busy with their various enterprises to be able or willing to participate in designing a study of themselves, the answer can only be that that is for them to decide. Moreover, a great deal depends on how they are asked.

Research *for* people

Who does the researcher in the human sciences do the research for? The notion of doing research for people does not identify a research method; it spotlights fundamental issues in the sociology of knowledge. Knowledge is power, and can be used for control as power over people, for sharing as power with people, and for delegation and giving away as power to people. But first, a bit more about who research is for.

You may do research for yourself, both because it is an intrinsically interesting process and because the knowledge it yields is interesting, useful or empowering to you. You may do research for others because the knowledge it yields is interesting, useful or empowering to them. This last statement is ambiguous. It could mean you do research for others because they can use it to enhance and empower their own lives and/or the lives of more people. Or it could mean you do research for others because it is useful to them in controlling, dominating and manipulating their subordinates.

You may do research for some funding agency or organization, in order to make money and acquire social status. And you may do research for your masters in a higher education institution such as a university in order to win their approval, advance your own academic career, and, above all, maintain the academic status quo. The influence on research of the academic status quo is what I want to discuss here in more detail.

The academic status quo

Research in the human sciences is very much an academic pursuit, based in and originating from universities. Universities are still Aristotelian institutions, committed to intellectual excellence as the highest end of man (not, for Aristotle at any rate, women). They are also committed to intellect as the controlling force in individual and social life, and to the preeminence of propositional knowledge, a set of intellectual statements published in systematic form.

Their educational model, with an increasing number of honourable exceptions in particular schools and departments, is still predominantly authoritarian. Staff unilaterally make all educational decisions on behalf of their students. They decide what their students shall learn, how and when they shall learn it, and assess whether they have learnt it. Undergraduate students have no say at all in determining the objectives and programme of learning, the teaching and learning methods to be used, the pacing of their learning, the criteria of assessment, or the conduct of assessment.

Universities have a strong vested interest in maintaining this unilateral social control of student learning and assessment. It secures incoming waves of anxious students compulsively seeking its *imprimatur*. Academic staff can float upon these waves exercising dissociated intellectual command and control. They do not need to acquire the kind of emotional and interpersonal competence necessary for empowering students (1) to learn more holistically and (2) to participate in educational decisions thereby becoming progressively more self-determining with respect to their objectives, programme, pacing, learning methods, and assessment.

Authoritarian collusion between teaching and research

This model of authoritarian control which staff use for educating their students is transferred unawarely into their research. They exercise the same kind of unilateral control and decision-making about the design and management of research on or about their human subjects, as they do about the design and management of teaching their students. Research and teaching are the twin pillars of academic life. If staff were to introduce self-determination among their subjects with respect to research design, they would be faced with the implicit challenge of launching it among their students with regard to the curriculum. The whole established structure of university *power over* would be threatened.

This is one of the reasons why quantitative methods entirely, and qualitative methods predominantly, do not use front-end political partici-pation, that is, the involvement of subjects in research design. The justification of this, quite apart from outmoded notions of bias and objectivity, is that the intellectual expertise involved is too sophisticated. This view, however, is patronizing to the subjects and either lazy or arrogant on the part of the researchers. And if it is literally the case that the design expertise is too esoteric for subjects to grasp, too complicated to honour their right to participate in decisions being made for gathering knowledge about them, then the fault lies with the alienated and alienating design.

Extension of human rights

We live in an age in which the doctrine of human rights is moving forward inexorably, if painfully and slowly, on diverse fronts all over the world. Human rights are basically about providing just conditions for the fulfil-ment of human well-being. They assert fundamental freedoms: the right to freedom of speech and expression; the right to freedom of association and contract; the right to political membership of the community, to participate in the framing and working of political institutions.

The right to political membership of the community is a special case of the all-pervasive general right, to which I have already referred, of persons to participate, directly or through appropriate representation, in decision-making that affects their concerns and the fulfilment of their human needs and interests. Most readers of this book will live in countries where this right is acknowledged in terms of local and national government. But when it comes to respecting this general right in other social areas, including higher education and research, there is still a long way to go.

In fact, there are deep anomalies. We consider that an 18-year-old has a right to vote, to participate in political decision-making, but has no right to participate in educational decision-making, that is, in staff government of his or her higher education. We consider that a person has a right to choose whether or not to take part as a subject in a research project, but has no right to have a say in choosing what it is about, how it will be conducted, and what conclusions will be drawn from it. There is, indeed, a long way to go.

Propositional bias

As well as universities sustaining a model of authoritarian intellectual control of students in education and subjects in research, they also sustain a strong Aristotelian bias in favour of propositional knowledge, that is, intellectual statements, both verbal and numeric, conceptually organized in ways that do not infringe the rules of logic and evidence. Propositional knowledge is regarded both as pre-eminent and self-sufficient. It rules over other kinds of knowledge, such as knowing how to do something, but does not depend on them. It is necessary only that it should observe those rules of logic and evidence which are internal to its own nature.

This bias has a huge influence on both the quantitative and qualitative research coming out of universities. This research rests on the unquestioned assumption that intellectual knowledge is the only valid and respectable outcome of systematic inquiry. This one-dimensional account of research outcomes offends a fundamental principle of systemic logic, the logic of whole systems, which is that the relative autonomy of the part is interdependent with the mutual interaction of parts within the whole.

Holistic knowledge and systemic logic

A multi-dimensional account of knowledge, and so of research outcomes, is one which I advance in this book. It rests on systemic logic, which holds that intellectual or propositional knowledge, together with the validating principles internal to it, is interdependent with three other kinds of knowledge: practical knowledge, that is evident in knowing how to exercise a skill; presentational knowledge, evident in intuitive grasp of the significance of imaginal patterns as expressed in graphic, plastic, moving, musical and verbal art-forms; and experiential knowledge, evident only in actually meeting and feeling the presence of some energy, entity, person, place, process or thing. These three other basic kinds of knowledge also have validating principles internal to them.

Valid knowledge, on the multi-dimensional view, means that each of the four kinds of knowledge is validated by its own internal criteria, and also by its interdependence and congruence with all the others within a systemic whole. The notion of validity as used here is defined in terms of a participative paradigm, not a positivist one, as discussed in Chapter 9.

In the chapters which follow I shall argue that this systemic whole is an interdependent up-hierarchy, a dynamic pyramidal process in which what is below supports, grounds and empowers what is above. Experiential knowing – direct, lived being-in-the-world – at the base of the pyramid, supports presentational or pattern knowing, which supports propositional or conceptual knowing, which upholds practical knowing, the exercise of skill. At the same time, what is above consummates and celebrates at a new level of relative autonomy what is below. Practical knowing, with the standards internal to it, consummates the propositional knowing which grounds it. Propositional knowing, with the standards internal to it, consummates the presentational knowing which grounds it; and so on. This holistic epistemology, first presented in Heron (1981a), is elaborated in substantial form in *Feeling and Personhood* (Heron, 1992), and I refer the reader to this work for a more detailed treatment.

Primacy of the practical

Practical knowledge, knowing how, is the consummation, the fulfilment, of the knowledge quest. It is grounded on and empowered by all the prior forms of knowing, and is immediately supported by propositional knowing, which it celebrates and affirms at a higher level in its own relatively autonomous way. To say that practice consummates the prior forms of knowing on which it is grounded, is to say that it takes the knowledge quest beyond justification, beyond the concern for validity and truth-values, into the celebration of being-values, by showing them forth. It affirms what is intrinsically worthwhile, human flourishing, by manifesting it in action. I elaborate this view in Chapter 9.

This kind of dynamic up-hierarchy is in marked contrast to the classical Greek down-hierarchy, in which the intellect is on top and controls everything below it in the psychological system, without being empowered by any of it. It also follows from it that practical knowledge, knowing how to exercise a skill, supported by propositional knowledge, is the primary kind of research outcome.

If this is so, then it inescapably underlines the importance of all or most of the researchers also being the subjects of their own research, since practical knowledge as a research outcome cannot be about anyone else, since it is not *about* anything and is not cast in propositional form. It can only be evident as a skill the researcher has cultivated as a consequence of being a co-subject within the research. As a research outcome it is also a researcher outcome. Nor can the secondary propositional knowledge, which is also a research outcome, exclude the researcher, since it is supportive of the practical skill which the researcher as co-subject has acquired. There is an important corollary that when this skill includes speaking out for others in the service of a liberatory truth, then the propositions which support it will also have this liberatory function.

In what follows I shall take the view that going for practical outcomes of an inquiry and going for propositional outcomes are complementary approaches; and while the deeper way, the route of primacy, is to choose practical outcomes supported by propositional ones, there is clearly a case for pursuing propositional outcomes supported by practical ones. They exhibit a fundamental interdependence characterized by a radical asymmetry, the primacy of the practical. I explain this in the next chapter in the distinction between informative and transformative inquiries.

This thesis about the primacy of the practical in research outcomes does pose a special challenge for university-based researchers, surrounded by an academic culture with an entrenched Aristotelian bias in favour of pro- positional outcomes. For a skill, knowing how to do something, can never be reduced to written descriptions of doing it. Being able to write such a description is no evidence of being able to perform the skill. The only evidence that you have the skill, and have it up to a certain standard of competence, is your demonstration of it. The only skill that can be demonstrated conclusively by writing a research report is the skill involved in writing such reports.

Thus the challenge to the academic research establishment of the primacy of the practical is that published research reports become entirely secondary to the researcher's demonstration of competence in action. I imagine that at least at one or two of the human science research conferences of the future, the main proceedings will be a variety of demonstrations, portrayals and dramatizations of different kinds of skill, variously combining physical, psychosocial, transpersonal elements. Also a range of training workshops in which others can acquire them or at least have a go at them in rudimentary form. And for all this the written papers will simply provide the supporting programme notes. And at conferences where there are only papers on offer, it will at least be acknowledged that they are offering second best, the programme notes without the performance.

3
Overview of Co-operative Inquiry

The purpose of this chapter is to give a general survey of co-operative inquiry. It includes: (1) the range of inquiry outcomes and topics, (2) ways of launching an inquiry, (3) the different types of inquiry, (4) an outline of inquiry stages, (5) an extended epistemology involved in the inquiry stages, (6) a summary of validity procedures and special skills. Items (1), and (4) to (6) inclusive, will be explored in more detail in later chapters. Basic issues from item (3) will keep cropping up throughout the book.

But first I offer a reminder from the opening of the last chapter, that the defining features of co-operative inquiry, as I see it, are:

- *All* the subjects are as fully involved as possible as co-researchers in *all* research decisions – about both content and method – taken in the reflection phases.
- There is intentional interplay between reflection and making sense on the one hand, and experience and action on the other.
- There is explicit attention through appropriate procedures to the validity of the inquiry and its findings.
- There is a radical epistemology for a wide-ranging inquiry method that can be both informative about and transformative of any aspect of the human condition accessible to a transparent body-mind, that is, one that has an open, unbound awareness.
- There are as well as validity procedures a range of special skills suited to such all-purpose experiential inquiry.
- The full range of human sensibilities is available as an instrument of inquiry.

And second I remind the reader that this is an account from my perspective. It is a personal reflection on, and articulation of, the nature of the inquiry process and of the given reality in which it participates. It is a contribution to a rational debate, a continued inquiry, an invitation to exploration, with my peers.

Inquiry outcomes

There are at least four main kinds of inquiry outcome, corresponding to the four forms of knowing: experiential, presentational, propositional and practical. Depending on the topic area, some aspect of each of the following can be an outcome:

- Transformations of personal being through engagement with the focus and process of the inquiry.
- Presentations of insight about the focus of the inquiry, through dance, drawing, drama, and all other expressive modes: these provide imaginal symbols of the significant patterns in our realities.
- Propositional reports which (1) are informative about the inquiry domain, that is, they describe and explain what has been explored, (2) provide commentary on the other kinds of outcome, and (3) describe the inquiry method.
- Practical skills which are (1) skills to do with transformative action within the inquiry domain, and (2) skills to do with various kinds of participative knowing and collaboration used in the inquiry process.

I take the view that the last two, the propositional and the practical, are interdependent, but that practical outcomes (1) have primacy, and I discuss this later in this chapter and more fully in Chapters 6 and 9.

The range of inquiry topics

I see co-operative inquirers as deeply engaged with the human condition, living and choosing with awareness. Each one uses the full range of her or his sensibilities as a composite instrument of inquiry, and as a group they interweave creative discussion with concerted action and openness to experience. Thus any aspect of the human condition, construed as a dialogue between fully embodied people, is available as a topic for inquiry.

It follows from the participative paradigm that the following topics of inquiry do not refer to different domains of objective reality, but to different subjective-objective articulations of reality, reality cut to our cloth, co-created by our mental shaping of it in the process of participating with it. And the category system of the list itself is a construct, which can be put together in many different ways. The first half of the list relates to what I call informative inquiries, which have propositional outcomes which describe and explain what is going on, or presentational outcomes which portray it.

- Participation in nature: from molecules, minerals and galactic clusters to microbes, protoplasm and all life forms in the biosphere.

  I believe that the development of a participative world-view requires an imaginative recognition of humanity's fundamental participation in the natural world, a recognition of the way the human mind is engaged in a co-creative dance with the primeval givenness of the cosmos. (Reason, 1994a: 15)

- Participation in art: from sculpture and painting to theatre and song.
- Participation in intrapsychic life: from sensations and moods to elevations and ecstasies.
- Participation in interpersonal relations: verbal and nonverbal, from

one-to-one encounters and face-to-face groups, to structured large group meetings.

- Participation in forms of culture: from environmental and economic arrangements to education and politics.
- Participation in other realities and altered states of consciousness: from telekinesis and extrasensory perception to cosmic consciousness and unitive awareness.

This second half of the list covers items for transformative inquiries, which have practical or skills outcomes, including their effects. This is the manifold arena of personal and social transformation, of liberatory praxis. It is obvious on inspection that the two halves of the total list are interdependent.

- Transformation of the environment: from local to planetary ecology; from architecture to permaculture.
- Transformation of social structure: social practices and rituals; organizational development; economic and political transformation; liberation of the disempowered and disadvantaged and of their oppressors; a self-generating culture.
- Transformation of education: from birth to death; including self-directed learning, peer and holistic learning.
- Transformation of professionalism: professional skills; peer review audit; creating a culture of competence; deprofessionalization, delegation and facilitation.
- Transformation of personhood: personal growth skills, interpersonal and transpersonal skills.
- Transformation of life-style: ranging from intimacy and domicile to occupation and recreation.

Each of these twelve major topic areas has within it a huge variety of more specific inquiry questions. Only a minute fraction of this vast agenda has ever been the subject matter of a co-operative inquiry, or even of tentative proposals for inquiry. And, thinking on the grand scale, the agenda as a whole is a participative approach to planetary transformation.

Launching an inquiry group

A group can be launched into an inquiry in three main ways, two of them involving initiating researchers and one without.

Initiators' call

This is the way in which all the inquiries I know of have been started. One or two initiating researchers, who have launched or participated in other co-operative inquiries or who have read about and reflected on the method, can put out a call, by some appropriate form of publicity, for interested people to join them in an inquiry in some broad topic area. This topic area will be one the initiating researchers are keen to explore. They will put out their call among people who are likely to share that keenness. The topic area is only broadly stated so that when the group forms, a more focused account of it can be co-operatively chosen.

The first meeting of respondents is for induction and selection. It may be for two hours (Traylen, 1994) or for one day (De Venney-Tiernan et al., 1994); in my view it needs plenty of time because it is the contracting stage. After the respondents have been welcomed and perhaps invited to share in small groups what has drawn them to the project, the initiating researchers:

- Talk more about their interest in the topic area.
- Spell out in detail what this co-operative inquiry might involve in terms of participative method, roles, time-structure.
- Make clear any selection criteria they consider relevant for inquiry membership.

After discussion and clarification of these three factors, the respondents use them to select themselves in or out of the inquiry group. Some may be ready to do this at the end of the meeting, others may want to sleep on it, so a further meeting may be needed.

Reason points out that the initiating researchers have, at this contracting stage, an important tension to manage. If they come on too emphatically about their aims and interests, they may generate dependency, resistance or alienation. If they are too vague and flexible, the forming group may flounder in confusion. He recommends both clarity and flexibility:

> The attitude of the initiators should be: 'This is our idea about what we want to look at together. This is an outline of a co-operative inquiry. Let's talk about all this and see if we have a basis for co-operation.' (Reason, 1988b: 25)

This launches the challenging task of initiating researchers: to create a community of shared values without either imposing them or compromising them. The initiators have a commitment to educate, and not indoctrinate, people in collaborative research method. I discuss the process of initiation in detail in the next chapter.

Shortly after the induction meeting, when people have contracted in, the group has its first inquiry meeting, and the initiating researchers start to introduce members to the inquiry method. In the early stages of the group forming, the contracting process continues, the joining contract being revisioned on the basis of experience. Eventually, and hopefully, everyone internalizes and creatively modifies the method and makes it their own, so that a group of co-researchers evolves.

An alternative approach here is that rather than call a new group into being, the initiating researchers may call on an existing group to join in an inquiry with them. Reason points out that an existing group may have competing priorities, may have a history and dynamics which take time to grasp, and suggests it is most likely to be a good inquiry group if it already has a current problem in need of solution, one which is well suited to the inquiry method (Reason, 1988b: 22).

Call for initiators

Conversely some already existing group, having a research topic in mind, and having heard about co-operative inquiry, might call in initiating researchers to join the inquiry and launch the method. This group itself will probably have been called into being by one or two people with a special interest in the topic. In 1982, one person in Dublin got together a group which invited me to launch with them a co-operative inquiry (unreported) into group energy.

Group bootstrap

A group may exist, or form, that chooses to be entirely self-initiating, and pull itself up by its own bootstraps into the practice of co-operative inquiry. It may do so by its members either reading a book like this, or by inventing and experimenting *de novo* with its own version of the process. While the latter approach is beset by the restriction of re-inventing the wheel, it is nevertheless a useful antidote to the formation of new orthodoxies in research, and to any assumption that there is some received, correct and established way of doing things.

   A bootstrap group, though it has all the disadvantages of not being able to benefit from people with prior experience of the method, is free of the main hazard of a group that is launched by initiating researchers. This is that group members fail to internalize the method and become dependent on, or resistant to, the initiating researchers, with the result that a truly co-operative inquiry never occurs. I don't know of any examples of a bootstrap group, but I hope and expect there will be many in the future, and I look forward to hearing news of them.

Types of inquiry

There are several different sorts of co-operative inquiry, and I haven't seen so far a systematic account of them. An overview of the various options is useful when anyone is contemplating launching a research group.

Internally or externally initiated

In an internally initiated inquiry the initiating researchers are internal to the inquiry focus of the group: they are personally engaged with the culture or practice which the research is about, and this means they can be full co-subjects.

   An inquiry by youth workers into how people learn was initiated by a youth worker (De Venney-Tiernan et al., 1994); and an inquiry by women staff in a university into sex and gender issues in the workplace was initiated by a woman member of staff (Treleaven, 1994). In both cases, the initiator was a full co-subject in the action phases of the inquiry.

In an externally initiated inquiry the initiating researchers are external to the particular culture or practice that is the research focus of the group, and so cannot be full co-subjects. There are, however, certain to be important areas of overlapping interest and practice, which enable them, to a greater or lesser degree, to be analogous or partial co-subjects.

The initiating researchers of a holistic medicine inquiry were not doctors, but they were practitioners in psychotherapy, and became analogous co-subjects, in the action phases, in this form of practice (Heron and Reason, 1985; Reason, 1988c).

The initiators of an inquiry into an organizational culture were not members of the culture, but were academics with a lot of experience in the field, and were partial co-subjects as participant, ethnographic visitors to the culture (Marshall and McLean, 1988).

The initiators in an externally initiated inquiry, once they have done their work of initiation and education, continue on as co-researchers, but *of lesser rank* than the main group. Their role as analogous or partial co-subjects, gives them only a reduced warrant to contribute relevant data to the descriptions and explanations of the reflection phases. This progression from higher rank as initiating researchers, to lower rank as peer co-researchers, is one they can proclaim at the outset. It affirms the democratization of the research process.

The progression, however, may never be complete. The initiators may retain some degree, hopefully reducing, of their initial higher rank status throughout the inquiry, as they make substantive prompts and reminders about key aspects of the inquiry method. This tension around the issue of authentic collaboration is often a major issue for the initiating researchers (Reason, 1994a: 201).

Full or partial form

This distinction overlaps with the previous one and was introduced in the last chapter. In full form inquiries, everyone is involved fully as both co-researcher and co-subject, once they have grasped and internalized the method. I suggest in an earlier paper (Heron, 1981b) that the fullest form means that the inquirers are working together in the action as well as in the reflection phase. This allows for the maximum amount of influence between reflection and action. This influence can occur within each person, and also between people in terms of feedback to another on their action, and learning from the action of the other. The full form, however, also includes inquiries where each person does the action phase on their own away from the group, although this is not so rich in terms of the number of feedback loops within and between people.

In partial form inquiries, all are involved fully as co-researchers and almost all are involved fully as co-subjects, the exceptions being the initiating researchers who are only analogously or partially involved as co-subjects, as explained in the previous section.

A partial form inquiry is the same as an externally initiated inquiry. A full form inquiry may be internally initiated, or it may be self-generated and self-directed by the group bootstrap approach.

Same, reciprocal, counterpartal or mixed role

These four sorts are to do with inquiries that focus on practice within a given social role. A same role inquiry is one in which co-inquirers all have the same role, such as doctor or health visitor, and are researching aspects of their practice within that role. Many of the inquiries cited in this book are of this sort.

In a reciprocal role inquiry, the co-inquirers are two or more people who interact intensively within a role of equal status, such as spouse, partner, friend, colleague, and inquire into that interaction. Peer relationships of this kind can readily be turned into ongoing co-operative inquiries, thus entirely closing the gap between research and everyday life. I know of unreported examples of this sort.

A counterpartal role inquiry is one in which the co-inquirers include, for example, both doctors and patients, or health visitors and some members of the families they visit, and the inquiry is about the practitioner–client relationship and what it is seeking to achieve. I don't know of any reported examples of counterpartal role inquiries. But they are extremely promising and are bound to occur sooner or later in the interests of client empowerment and practitioner deprofessionalization.

Finally, a mixed role inquiry is one that includes different kinds of practitioner. If they don't work together, then they may explore similarities and differences in their several modalities of practice. If they collaborate, then they may focus on aspects of this:

> This was the case in the pioneer work of Peter Reason in this field: he launched an inquiry involving general medical practitioners and different complementary therapists into issues of power and conflict involved in their collaboration (Reason, 1991).

Inside or outside

This option depends on what the inquiry is about and where, therefore, the action phase is focused. Inside inquiries are those in which all the action phases occur in the same place within the whole group: they include group process inquiries and group-based inquiries.

A group process inside inquiry is looking at what goes on within the inquiry group: members are studying their individual and collective experience of group phenomena. So the group stays together during the action phases, since that is what the inquiry is all about.

In a three-day inquiry in 1982 in Dublin, which remains unreported, a group which I was invited to launch chose to explore the vague notion of 'group energy'. In the first reflection phase we gave it a provisional meaning and devised a structured group exercise to check this out. After the first action phase doing the exercise, we had a second reflection phase to make sense of the exercise, to modify the group energy notion, and to devise a second group exercise to check out the modified meaning. And so on.

A group-based inside inquiry is rather more varied in its format. All the action phases occur when the whole group is together in the same space, but some phases may involve each person doing their own individual activity side by side with everyone else; or there may be paired or small group activities done side by side. Other action phases may involve the whole group in a collective activity.

A full form inquiry into altered states of consciousness was group-based using this sort of combination: of the six action phases, two involved people doing individual activities side by side, and four involved collective activity (Heron, 1988c).

An outside inquiry is about what goes on in group members' working and/ or personal lives, or in some special project, outside the group meetings. So the group come together for the reflection phases to share data, make sense of it, revise their thinking, and in the light of all this plan the next action phase. Group members disperse for each action phase, which is undertaken on an individual basis out there in the world.

A group of health visitors had six reflection meetings over a four-month period to consider strategies used individually on the job with families in the action phases between these meetings (Traylen, 1994).

Similarly with the inquiry into the principles and practice of whole person medicine: the principles were refined in the whole group at weekend reflection meetings, every six weeks, from data generated by individual professional practice in the six-week action phase (Heron and Reason, 1985; Reason, 1988c).

A group of co-counsellors decided to explore their handling of distress-driven reactions in everyday life: they met together once a week for several weeks to reflect together on the data each person had generated during his or her individual week-long action phase, and in the light of that to plan the next action phase (Heron and Reason, 1982).

An outside inquiry could also involve elements of an inside inquiry: for example, a group of people who work in some organization as a team, and who are inquiring into the work of the team within the organization. In this case the action phase would include a good deal of interaction between group members as they go about their teamwork on the job.

The inside and outside option is the same as Cunningham's distinction between Type I and Type II kinds of collaborative research (Cunningham, 1988). He points out that an outside or Type II inquiry may *also* choose to do some inside, group process or Type I inquiry. But whether or not an outside inquiry chooses to explore its inside processes as an extension of its formal inquiry, it will certainly need to take some time out to uncover and heal interpersonal tensions and related processes within the group so that they do not accumulate and distort the inquiry process. This kind of validity procedure is discussed in Chapter 8.

Closed or open boundary

Closed boundary inquiries are concerned entirely with what is going on within and between the researchers and do not include, as part of the inquiry, interaction between the researchers and others in the wider world. Open boundary inquiries do include such interaction as part of the *action phases* of the inquiry. So they are usually outside inquiries; but an outside inquiry does not necessarily have an open boundary, since action phases out there in the world apart from the inquiry group need not involve interaction with other people.

> The youth worker inquiry into how people learn had a closed boundary: the inquirers focused exclusively on their own learning processes in subgroups and the whole group (De Venney-Tiernan et al., 1994). Also the first co-counselling inquiry: it involved pairs of co-counsellors exploring client states and strategies, with no reference to anyone outside the inquiry group (Heron and Reason, 1981).

> The inquiry into health visitors' practice in working with families had an open boundary (Traylen, 1994). And the holistic medicine inquiry in which GPs were engaged with the practice of holistic medicine with their NHS patients (Heron and Reason, 1985; Reason, 1988c). Also the second co-counselling inquiry (Heron and Reason, 1982), which explored how the group members managed the restimulation of old emotional hurt in their contact with people at work and at home.

The main issue for open boundary inquiries is whether to elicit data and feedback from people at the open boundary with whom the inquirers interact in the action phases, but who are not themselves part of the inquiry. If no data is generated, a valuable source of relevant feedback and information is ignored. If the data is generated, but the people by whom it is generated remain outside the inquiry and have no say in how it is explained and used, then a norm of co-operative inquiry is infringed. One solution is to include some of them, or their representatives, within the inquiry group, which will, of course, radically shift the whole focus of the group.

None of the three open boundary inquiries mentioned above really got to grips with this issue. Some doctors in the holistic medicine inquiry made some attempts to elicit data from selected patients, but this data was minimal and little use was made of it.

Some inquiries have an open boundary in the *reflection phases*.

In the holistic medicine inquiry we invited to several reflection meetings a visiting luminary to give a talk to the whole group, to participate in the reflection process and give us feedback on it. These luminaries were invited

> to inject new perspectives, refresh our thinking, contribute to our programme design, and challenge the limitations of our inquiry. (Reason, 1988c: 105)

The women university staff inquiry on gender issues in the workplace invited external participation: women beyond the group were invited to share their stories with the group.

> With external participation, it is possible to avoid several of the implicit dangers of collaborative inquiry. Participants are not assumed to fully resource their own inquiry but are able to draw on knowledges beyond the group. External voices can also present a challenge to the paradigms within which the inquiry/co-researchers are located. (Treleaven, 1994: 156)

Apollonian or Dionysian

Nietzsche applied the Apollonian–Dionysian distinction to Greek drama in his first book, *The Birth of Tragedy*, published in 1872. He took Apollo as a symbol of the rational, controlled and lucid aspects of Greek culture, and Dionysus as a symbol of the opposite. Ruth Benedict used the terms to distinguish two 'patterns' of culture, one like the Zuni Indians encouraging control in social responses, the other like the Kwakiutl Indians' more emotional expression. Evans-Pritchard called this 'the rustling-of-the-wind-in-the-palm-trees' kind of anthropology. For Jungians, the mythical and archetypally correct opposition to Dionysus are the Titans (Lopez-Pedraza, 1995).

Be that all as it may, I use the terms to refer to two different and complementary co-operative inquiry cultures. The Apollonian inquiry takes a more rational, linear, systematic, controlling and explicit approach to the process of cycling between reflection and action. Each reflection phase is used to reflect on data from the last action phase, and to apply this thinking in planning the next action phase, with due regard to whether the forthcoming actions of participants will be divergent or dissimilar and convergent or similar. This is the rational cycle of sequenced steps – plan, act, observe and reflect, then re-plan – familiar in action research (Kemmis and McTaggart, 1988). The two co-counselling inquiries, and the whole person medicine inquiry, all initiated by myself and Peter Reason, have been Apollonian inquiry cultures (Heron and Reason, 1981, 1982, 1985).

The Dionysian inquiry takes a more imaginal, expressive, spiralling, diffuse, impromptu and tacit approach to the interplay between making sense and action. In each reflection phase, group members share improvisatory, imaginative ways of making sense of what went on in the last action phase. The implications of this sharing for future action are not worked out by rational pre-planning. They gestate, diffuse out into the domain of action later on with yeast-like effect, and emerge as a creative response to the situation.

Treleaven's inquiry with a women's staff development group in a university is a powerful example of this kind of culture. The group used story-telling to share and illumine experiences of gender issues in the workplace, which was the focus of the inquiry. They made space to speak about their bodies and allowed themselves to express the emotions that accompanied their stories. These kinds of sharing were catalysts to new understanding and action.

> As emergent processes within different individual stories have unfolded, changes have been produced in the everyday lives of some of the women, in the way the group conducts itself, and more widely in the horizontal diffusion into parts of the organization. This centrifugal process of diffusion has brought stories of action research cycles which could be described as spiralling outward, connecting women within and beyond the group. (Treleaven, 1994: 149–50)

She uses a metaphor of spot fires to illumine this process of organizational change through the diffusion of action by group members:

> The process of horizontal diffusion seemed to be well described by the metaphor of sparks being ignited in joint collaboration, starting another fire at some distance separate from but connected to the same source of energy; of the fires clearing heavy loads of undergrowth, forcing seeds open to the heat, and encouraging the cycle of bush regeneration. (Treleaven, 1994: 151)

Marshall and McLean, who inquired into the organizational culture of a local district council with a group of people working in it, were from a university department and had Apollonian research propensities. The inquiry group evolved a much more Dionysian research style, consistent with their organizational culture. Marshall and McLean give an interesting account of this tension:

> The group seemed to be taking its own line, doing what was intuitively right rather than carefully discussing and planning the research process. The emphasis was more on *reflection in action* than on addressing each as distinct and separate. Once more we realized that here was an expression of a cultural quality; in this case, what came to be called the 'right brain' property of the culture. Things tend to happen as a result of intense and at times chaotic activity and less as a tidy culmination of systematic planning . . .

The dilemma that this posed for us was whether we should be pushing the group for more discussion of research methods or moving forward with what 'felt right', allowing process issues to emerge *as they become relevant to the group*. We had some confidence in taking the latter approach as this seemed to be how the group was already working *and* had resulted in discussions of possible collusion, confidentiality and so on. We felt that they had 'a fund of knowledge' about how to do research which our presence was helping them to tap . . .

We admitted to each other being impressed by the culture, despite ourselves and despite an initial scepticism. This was a particularly interesting struggle between feeling that we were becoming acculturated – and simultaneously seeking to retain a detached and more discriminating view. (Marshall and McLean, 1988: 213–14)

Whether inquiry cultures are Apollonian or Dionysian, what they have in common is the intentional interplay between making sense and action, and the realization that both the meaning and the action need progressively to emerge as the inquiry proceeds. The content of the inquiry as a whole, with all that goes on in its phases of reflection and action, cannot be preplanned; and the preplanning of an action phase in the Apollonian cultures is piecemeal, done one at a time, each plan emerging from what has gone before. So there is a sense in which any inquiry in its overall format has a predominantly emergent or Dionysian format.

One weakness of the rational preplanning of action in the Apollonian culture is that this does not allow action to gestate and germinate in its own good time after the sharing of the reflection phase, to emerge in creative response to unfolding events in the domain of application. A weakness of the Dionysian culture is the ambiguity of the connection, in some instances, between the actions out there and the sharing that has gone on in the group.

I take the view that the two cultures are not separate, independent entities between which a choice must be made, but rather bipolar and inter-dependent values and processes within any inquiry culture. The polarity is between the mental and the vital, between prior shaping by thought and imaginative openness to living, creative impulse. This is a complementarity at the heart of all human endeavour.

There is thus a creative tension between the Apollonian and Dionysian principles which fluctuates depending on the pole the inquiry inclines towards. An excess of the Apollonian tendency to make everything controlled and explicit, and the inquiry will lose depth, range and richness, will overfocus and miss the point. An excess of the Dionysian propensity to allow for improvisation, creative spontaneity, synchronicity, situational responsiveness and tacit diffusion, and the inquiry will lose its focus and cease to be an inquiry. Any effective inquiry will have some elements of both, even when the emphasis is clearly towards one pole rather than the other. An inquiry could also move between the poles quite explicitly, some research cycles being Apollonian, some Dionysian, in style; and could seek on other cycles to find an equipoise between the two.

Informative or transformative

This is a fundamental distinction and picks out the primary poles of co-operative inquiry, its complementary supporting pillars. Will the inquiry be descriptive of some domain of experience, being informative and explanatory about it? Or will it be exploring practice within some domain, being transformative of it? The descriptive and the practical are interdependent in various ways. Holding a descriptive focus means you have to adopt some practice that enables you to do so. Here the information you are seeking to gather about a domain determines what actions you perform within it. Having a practical focus throws into relief a lot of descriptive data. Here the transformative actions within a domain are your primary intent and the information you generate about their domain will be a secondary offshoot of them.

If the inquiry is mainly descriptive and explanatory, the primary outcomes will be propositions about the nature of the domain. Secondary outcomes will be the skills involved in generating the descriptive data. If the inquiry is mainly practical, the primary outcomes will be skills, that is, the practices acquired, and the situational changes they have brought about. Secondary outcomes will be propositions which (1) report these practices and changes, and evaluate them by the principles they presuppose; and (2) give information about the domain where the practices have been applied, information which is a consequence of this application.

An inquiry may aim to be both informative and transformative, one before or after the other. It can be descriptive first in order more effectively to be practical and transformative. Or it can be practical and transformative first, in order to be richly descriptive, like cleaning a painting to find out what is there. In between these poles, it may be informative-transformative in balanced measure.

In Chapter 6 on outcomes I advance the view that you get richer descriptions of a domain if your primary intent is to be practical and transformative within it, than you do if you pursue descriptions directly. To put it crudely, the world needs cleaning up and we get a better and deeper view of it when we set out to acquire skills to transform it. In general, throughout this book I suggest the interdependence of the informative and the transformative, while also asserting the primacy of the latter. However, it is not wise to be doctrinaire about this primacy, and various kinds of sequencing and blending between the informative and the transformative will have a claim, depending on the circumstances.

Of the several inquiries I have so far referenced, the health visitors', the youth workers', the holistic medicine, the second co-counselling inquiries were all transformative, being concerned with changes of practice in daily life or on the job. The altered states inquiry was transformative of states of mind through a variety of practices, generating incipient information about another reality. The women's university staff inquiry was informative and transformative in mutual interplay: by members telling their stories depicting gender issues they generated transformative initiatives on the job. The organizational culture inquiry was informative with transformative implications for the future. The first co-counselling one was primarily informative, being descriptive of client states, with a secondary attention to transformative strategies that bring about changes of state. The greater thrust of this sample is toward the transformative.

An outline of inquiry stages

An inquiry starts off moving through four stages, which make one complete cycle that goes from reflection to action and back to reflection again, and there are choices to be made within each of them. What goes on in these stages is explicit in the more formal, controlled Apollonian inquiry, whereas in the Dionysian inquiry it will be more tacit. The next chapter starts off with a fuller account of this brief outline and then discusses all the items in it in much greater detail.

And may I again remind the reader that I do not consider that adopting these stages, explicitly or tacitly, is *the* way to do a co-operative inquiry; it is only *a* way. There cannot be in this field such a thing as the one and only right, proper or correct method. There can only be my, or your, or our view as to what is a good method. What follows is currently my view, based on prior dialogue, and put forward as a contribution to future dialogue.

Stage 1 The first reflection phase for the inquirers to choose

- The focus or topic of the inquiry and the type of inquiry.
- A launching statement of the inquiry topic.
- A plan of action for the first action phase to explore some aspect of the inquiry topic.
- A method of recording experiences during the first action phase.

Stage 2 The first action phase when the inquirers are

- Exploring in experience and action some aspect of the inquiry topic.
- Applying an integrated range of inquiry skills.
- Keeping records of the experiential data generated.

Stage 3 Full immersion in stage 2 with great openness to experience; the inquirers may

- Break through into new awareness.
- Lose their way.
- Transcend the inquiry format.

Stage 4 The second reflection phase; the inquirers share data from the action phase and

- Review and modify the inquiry topic in the light of making sense of data about the explored aspect of it.
- Choose a plan for the second action phase to explore the same or a different aspect of the inquiry topic.
- Review the method of recording data used in the first action phase and amend it for use in the second.

These four stages complete the first full cycle from reflection to action to reflection.

Subsequent stages will

- Continue the inquiry, in cyclic fashion, with the second action phase, full immersion in it, the third reflection phase, the third action phase, full immersion in it, and so on.
- Involve from five to eight full cycles of reflection–action–reflection (including the first) with varying patterns of divergence and convergence, in the action phases, over several aspects of the inquiry topic.
- Include a variety of intentional procedures, in the reflection phases, and of special skills in the action phases, for enhancing the validity of the process.
- End with a major reflection phase for pulling the threads together, clarifying outcomes, and deciding whether to write a co-operative report.
- Be followed by post-group collaboration on writing up any agreed form of report.

Figure 3.1 shows the four stages of the inquiry cycle, and is a model of a full form, inside inquiry, in which everyone is fully involved as both co-researcher and co-subject, and in which people interact with each other in the action phase, hence the stage 2 arrows are both within each participant and between participants.

After the four stages of the first complete cycle, the inquiry continues through several more reflection–action–reflection cycles, the concluding reflection phase of one cycle being continuous with the launching reflection phase of the next. The assumption of this kind of research cycling is that the research outcomes are well-grounded if the topic of the inquiry, both in its parts and as a whole, is taken through as many cycles as possible by as many group members as possible, with as much individual diversity and collective unity of approach as possible. This assumption can only be very partially realized by any one inquiry group, working amidst the exigencies and limitations of everyday human existence.

Positively, research cycling – with its two-way impact between reflection and action – refines, clarifies, extends and deepens the focus of the inquiry, whether informative or transformative. Negatively, such cycling checks,

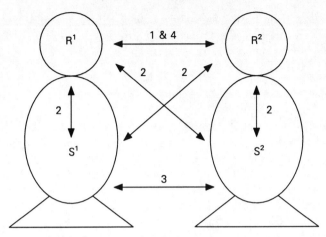

R¹,R². . . Rⁿ = participants as co-researchers
S¹,S². . . Sⁿ = participants as co-subjects

Figure 3.1 *Four stages of the inquiry cycle*

corrects, amends, deletes what the inquirers find ill-grounded about the way they have been framing or practising the focus. The inquirers achieve these effects, in the movement between reflection and action, by exploring the interplay among a few basic parameters of research cycling.

These parameters of research cycling, combined with whatever number of cycles an inquiry group may choose, yield a plethora of possible research designs. I discuss this logic of method initially in section Stage 1 (3) of Chapter 5, and more fully in Chapter 8. In the former, I make the point that Dionysian inquirers will not want to plan their cycles intentionally using research logic. They will prefer to let the logic emerge by tacit infusion from cycle to cycle. Later in Chapter 5, I suggest strongly that the logic of method, for Apollonian inquiries, is secondary to, and supportive of, the interaction between emotional arousal and creative imagination in planning successive cycles and in sustaining the forward thrust of a co-operative inquiry.

Even in the most Apollonian inquiry, it is highly unlikely that the design of a whole series of cycles will be undertaken beforehand. The inquiry and its detailed design is an emergent process. What is done next is a function of what has been learnt about what was done last. You cannot plan too far in advance how usefully to traverse unexplored territory. Too much routinization and prior elaboration of method is likely to miss the point and avoid a deep experiential grounding of the inquiry outcomes.

What every inquiry *will* need to map out in advance is its overall time structure: how many hours, days, weeks or months it will last; how many cycles of reflection and action; and when and for how long the reflection meetings will occur. This is simply so that people can get their diaries organized and make sure the inquiry has a place among their other commitments. For both inside and outside inquiries, somewhere between five and eight major cycles of reflection and action seem to offer enough scope for fruitful outcomes, to judge from use of the method so far.

Extended epistemology and the inquiry cycle

At the end of Chapter 2, I introduced a model of holistic knowing which holds that propositional knowing, expressed in statements that something is the case, is interdependent with three other kinds of knowing: practical knowing, or knowing how to exercise a skill; presentational knowing, an intuitive grasp of the significance of patterns as expressed in graphic, plastic, moving, musical and verbal art-forms; and experiential knowing, imaging and feeling the presence of some energy, entity, person, place, process or thing.

Experiential knowing means unrestricted perception and radical meeting. The former is the creative shaping of a world through the transaction of imaging it. The latter is participative empathy, through which we commune with the inner experience of beings, their mode of awareness. The transaction of imaging a world is not restricted to sense perception, but includes productive imagination and extrasensory perception.

The pyramid and circuit models

I suggested that these kinds of knowing are a systemic whole, a pyramid of upward support in which experiential knowing at the base upholds presentational knowing, which supports propositional or conceptual knowing, which upholds practical knowing, the exercise of skill. This is shown in Figure 3.2.

They can also be construed as a circuit of knowing in which the last, skilled action, leads over into enriched encounter, with a resultant deeper and wider imaginal expression of the patterning of events, thence more complex and comprehensive conceptual models of our reality, and so into more far-reaching and advanced skills; and so on. This circuit is seen in Figure 3.3.

The circuit can further be seen as a spiral, which expands if our knowing is free and unfettered, or contracts if our knowing is psychologically and socially damaged, especially in early life. This model of holistic knowing is elaborated in my book *Feeling and Personhood* (Heron, 1992), and I refer the reader to that for a more substantial account.

Four kinds of belief

Before knowledge comes belief. A belief is beyond mere arbitrariness of mind. It has some sort of warrant that makes it plausible. The claim to know something has a stronger warrant which makes the claim not merely plausible but well-founded. Research cycling seeks to convert plausible

Figure 3.2   *The pyramid of fourfold knowing*

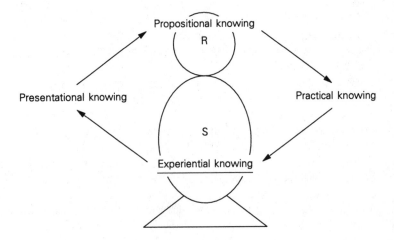

Figure 3.3   *The circuit of fourfold knowing*

belief into well-founded knowledge. It may, of course, make limited progress, and only convert plausible into more plausible belief. The warrant is extended but not enough to substantiate a claim to knowledge.

Just as there are four kinds of knowledge, with the word used in different senses in each case, so there are the equivalent four kinds of belief, with the word 'belief' being used not only in the sense of propositional belief in some statement, but also in the sense of presentational belief as a hunch about, rather than a full intuition of, significant pattern; of practical belief as the process of acquiring a skill rather than knowing how to do it; of experiential belief as inchoate participation in the presence of something rather than a richly fulfilled resonance with it.

This extension of the notion of belief is related to the distinction between 'belief that' and 'belief in'. Propositional belief is belief that something is the case. Presentational belief is belief in one's intuitive feel for a meaningful pattern. Practical belief is belief in one's developing skill. Experiential belief is belief in one's dawning sense of a presence. These forms of believing in, all carry elements of trust and the commitment of faith, as well as their different kinds of provisional and tentative, but not fully substantive, knowing.

With this model of four kinds of cognition, each distinct in its own mode, each with a stage of belief preceding a stage of knowledge, and each interdependent with the others both in terms of grounding and of an empowering circuit, we can get more insight into the four stages of the inquiry cycle.

Four cognitive modes and stages of the inquiry cycle

Stage 1, the first reflection and planning stage, involves mainly propositions. It can also contain important kinds of presentation as group members use their imagination in one or more art-forms, in story and phantasy, to articulate their interests, choose an inquiry focus and plan the first action phase to explore it. This stage, then, includes both *propositional belief* and *presentational belief* regarding what it may be fruitful to inquire into and how to start to do so.

Stage 2, the first action phase, involves a range of special inquiry skills. In informative inquiries, these skills include being fully present with imaginal openness; bracketing off different kinds of imported conceptual frameworks; and generating and holding in mind alternative frameworks. In transformative inquiries, to do with practice, the skills include dynamic congruence among all the components of the practice; spotting and interrupting compulsive or conventional behaviours; being non-attached to the form of one's action; and open to using alternative action frameworks.

Stage 2 then involves *practical belief*: the researchers may not yet *know* how to do all these things; they are learning how to do them. Their competence is not yet well-founded and well-formed, but rudimentary and provisional. Practical belief is belief in my growing ability to exercise a skill. It is a necessary precursor to practical knowledge, which is a well-rehearsed and competent skill.

Stage 3, as I said earlier, is the state of deep immersion in the action phase, a full engagement with the relevant experience or practice, a great openness of encounter with the chosen domain. This stage is the bedrock, the touchstone of the inquiry process, and mainly involves, in the first action phase, *experiential belief* as the precursor to experiential knowledge in later phases.

Experiential knowing is participative knowing, through empathy, resonance, attunement with what is present, in and with the process of radically imaging it, perceptually and in other ways. I know what is present when it declares itself to me through my participative compresence with it. By analogy, experiential belief is tentative, provisional participation, the first inchoate declarations of attunement and resonance, and of deeper imaginal enactment.

In informative inquiries, experiential belief relates to the domain about which knowledge is sought, in transformative inquiries it relates to transformations of a domain brought about by one's practice within it. It can be symbolized in creative presentational form through graphics, colour, sound, movement, drama, story, poetry – which disclose the significant imaginal patterns that manifest the presences with which it tentatively connects.

Stage 4 is the second reflection phase, which makes sense of data generated in the first action phase. There is an interplay between presentational and propositional processes, now having reference to and grounded in prior experience and practice. This leads over into preparing to extend and deepen experience and practice in the next action phase. This interaction between the four cognitive modes launches the shift from opening belief to concluding knowledge, or at least to belief that has better warrants than its opening form.

Through variations of content and method, as the research cycle is repeated several times, the four forms of belief metamorphose through mutual impact into four forms of knowledge, each interdependent with the other. It is the grounding of practical, propositional, presentational and experiential knowledge on each other, as they are brought repeatedly to bear upon each other in a variety of forms over a series of cycles, that makes the research outcomes well-founded, with a well-formed warrant to lay claim to knowledge. The whole process is symbolized in Figure 3.4.

> Ideas and discoveries tentatively reached in early phases can be checked and developed; investigation of one aspect of the inquiry can be related to exploration of other parts; new skills can be acquired and monitored; experiential competences are realized; the group itself becomes more cohesive and self-critical, more skilled in its work. Ideally the inquiry is finished when the initial questions are fully answered in practice, when there is a new congruence between the four kinds of knowing. It is of course rare for a group to complete an inquiry so fully. (Reason and Heron, 1995: 127–28)

An alternative way of mapping out the same process is shown in Figure 3.5. In this model the presentational mode is shown with a full role in the cyclic process. It gives first form to the data from the experiential and practical stages, being an intermediary between these and making sense of the data in propositional form.

I also take the view that the congruence between the forms of knowing has a bipolar form. There is the grounding of one form of knowing on those below it, and this is to do with validity and truth-values. And there is the consummation, by the relatively autonomous emergent form above, of what lies below it. This is about fulfilment, the celebration and manifestation of being-values, ultimately, at the apex, the intrinsic value of human flourishing in emancipated social practice. So congruent knowing is not just about validity and truth. It is also about affirming in action what we deeply value for its own sake. This bipolarity is shown in Figure 3.6, and explained further in Chapter 9. When the bipolar congruence is conceived as a dialectical process, with one aspect flowing into the other, we have Figure 3.7.

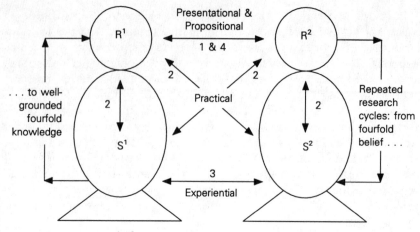

$R^1, R^2 \ldots R^n$ = participants as co-researchers
$S^1, S^2 \ldots S^n$ = participants as co-subjects

Figure 3.4   *Four cognitive modes and stages of the inquiry cycle*

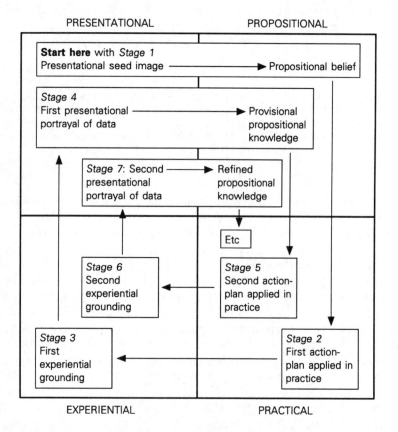

Figure 3.5   *Four cognitive modes and stages of the inquiry cycle (version 2)*

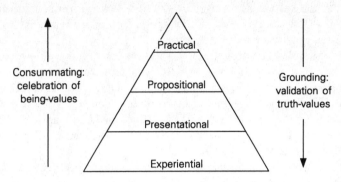

Figure 3.6   *Bipolar congruence*

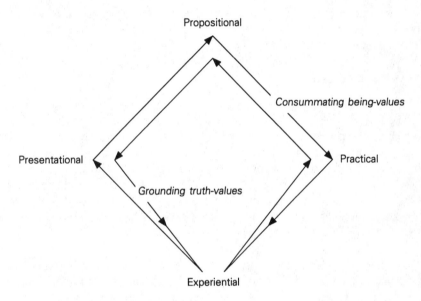

Figure 3.7   *Bipolar congruence as dialectical process*

Validity, special inquiry skills and validity procedures

In Chapter 1 I explained why I think it is essential to retain and redefine terms like 'validity' and not abandon them because of their epistemological and political abuse within positivism. What I basically mean by validity is well-groundedness, soundness, having an adequate warrant.

I think that the outcomes of a co-operative inquiry are valid if they are well-grounded in the forms of knowing which support them. And I believe that the forms of knowing are valid if they are well-grounded in the procedures adopted to free them from distortion, and in the special skills involved in the knowing process. The validity of each form of knowing also depends on how sound it is in the light of standards internal to it, of autonomous criteria at its own level.

So, for example, when practice is a valid outcome, it is well-grounded on propositional knowing by being evaluated in terms of a range of verbally stated criteria of sound practice. These include executive, technical, psychosocial, intentionality and value criteria, as defined in Chapter 9. And a valid practice is one that is sound by its own internal standard, which is having the knack, an inherent knowing of the excellence of its doing. I discuss this notion of a knack in Chapter 6.

I take the view that validity itself, concern with the justification of truth-values, is interdependent with that which transcends it, the celebration of being-values, of what is intrinsically worthwhile in our experience. This is discussed in Chapter 9.

Next I present a simple overview of special inquiry skills, and of validity procedures. Chapter 7 elaborates on the skills, Chapter 8 on the procedures and Chapter 9 on validity as such.

Special inquiry skills

I have in mind here the special skills involved in the forms of knowing used in the action phases of the inquiry, when people are busy with the particular kind of experience or action that is the focus of the research. A bald list of these skills looks daunting. In fact, I believe they start to develop simply by being engaged in a committed way with the cycle of inquiry.

The first group relate to radical perception in informative inquiries where the purpose is to be descriptive and explanatory of the inquiry domain. All these skills relate to what is going on in a person when he or she is actually there, engaged with the experience.

Being present   This is to do with empathy, with meeting and feeling the presence of people and a world. The skill is about harmonic resonance and attunement, participating in the inner experience of people and the mode of awareness, the prehension, of things. It is indwelling the inward declaration made by the being of the other. It is necessarily associated with the next.

Imaginal openness   This is to do with being receptive to the meaning inherent in the total process of shaping people and a world by perceptually imaging them with sensory and nonsensory imagery. I enact and participate in their appearing and intuit its meaning. The skill is about imaginal grasp, the intuition of pattern meaning.

Bracketing   This is to do with managing the conceptual labels and models embedded in the process of perceiving people and a world. The skill is about holding in abeyance the classifications and constructs we impose on our perceiving, so that we can be more open to its inherent primary, imaginal meaning.

Reframing This is to do with the conceptual revisioning in perceiving a world. With this skill we not only hold in abeyance the constructs being imposed on our perceiving, we also try out alternative ones for their creative capacity to articulate an account of people and a world. We are open to reframing the assumptions of any conceptual context or perspective.

The second group relate to radical practice in transformative inquiries where the purpose is to engage in some action that seeks change within its domain. Again, all these skills relate to what is going on in a person when he or she is engaged with the action, busy doing it.

Dynamic congruence This is about practical knowing, knowing how to act. The skill goes way beyond ordinary competent action. It means being aware, while acting, of the bodily form of the behaviour, of its strategic form and guiding norms, of its purpose or end and underlying values, of its motives, of its external context and supporting beliefs, and of its actual outcomes. At the same time it means being aware of any lack of congruence between these different facets of the action and adjusting them accordingly.

Emotional competence This is the ability to identify and manage emotional states in various ways. These include keeping action free from distorted reactions to current events that are driven by the unprocessed distress of earlier years; and from the limiting influence of inappropriate conventions acquired by social conditioning.

Non-attachment The ability here is to wear lightly and without fixation the purpose, strategy, form of behaviour and motive which have been chosen as the form of the action. This is the knack of non-attachment, not investing one's identity and emotional security in the action, while remaining fully intentional about it and committed to it.

Self-transcending intentionality This skill involves having in mind, while busy with one overall form of action, one or more alternative forms, and considering their possible relevance and applicability to the total situation.

Validity procedures

The purpose of these procedures is to free the various forms of knowing involved in the inquiry process from the distortion of uncritical subjectivity, that is, a lack of discriminating awareness. This occurs when, for example, the mind fails to do justice to the claims of the given cosmos in which it participates, to the claims of appropriate method, and to the claims of dialogue and engagement with other minds involved in the same arena of participative knowing. All the following validity procedures need to be planned for, or applied, within the reflection phases.

Research cycling If the research topic as a whole, and different subwholes and parts singly and in combination, are taken round several cycles of reflection and action, then experiential and reflective forms of knowing progressively refine each other, through two-way negative and positive feedback.

Divergence and convergence Within the action phase of any one cycle, or as between the action phases of two adjacent cycles, the co-inquirers can diverge over different parts or subwholes of the topic, or converge on the same part or subwhole, or on the whole. This gives rise to innumerable combinations of divergence and convergence which, expressed through research cycling, can enable all forms of knowing to articulate the research topic more thoroughly.

Reflection and action Since reflective and experiential forms of knowing refine each other through cycling to and fro between reflection and action phases, then this effect also depends on getting a right balance between these two phases, so that there is neither too much reflection on too little experience, nor too little reflection on too much experience.

Aspects of reflection Within the reflection phase, there is a balance between presentational (expressive or artistic) ways of making sense and propositional (verbal/intellectual) ways. And within intellectual ways, there is balance between four mental activities: describing, evaluating descriptions, building theory, and applying what has been learned in one cycle to the management of the next.

Challenging uncritical subjectivity This is done with a simple procedure which authorizes any inquirer at any time to adopt formally the role of devil's advocate in order to question the group as to whether one of several forms of uncritical subjectivity is afoot. These forms include: not noticing, or not mentioning, aspects of experience that show up the limitations of a conceptual model or programme of action; unaware fixation on false assumptions implicit in guiding ideas or action plans; unaware projections distorting the inquiry process; lack of rigour in inquiry method and in applying validity procedures.

Chaos and order This is not so much a procedure as a mental set which allows for the interdependence of chaos and order, of nescience and knowing. It is an attitude which tolerates and undergoes, without premature closure, inquiry phases which are confused and disorientated, ambiguous and uncertain, conflicted and inharmonious, generally lost and groping. These phases tend in their own good time to convert into new levels of order. But since there is no guarantee that they will do so, they are risky and edgy. Tidying them up prematurely out of anxiety leads to pseudo-knowledge.

Managing unaware projections The group adopts some regular method for surfacing and processing repressed templates of past emotional trauma, which may get unawarely projected out, distorting thought, perception and action within the inquiry. The very process of researching the human condition may stir up these templates and trigger them into compulsive invasion of the inquiring mind.

Authentic collaboration   Since intersubjective dialogue is a key component in refining the forms of knowing, it is important that it manifests through authentic collaboration. One aspect of this is that group members internalize and make their own the inquiry method so that they become on a peer footing with the initiating researchers. The other aspect is that each group member is fully and authentically engaged in each action phase and in each reflection phase; and in each reflection phase is fully expressive, fully heard, and fully influential in decision-making, on a peer basis with every other group member.

4

Initiating an Inquiry Group

The purpose of this chapter is to review some of the issues involved in enabling members of an inquiry group to become authentic and effective co-researchers. In all the co-operative inquiries I know about, this enabling has been undertaken by one or two initiating researchers who have some prior knowledge or experience of the method. However, I must point out that this is not necessary. A new inquiry group can be entirely co-operative and peer directed from the start. This is the bootstrap group mentioned in Chapter 3.

One reason for my writing a book like this is so that all the members of a bootstrap group can read it, reach agreement about how to modify the method to suit their own needs and interests, and then set about putting it into practice. From the very outset they can rotate among themselves any special roles which look after different important strands of the inquiry process. I imagine this will happen more and more as time goes by, and look forward to it.

However, there is little doubt that many inquiry groups will occur because one or two initiating researchers call them into being; and that such groups will find it convenient and helpful for the initiators to guide them into use of the method while they gradually make it their own. So the role of the initiating researcher is likely to be with us for quite a while, with all the creative tensions that go with it.

This chapter is therefore written for and from the standpoint of the initiating researcher. But any bootstrap group can equally well take advantage of it and find its own imaginative ways of dealing with the issues raised. I would be interested to hear from any such group how it gets on.

What follows is presented in an orderly and systematic manner. What happens in the living presence of a group will be much more creatively delightful, disorganized, incomplete and distraught.

Three-stranded initiation

The initiating researchers of a co-operative inquiry group have, from the outset, three closely interdependent and fundamental issues to consider:

- The initiation of group members into the methodology of the inquiry so that they can make it their own.

- The emergence of participative decision-making and authentic collaboration so that the inquiry becomes truly co-operative.
- The creation of a climate in which emotional states can be identified, so that distress and tension aroused by the inquiry can be openly accepted and processed, and joy and delight in it and with each other can be freely expressed.

The first of these is to do with cognitive and methodological empowerment, the second with political empowerment, and the third with emotional and interpersonal empowerment. Initiating researchers need some skills in all these three ways of empowering others. The combination is familiar to the whole person educator whose analogous concern is to facilitate:

- Self-directed learning by students of some content and method.
- Increasing student participation in all aspects of educational decision-making: the objectives, topics, resources, methods, programme and pacing of learning; the assessment of learning, and the evaluation of the course.
- Integration of cognitive with emotional and interpersonal aspects of learning.

At the induction meeting, the initiating researchers will be wise to make clear that the three strands are basic to the inquiry process, and to invite only those to whom the three strands appeal to join the project. Then they seek a contract in which everyone who wants to join makes a commitment to bring the strands into being.

It is pretty important that this contract is not the result of either rapid conversion or persuasive coercion. It needs to be a fully voluntary and well informed agreement to realize the values of autonomy, co-operation and wholeness which underlie the three strands. A co-operative inquiry is a community of value, and its value premises are its foundation. If people are excited by and attuned to these premises, they join, otherwise not. Getting clear about all this at the outset makes for good craftspersonship later.

Suppose there are two initiating researchers. Once the inquiry gets under way they may nurture the strands by the following sorts of strategy:

- They co-facilitate the emergence of all three strands, or they divide the three strands among themselves, each taking responsibility for one or two of them.
- As facilitators of any strand, they move along an intentional gradient from presenting conceptual models and making directive proposals to which assent is sought, through prompting and fully consultative processes, until autonomous collaborative initiatives take off. This is a basic sequence in which the facilitators move from hierarchy, deciding for participants, through co-operation, deciding with participants, to autonomy, in which decision-making is transferred fully to and taken over by participants. A good deal of material about the use of these

three decision-modes is given in *The Facilitators' Handbook* (Heron, 1989).

- As part of this process they may invite, and offer supervisory guidance and support to, different individuals or subgroups to take responsibility for each strand. Those people will then alert the group to relevant issues, and propose and facilitate ways of dealing with them. These facilitator roles can be rotated around the group as the inquiry proceeds, starting with those group members who already have the appropriate kind of skills.
- As the initiating researchers' active facilitation, or supervisory facilitation, on each strand progressively decreases, they participate more and more on a par with everyone else.
- They may make it clear at a certain point that they are retiring from the primary facilitator role entirely. Or they may still formally maintain, with the assent of the group, a residual primary facilitator profile. In this case, they occasionally exercise the role when it seems appropriate and necessary to do so, for example facilitating the current group member facilitator in some crisis of omission or commission.

The initiating researcher of the youth workers' inquiry into their own learning processes launched the group, on its induction day, into identifying and choosing roles. Thus the roles were in place from the first day of the inquiry proper. These roles included: group facilitators to plan and run the whole group reflection meetings; organizers to deal with written communications between these meetings; group recorders to take notes of the whole group process; personal recorders (everyone keeping a diary of their own inquiry experience); distress managers (everyone available to play this role for anyone in need); two people to brief absent members about what they missed. Although the group members started to plan and facilitate group reflection meetings from the very outset, they still needed the guidance and support of the initiating facilitator, who thus remained in role as superordinate facilitator for the early sessions.

> At the start of the research project, there was obviously a high level of dependency upon Annette [the initiating researcher], primarily regarding the research methodology. This diminished as we learned through our own experience of the project that the initiator meant what she said, that is, that *our* experiences, ideas and feelings were as important as hers.
>
> It also diminished as we perceived the initiator less as an expert and more as an equal co-researcher. A major turning point in this was 'The Issue of the Questionnaire' as it became known. This led to co-researchers using each other for support and to answer queries, rather than addressing these solely to Annette as had occurred in the first four to six weeks of the project.
>
> Similarly, the six co-researchers who had taken on the role of facilitator or co-facilitator of the whole group days experienced a dependency on Annette for the planning of the earlier ones. However, as we gained more confidence in this role, and our understanding and knowledge of the process deepened,

this dependency diminished to the extent that Annette was not involved in helping to plan or facilitate any part of our Days 5, 6 or 7. (De Venney-Tiernan et al., 1994: 132)

This quote is from a part of the report written by group members, who assert strongly here and elsewhere that they moved beyond the stage of dependency into a genuine collaborative ownership of the project. By contrast, here is a quote from the two initiating researchers of an inquiry into supervision in child protection agencies. They are commenting on the sixth and final reflection meeting in which

the discussion was rambling and endless. Reiterating the agenda failed to focus the group, as did reminding them of the time remaining. Our distress was clear in the post-session tape: 'I was in absolute panic half-way through . . . they kept losing their way . . . none of them were being concise or crisp and they knew we only had today . . .' The burden of ownership is evident from our transcript. We had considerable doubts about whether it was still willingly shared by the group. There seemed to be a lot of unfinished business about. (Cosier and Glennie, 1994: 116)

So it is a knife-edge business. When initiating researchers launch an inquiry it is the nature of the case that there can be no absolute parity of influence between them and their co-opted inquirers. They can move from appropriately strong and primary influence, to significant peer consultant influence; and on the way may degenerate into either over-control or under-control. It is a mistake to suppose that there can be a simple parity of influence and to try to achieve it; or to imagine that it has ever been fully achieved in an inquiry involving from five to eight full research cycles. What undoubtedly can be achieved as the inquiry proceeds is a sufficient degree of non-dependent collaborative reflection and management, for the research to be genuinely *with* people, and not about them or on them. I pick up this theme again in Chapter 8.

The inquiry strand

Facilitators of the inquiry strand have some fairly obvious tasks. The first is conceptual, to enable people to grasp the method. Fortunately, the idea of the method is not only radical, it is also very simple, however challenging it may be to practise. The basics can be simply explained and readily understood, since they speak directly to the human condition. The initiating researchers can prepare explanatory handouts, and can recommend selected readings, such as parts of *Human Inquiry in Action* (Reason, 1988a), of *Participation in Human Inquiry* (Reason, 1994a), and of this book.

The approach of Dionysian and Apollonian initiators to the inquiry strand will differ. The former will stress more the way in which action emerges by diffusion from the reflection phase, being improvisatory and situation-responsive. The latter will stress more the intentional preplanning of action phases in the prior reflection phases. Other initiators may present these as bipolar interweaving aspects of one inquiry culture, and encourage the group to find its own cultural identity.

At the induction day, the initiators can expound the basic ideas, with supporting visual aids and discussion. They can help people ground them in a series of mini-cycles of reflection and action, done in pairs, on some immediately accessible topic, like the distinction between action and intention, or between the eyes and the gaze. They can also outline some of the basic validity procedures, and again invite people to have a mini-experience of them. The importance of emotional processing can be explored by people in pairs taking turns to share any anxieties and fears evoked by the thought of participating in the inquiry.

Once the inquiry is under way, in the earlier sessions there will need to be:

- Intermittent and brief presentations, with discussion, as reminders of various aspects of the method.
- Well-timed prompts, which suggest in a consultative mode what it may or may not be appropriate to do at different stages of a reflection meeting; and, as a complement to this . . .
- Well-timed invitations to group members to reflect on what they are now doing, and to identify for themselves what it may or may not be appropriate to do next.
- Occasional coaching over the shoulder of a group member who has taken on the role of facilitating the inquiry process.

There are certain key aspects of the inquiry process which represent a major challenge to its initiators. It is only too easy to collude with a group not wanting to know about them. Some of these are:

- Evaluating, in the light of appropriate criteria, descriptive accounts shared in a reflection phase, when making sense of the prior action phase. The tendency is for people to stay at the level of a description without rising out of it to the level at which they can start to evaluate its soundness.
- Being clearly intentional, in an Apollonian inquiry, in applying the learning from the prior action phase to planning the next action phase. This item tends to follow from the previous one. Without *evaluating* data from the last action phase you haven't got much of a warrant for planning the next one.
- Being clearly *intentional*, in a Dionysian inquiry, about *not* preplanning the next action phase. A Dionysian inquiry is not sleepwalking. It is very aware about its use of creative pregnancy.
- Assessing at regular intervals various aspects of the soundness of the inquiry process.

The last point is crucial. We live in a culture in which no-one is educated in the art of self and peer assessment. Through long years of social conditioning to its absence, there is malaise, impotence, confusion and bewilderment about adopting it. The group needs some skilled facilitation to help it discover the excitement of taking the process on board, and to realize that an inquiry which doesn't question its own soundness is simply not an inquiry. There are several validity procedures which a group can adopt for this kind of ongoing assessment, and these are discussed in Chapter 8.

Initiating research facilitators are busy with the paradox of leading people into freedom. They are coaching people in a discipline of method, of liberatory praxis, and are articulating it in some detail. If they coach in a way that is continually sensitive to how what they do and when they do it is respectful of human autonomy and empowering of it, then all will be well. People will take the method on board, and reinvent it to express their own creativity. If they coach in a way that is possessive of an orthodoxy to which others must subscribe, they launch yet another generation of researchers who are oppressed, and will oppress others, by the use of 'proper method'. This will produce conformist, but certainly not co-operative, inquiry.

The collaboration strand

This strand is about how much each individual contributes to the inquiry and is open to listen to, learn from, share with and negotiate with others. This applies mainly to the reflection phase, both in making sense of what has been done and in planning what to do next. If people get fully involved in these matters, their involvement in the action phase will follow. There are some simple guidelines the facilitator of this strand can follow. With respect to making sense of the data from the last action phase, the facilitator can:

- Make space for each person to present his or her own data to the others, in the whole group or in subgroups, to reflect on it out loud and discuss it with the others.
- When the group is discussing and reflecting together on all the presented and collated data, make space for everyone to have a fair amount of air time. Ensure that high contributors do not dominate the proceedings constraining the others to be medium or low (or nil) contributors. This can be done by:
  - Raising consciousness of the issue by giving the group feedback on its pattern of contribution rates.
  - Inviting everyone to be responsible for managing contributions equitably: by speaking out, by reaching out to bring each other in and draw each other out, by practising restraint if one is a compulsive and competitive high contributor.
  - Simple verbal and nonverbal facilitation methods of bringing low contributors in, drawing them out and of shutting high contributors out.

- The occasional use of a round, especially for an important issue, in which each person takes a turn to express their views on it.
- The occasional use of the ground-rule that no-one speaks twice until everyone has spoken once.
- The occasional use of procedures such as: no-one speaks until handed the mace by the current speaker; no-one speaks until sitting in a fish-bowl in the centre of the group, and no-one stays there talking with others in the bowl for too long.
- The occasional use of three subgroups, one of high contributors, one of medium and one of low contributors.
- Remember the importance of story-telling, dramatized accounts, role-plays, poetry, the free use of metaphor and analogy; and of the whole range of presentational methods, including photos, film, drawings, graphics, paintings, sculptures, music, song, dance, movement, mime. Remember how these can be used powerfully as a first step in data presentation; and as part of an ongoing dialectical interplay with conceptual, analytic accounts. I discuss this in more detail in Chapter 5.
- Make sure that you or someone else has the role of maintaining a visual aid that shows the key themes, issues and outcomes of the group's reflection.

When the group is planning the first action phase, the facilitator needs to raise the consciousness of the group about what method of decision-making they are going to use. This means:

- Present to the group a range of decision-making methods such as:
  - Unanimity.
  - A percentage majority vote, such as a seventy-five percent majority.
  - A simple majority vote, that is, any percentage majority above fifty.
  - Consensus: the contract here is that when the minority realizes it has been heard, understood and still disagreed with, it yields to the majority.
  - Gathering the sense of the meeting: anyone may gather at any time and if the gathering doesn't take, then the cycle of discussion and gathering is repeated until a gathering does take.
  - An elected leader negotiates with people to integrate his or her proposals with theirs, then seeks assent by consensus or gathering the sense.
  - An elected leader follows his or her own light after hearing everyone's preferences and proposals.
  - An elected leader follows his or her own light after collecting in relevant information only.
- Discuss these with the group and help people to choose one that seems best suited to their inquiry needs. Suggest they use it for an agreed period, then review it.
- In the discussion of options, issues and possible outcomes prior to

making a decision, bear in mind all the strategies listed above f
managing contribution rates.

- Propose an absolutely basic ground-rule that before any decision, each
  person states out loud their personal preference before participating in
  any group choice. This is based on the principle that no-one can be
  genuinely co-operative until they have established their autonomous
  position. People who do not really know where they stand on an issue
  have no proper ground for co-operation, and can only huddle together
  in the middle of a fudge. The first step for someone to find out where
  they stand is to identify the different emotional values the options have
  for them, since this will lead them to their preference.
- When facilitating the final decision-making, use the chosen model,
  remind people of it and gently but firmly keep everyone on track.

One fundamental anxiety for any community or co-operative group is
generated by the challenge of realizing personal autonomy in the context of
a fully collaborative venture. Meeting this challenge means the celebration
and affirmation of differences both when they are compatible with
collaboration and when they are not. A classic symptom of the anxiety at
work, and of the challenge unmet, is the group demand for unanimity in
decision-making. The youth workers' inquiry into their own learning processes uncovered this one.

> Another early but major dependency was the group's need to have a 100 per cent
> consensus on every decision – majorities, however overwhelming, were not
> sufficient. It was only on Day 3 that this was articulated by some co-researchers
> to be a block to progress, creating frustration and eating up valuable group time.
> Once the dependency was identified we could talk it through and came to the
> conclusion that unanimity in decision-making would be sought, but where it
> proved to be unobtainable in the time available, a majority decision would be
> taken. With the additional mechanism that individuals could renegotiate the
> decision on the following whole group day, this proved to be a constructive way
> forward. (De Venney-Tiernan et al., 1994: 132)

The emotional and interpersonal strand

The facilitator of this strand needs a general overview of the stages through
which an effective co-operative group moves. Each stage has a different
emotional climate. Reason suggests there are three primary ones. The first is
about safety and inclusion, the second about difference and disagreement,
the third about authentic collaboration between respected individuals.

For the first stage, the facilitator needs to offer

> ways in which people can get to know each other and feel comfortable with each
> other, and get some measure of clear agreement about the nature of the task.

The facilitation task in the second stage is

> to allow and encourage the expression of different opinions, to help people listen to each other, give and receive negative and positive feedback, and to help the group find ways of working which include these diverse perspectives.

Then the group may establish

> a more open network of affectionate relationships, in which each individual has a unique place and is seen as making a unique contribution to the group. The group is able to engage in a mature way with its task, using fully the contribution of each member. Facilitation of the group and its task becomes more fully shared, so there is less need for a normal facilitation role. (Reason, 1988b: 27–8)

The facilitator, through all these stages, is supporting the group to manifest a basic level of competence in both identifying and managing emotional states. I discuss the notion of emotional competence, nowadays called emotional intelligence (Goleman, 1995), in more depth in Chapter 8. One important thing it includes is having some skill in dealing with emotional distress from past trauma and oppression, so that it is not unawarely displaced into current activities in ways that distort attitudes to self, to others and to the task.

The importance of this strand needs to be affirmed at the induction meeting, and its unconventional nature in an emotionally repressive society made clear. People are then invited to make a conscious choice and commitment about joining an inquiry where it will be openly explored. If you launch an inquiry without a contract to work with emotional processes and interpersonal tensions, you will have no warrant to address and resolve distressed distortions of the inquiry process, such as consensus collusion, lack of rigour and so forth.

Once such a contract is in place, then the facilitator of this strand can:

- Propose, as a regular feature of reflection meetings, whole group rounds, or small group or pair exchanges, in which everyone takes time to report on current and recent emotional states accompanying the inquiry process. The simple business of identifying, owning, accepting and sharing such states, if they are distress states, may be sufficient to defuse any distorting effect they may have. If the states are positive, affirming them will strengthen motivation and involvement, and make the inquiry radiant.
- Propose the same thing when the group process is lurching about with a lot of unowned and unidentified agitation and tension. The essential ground-rule here is that each person owns and reports their state without blaming or attacking anyone else in the group.
- Keep an eye out for the appropriateness and relevance of doing more in-depth work with people, using breathing, bodywork, uncovering memories, psychodrama. This is in order to abreact hidden distress and get some insight into how it has been distorting current attitudes and

behaviour. This assumes that you are competent and willing to facilitate such work.

- Find out who else in the group is competent to do this kind of in-depth work, and seek a contract that their skill is available to the group.
- Seek a contract that each person in the group is available at any properly negotiated time, on a one-to-one basis, for one-way or reciprocal processing of emotional states, by whatever method is mutually agreed.
- Seek a contract to complement the discharge of distress emotion by two methods of transmuting and transforming it. The first is through simple, non-contentious, transfiguring ritual, and meditative practices of inner centring and expansion of consciousness; the second is through symbolic rendering in presentational forms, through drawing, painting, movement, sound, music, drama, story.

Where strong interpersonal tensions and animosities build up between people in the group, they need addressing openly, otherwise real co-operation is undermined. The facilitator here needs to help the parties involved to differentiate clearly between actual present-time issues, and projected unfinished painful business from the past. There may be very real issues in the present that need dealing with in their own terms, in which case any past associations are of secondary import. On the other hand, there may be virtually nothing at work but strong projections from the past. In this case, especially, the simple reciprocal method used by co-counsellors, whereby two people can check for hidden projections on each other, is invaluable. Each person asks the other these four questions:

- Who do I remind you of? It may be necessary to repeat this question several times until the association surfaces.
- How do I remind you of this person? This invites the other to identify whatever aspect of appearance, manner or role triggers off the association.
- What is it you still need to say to this person? This invites the other to slip into a psychodrama and speak directly to the person from their past, and so bring into conscious awareness the emotional charge that is running the projection.
- How am I different from this person? This invites the other consciously to withdraw the projection, and state clearly a positive difference that affirms the reality of the present person.

Facilitators of this strand need to make a fundamental distinction between the disruption of the inquiry process by emotional and interpersonal distress, and the chaos, disorder and confusion that is an integral part of the inquiry process. It would be a great mistake to try to clean up and get rid of the latter by the methods appropriate to the former. When the group is in the midst of chaos that is the harbinger of a new kind of order which may eventually emerge from it, members need to be encouraged to tolerate the anxieties and frustrations involved, to stay with them and undergo them. To climb out of these states as soon as they occur by some kind of emotional processing would simply produce premature closure and spurious order, and this would undermine the inquiry. I discuss this relation between chaos and order in Chapter 8.

Initiators, academia and reports

Some initiating researchers may be academic staff, some may be post-graduate research students, some may work in other professional settings, and others may be part of some special interest group in society that has no institutional form. For those who work in academia there are particular challenges.

There are strong forces at work in the academic world that uphold four traditions into which students are initiated in their secondary, and especially in their tertiary, education: the importance of individual work, the importance of the written word, the importance of external validating standards, and the importance of expert assessment. What you do you do on your own, after proper tutoring. You are not considered to have done it until you write it all up thoroughly on your own. You do so to a validating standard indicated by your tutors. And what you write is assessed unilaterally by an expert in the field.

Co-operative inquiry runs counter to these four traditions. It is research work that is done co-operatively. Written outcomes may be secondary to other outcomes to do with practice; and the writing up may be done co-operatively. The standards by which it is to be assessed are internal to each inquiry group. The expertise is internal to each inquiry group and is manifest through self and peer assessment.

If you are an initiating researcher and the inquiry is part of your postgraduate research project, no doubt there are various accommodations and mild compromises that can be made to meet the demands of the academic system. But there is clearly a limit, and to go beyond it will mean a basic breach of faith with your co-inquirers. So get clear where you stand, and rather than undermine the method by collusion with the system, press the system to yield to the method.

5

Stages of the Inquiry Cycle

My purpose in this chapter is to discuss in more depth the main issues and choices facing a group of researchers in the four stages of the first inquiry cycle. To start I will repeat in slightly fuller form the outline of these stages introduced in Chapter 3. Then I will go through various items in this fuller outline in greater detail. The summary of stages that follow is cast in Apollonian form. I will raise Dionysian issues in and among as I elaborate the stages.

Stage 1 is the first reflection phase when the co-researchers have several things to choose:

- The focus or topic of the inquiry and the type of inquiry. Will the focus be informative or transformative or some combination of the two? Will the type be full or partial form, inside or outside, with open or closed boundaries, Apollonian or Dionysian or some combination?
- A launching statement. How can the focus of the inquiry be framed in an opening statement that will be fruitful for launching the inquiry process?
- A plan of action for the first action phase. What aspect or aspects of the inquiry focus will the co-researchers choose to explore experientially? Will the group be divergent or convergent or some balance of the two? Will individuals be holistic or partitive or some balance of the two? How long will the action phase last, before the next reflection phase? How many cycles of reflection and action will be planned and with what time-structure?
- A method of recording for the first action phase. There are standard and presentational methods, preceded by the exercise of radical memory, informative and transformative. Which methods will be used? When will the recording be done?

Stage 2 is the first action phase when the co-subjects are:

- Exploring in experience and action the selected aspect or aspects of the inquiry focus.
- Applying an integrated range of inquiry skills.
- Keeping records of the data generated.

Stage 3 is a state of mind and being that is fully immersed in stage 2, bracketing off preconceptions, and at the forward edge of openness to experience and practice:

- Will the inquirers break through into new experience and transformative practice?
- Will they lose their way and 'fall asleep' to the inquiry process?
- Will they jump into transcendence of the inquiry format?

Stage 4 is the second reflection phase when the co-researchers come together to share the data generated in the action phase. They will:

- Review how they now see the selected aspect of the inquiry focus in the light of their experiential exploration of it, and as a result modify, develop or reframe it; and review the overall launching statement in the light of this, and likewise modify, develop or reframe it.
- Choose, for the second phase of action, the same aspect of the inquiry focus, taking the reframed account of it back into experience for further development; or select a different aspect for the next action phase; and bear in mind the same divergent–convergent, holistic–partitive issues as in the first reflection phase.
- Review, in the light of the sort of aspect chosen and of experience in the first action phase, the inquiry procedures: the format of action, ways of generating and recording data, the duration of the action phase; and choose what to repeat, alter, add or delete.

Stage 1 (1)   Focus and type of inquiry

If initiating researchers have recruited a group in terms of some broad topic idea, once the group has convened, its members will need to rework this idea, make it fully their own and bring it to more of a focus. It may be that the use of graphics, phantasy, story-telling, dramaturgy and role-play, and other expressive methods will help people bring forward a well-grounded sense of a focus that really speaks to their condition. To agree on the focus of the inquiry, what it is to be about, is also to start thinking about what possible outcomes it will have. In these deliberations on the topic and possible outcomes it will be helpful to bear in mind the two basic pillars of the inquiry process, its informative and transformative dimensions, as discussed above.

If the inquiry is informative and descriptive of its domain, the primary outcomes are going to be propositional and presentational; if it is transformative, they will be forms of practice, with written reports and presentational forms as secondary.

It also makes sense when agreeing on the focus, for the group to start to clarify what other features their inquiry is going to have, and to consider their implications. Is it full form or partial, is it inside or outside, does it have closed or open boundaries, is the culture going to be Apollonian or Dionysian or some equipoise of the two?

Stage 1 (2)   A launching statement

Whether the focus of the inquiry is descriptive or practical, informative or transformative, or some combination of the two, it needs to be stated as an assumptive model. In an informative inquiry, this model is about the nature of the inquiry domain. In a transformative inquiry, it is about principles of action and strategic issues of practice. In a combined inquiry, it is about both of these.

The health visitors started off with strategic issues of practice to do with feedback, hidden agendas and confrontation (Traylen, 1994).

The youth workers began with the strategic issue of how people learn, to be researched through their own processes of learning (De Venney-Tiernan et al., 1994).

The women's university staff group chose both story and strategy to do with issues of sex and gender in a university (Treleaven, 1994).

The whole person medicine project worked out at its first meeting a five-part model which was a set of possible strategic principles for the practice of holistic medicine (Heron and Reason, 1985; Reason, 1988c).

The altered states inquiry began by assuming both a descriptive model of two worlds and the strategic possibility of functioning awarely in each world at the same time (Heron, 1988c).

The co-counselling inquiry on client states started out with a general descriptive map of client states prevalent in co-counselling culture at the time (Heron and Reason, 1981).

The launching statement is often broadly framed, embracing many aspects of the inquiry focus. Then there is scope for a variety of different ways of exploring it in more specific detail. The inquirers may discover, after a certain amount of divergence among these aspects in the early stages of the research, which ones they want to converge on in the later stages. In this way the really significant issues can emerge from creative interaction with a domain, rather than be imported into it from the outset.

The doctors exploring holistic medicine framed a very broad model of holistic practice with five main parts covering many subparts. This allowed for widely divergent forms of practice in the early action phases. Later on, there was a need to converge on just two main kinds of practice (Heron and Reason, 1985; Reason, 1988c).

Stage 1 (3)   The first action plan

Once the launching statement is decided the inquirers' next step is to consider how to explore it in more detail. They need to consider the many aspects of the topic and to agree which to choose to explore in the first action phase, in order to get the inquiry going in some specific direction. What information about the research domain will be gathered and how? What practice will be applied within it? It may be useful for the group to brainstorm a wide range of options, from the sober and realistic to the extreme, outrageous and bizarre, before winnowing through them to make a choice.

> This is a time for creative thinking and practical support. If the inquiry is into innovative practice in some field, it will be important for the group to find ways of thinking past the limitations of current practice towards the truly creative. This will be experienced as more or less risky by group members, and some may need the support and encouragement of their colleagues . . . It is helpful to have group members make some form of contract with their colleagues. (Reason, 1988b: 33)

In choosing what to do, there are some basic options about the sorts of choices being made. These are, for the group, whether to be divergent or convergent, and, whichever of those is chosen, whether to be partitive or holistic about the inquiry topic and its aspects.

Divergent and convergent

If the first action phase is divergent, the inquirers will go off and each do something different, finding out different things, or trying out different practices. If it is convergent, they will all find out the same thing, or try out the same practice. Between the extremes of all diverging and all converging, there are numerous gradations: thus there can be a number of subgroups, the members of any one subgroup converge on the same thing, and the subgroups diverge in different directions. This account of divergence and convergence is to do with what goes on *within* an action phase.

Divergence and convergence are also about what goes on *between* action phases: whether in the next action phase people do something different to, or the same as, they did on the previous action phase. The combined *within* and *between* accounts make up the simple logic of inquiry cycles.

Total combined divergence over several cycles means that everyone does something different within every action phase, and no-one repeats in a later action phase anything they have done in an earlier one. This generates data that gives the maximum diversified overview of a topic. But this overview is entirely impressionistic, since every part of the topic has only been attended to once by one person. It is also low in coherence, since no-one has attended to how the parts of the whole work together.

Total combined convergence over several cycles means that everyone does the self-same thing on every cycle. This generates data that gives a progressively refined and in-depth account of one aspect of the topic. This account, however, becomes suspect because there is no complementary view of how that aspect integrates with, and is influenced by, any other part and the whole.

The intermediate model seeks to maximize the benefits of both convergence and divergence and minimize the deficits of the extremes of each.

One version is for several subgroups to diverge within an action phase. Each subgroup takes on a different aspect of the inquiry topic. The members within one subgroup converge on the same aspect. Each subgroup sustains the same focus over several cycles.

> The youth workers inquiring into their own learning processes divided into small groups, each group converging on a specific skill and method, each group having a different focus from the other groups, and with intermittent whole group meetings for sharing and collating among the subgroups (De Venney-Tiernan et al., 1944).

> The doctors in the holistic medicine inquiry after diverging strongly over the first two cycles, each doctor exploring something different, then opted in the last four cycles to form two subgroups, each converging on one area of shared interest, with a final reflection weekend to draw the threads together (Heron and Reason, 1985; Reason, 1988c).

It is as well for Apollonian inquirers to get some feel for this logic of research cycling before planning the first action phase. Then they can start to be intentional about the way they are going to play the logic out over the whole series of cycles. There are, of course, innumerable variations of play, remembering how divergence and convergence can apply both within any action phase, and between successive action phases.

It is too early in the use of the research method to come up with any golden rules. From the limited experience so far available it does look as though divergence early on, both within and between action phases, is fruitful. As mentioned above, it allows for diverse interactions with a domain, as a basis for the later emergence of well-grounded convergence. It encourages individual interest and initiative at the start of the inquiry, and gets everyone motivated and involved. This avoids conformity and following behaviour, which is the absence of true co-operation.

> Allowing and encouraging idiosyncratic behaviour during the research process allows the researchers later to come together with their differences. It is essential that different approaches to the topic are taken, because often these are complementary: thus in this project state maps and process maps complement each other. It is important that people have space to discover their particular unique identities and contributions to the project. Thus to an extent we can argue that the validity of the process rests in the inquiry group – whether enough divergence and idiosyncrasy has been built up for the group to become supportively confronting and test each other's ideas strongly . . . We argue that allowing and encouraging divergence and chaos will lead to a richer convergence, greater creativity, novelty and excitement, and to a greater validity in the research. (Heron and Reason, 1981: 51)

So there may be a case for moving from divergence in the opening cycles, through an intermediate model in the middle cycles, to convergence in the closing cycles. But it would be a great mistake to turn this into a procedural rule. The field is wide open for meta-inquiries into the different variations.

Dionysian inquiries won't consider it appropriate to be as intentional as this about research logic. Instead, they will be intentional about letting issues of divergence and convergence play themselves out in an impromptu fashion through their tacit diffusion from the reflection phase into the action phase. The justification for this is that it allows for action:

- To be born following creative gestation after the reflection phase.
- To be influenced by intuitive, imaginal, emotional and sensory states occurring in the field.
- To take account of implicit structures and synchronicities in the field.

However, Dionysian inquiries may well choose to consider retrospectively the pattern of divergence and convergence that has emerged over several cycles.

Part and whole

Divergence and convergence are to do with how different members of the group address the topic area in a given cycle and over a series of cycles. Will we all, or some of us, do the same thing or something different? But whether the thing we do is the same or different, there is also the further question of whether it represents only a part of the topic area, a subset of parts (a subwhole), or the whole of it. This is another option facing inquirers when choosing what to do for their first action phase.

> I launched an inquiry with a group of dentists to monitor and modify their professional practice in the light of mutually agreed criteria (Heron, 1979). Their job can be divided into several main areas: clinical/technical, communication with patients, managing staff, financial, legal, educational, and so on. Each of these can be further subdivided. Thus the clinical area covers examinations, bitewing X-rays, amalgams, extractions, dental hygiene, and so on. Again, any one of these has its component parts. So amalgams include removing decay, undercutting, implanting, contouring, and more.
>
> What the dentists choose to monitor in any one action phase can range from the very partitive to the very holistic. They can choose to look only at how they do only one part of one main area, or they can opt to monitor the job as whole including all its main areas; and between these two extremes there is a graded series of selections of increasing scope, with many different possible combinations at each step in the series. In the inquiry mentioned, the dentists started off by looking only at their work on amalgams (fillings), which is just one part of the clinical area, which is a subwhole of the job.

The part–whole dimension is relatively independent of the divergence–convergence one. So if a group plans to be divergent for the next action phase, it can look at a different part, or at a different subwhole, or at the whole in terms of different assumptions – for example, in terms of a hierarchy in which a different part or subwhole is primary. (Whether underlying assumptions are different or the same brings in another dimension, that of heterogeneity–homogeneity: see Chapter 8.) If the group plans to be convergent it can look at the same part, or at the same subwhole, or at the whole in the same way. The holistic and the convergent ultimately merge at some ideal or infinite limit. If each individual is looking at the whole in an integration of all possible ways of looking at it, then the group is fully convergent.

Dionysian inquirers will understandably protest that all this is starting to lose sight of the synthetic wood for the analytic trees. I sympathize with them, and at the same time consider that it will benefit the processes of a Dionysian inquiry if its members have grasped the underlying logic of research method, even though they choose not to apply this logic explicitly in making decisions about what they do in the action phases. I give a complete account of the bipolar parameters of the logic of cyclic method in Chapter 8.

Length of the action phase

In an inside inquiry the group is doing all its work together in a special place where both reflection and action phases follow directly on from each other. The whole meeting, including several complete cycles of reflection and action, may be anything from two to five days. Depending on the topic, an action phase may last for anything between some minutes and some hours. The length allocated needs to include enough time for each subject to record their own experience, and where relevant, record some observations of other co-subjects working with them.

In an outside inquiry, the action phase will be done by each inquirer on their own in their place of work and/or in their personal life. It is likely that each action phase will last for several days or weeks.

For the doctors in the holistic medicine inquiry each action phase lasted for six weeks, and this is probably an outer limit for any action phase (Heron and Reason, 1985; Reason, 1988c).

The length partly depends on the focus of the inquiry and the amount of time needed to generate sufficient data for fruitful reflection. If the topic is a particular aspect of professional practice, this aspect may occur at irregular and unpredictable intervals, in which case weeks may be needed. The length also depends on concerns external to the inquiry. Busy people can only arrange to meet every so often for the reflection phases, because of other commitments, which therefore have an influence on the length of the action phases.

For any given topic, there is probably some best ratio between the lengths of the reflection and action phases of any one cycle, a ratio that makes them each as fruitful as possible. And for a given topic in the hands of a particular group, there is probably some optimum total of inquiry cycles which make for a fruitful inquiry. It is difficult to estimate at the start of an inquiry what these ideal numbers are; and if one did know, they would still probably need to be modified by other considerations. Nevertheless, the basic outline of the inquiry cycles

> needs to be worked out fairly early on: it is most important, at this stage, to arrange the project so that several stages of action and reflection can be undertaken. Inevitably this involves some pragmatic guesswork in arriving at an appropriate balance between action and reflection. (Reason, 1988b: 26)

Three would seem to be an absolute minimum for the total number of inquiry cycles. Somewhere between five and eight cycles gives enough scope for something fruitful to emerge.

> The youth worker inquiry into learning processes had eight one-month cycles for the whole group, with subgroup cycles of one week – making over thirty of these (De Venney-Tiernan et al., 1994).

> The holistic medicine inquiry had six six-week cycles (Heron and Reason, 1985; Reason, 1988c).

In this, as in every other aspect of the method, there are no rules, only exploratory choices.

Stage 1 (4)   Data generation methods

Standard methods

The final thing the inquirers need to do in the first reflection phase is to choose how they will keep a record of their forthcoming action, so that they can bring the data to the second reflection phase. Depending on the activity and its context there is a wide array of options here. There are descriptive notes, conceptual maps, theory outlines, journal entries of self or other, observational data and feedback notes, questionnaires and rating scales filled in by self or other, interview notes, audio and video tapes, photos, documents of self or other (letters, minutes, memos, records, reports), physiological measures. This list includes most of the standard data generation approaches of qualitative research (Creswell, 1994).

The primary purpose of data generation in co-operative inquiry is for each person to provide information about his or her own action and experience, to formulate data about oneself as a subject, not about someone else as a subject or 'informant'. A subordinate use, where two or more co-subjects are working and interacting together in the action phase, is for each person also to record data about the other co-subjects.

When no other co-subjects are present, non-inquiry people who are involved can be asked to generate data about the active inquirer and his or her context (but if these people have no say at all in how the data they provide is presented and used, this infringes a norm of co-operative inquiry). This data from others about the inquirer or context complements his or her self-report.

Presentational methods

Towards the end of Chapter 2 and again in Chapter 3, I presented a fourfold holistic model of knowledge which included presentational knowing, intuitive pattern knowing, expressed in graphic, plastic, moving, musical and verbal art-forms. I also suggested that this kind of knowing supports propositional or conceptual knowing. On this account of knowledge, there is a strong case for including, as forms of data generation, expressive records which reveal an imaginal grasp of significant pattern in the inquiry domain, including actions taken within it. These include: drawings, paintings, photos, film, sculptures, musical forms, choreography, ritual, thick multi-sensory descriptions, poetry, story, allegory, drama. Such presentational methods can be used as a precursor to and complement of the more literal, prosaic and conceptual forms. They may well be relevant as the first way of symbolizing the data from two radical kinds of memory I now discuss.

Radical memory

Since the inquirers are also their own subjects, their data about their own perceptions and actions is necessarily recorded retrospectively, anything from minutes to hours to a day or more after the event. Hence any record is actually a secondary form of data generation. The primary form, which indeed is at the very point of generation, is memory.

In Chapter 7 I discuss the use of memory in generating data. I suggest that reliable memory is born at the moment of focal perception or action through paying heed, giving careful attention to what is going on. I also distinguish between paying heed in the ordinary way, and paying heed to perception or action in an extraordinary way, which generates radical memory. Such radical memory is at the heart of data generation. It has two complementary, interrelated and different forms. One yields data for informative statements about an inquiry domain; the other yields data on transformative practice within a domain. See Chapter 7 for a full account of this summary paragraph.

I include radical memory in this discussion of the first reflection and planning phase, because it makes sense to prepare for it, reflect on it, maybe practise it in the group with short exercises; and because it is presupposed by all the other self-report data recording methods. I underline again the simple and central point that for research using one's own experiences and behaviours, the basic data about them is memory data, which is generated with them at their points of origin.

Stage 1   Inquiry culture

The whole of stage 1 – the choice of focal idea, of the launching statement, of first action plan, of data generation methods – can be carried through mainly in a conceptual, linear and logical manner. This may be leavened by the secondary and supportive use of presentational methods, with creative explorations of options through metaphor and analogy, using active imagination through phantasy futures, myth-making, story-telling, dramaturgy, drawing, movement, etc. This is the approach of the Apollonian inquiry culture. A Dionysian inquiry will reverse this balance. Expressive, presentational modes of exploring the options will lead the way, complemented by creative conceptual formulations. The intermediate culture will seek a continuous dialectic interplay between the conceptual and the imaginal.

Stage 2   The first action phase

The co-researchers now become experiential inquirers, each ready to implement his or her action plan. In an outside inquiry, they leave the group reflection meeting and go off into the outer world to do whatever it is they have undertaken to do in the first action phase, to generate data on this through the cultivation of radical memory, and to record this data in whatever ways they have chosen. This engagement with experience for the purpose of inquiring into it requires a range of special skills, some of which relate to perception and the informative inquiry pole, while others concern practice and the transformative pole. I give a summary of these in the next two paragraphs. A brief description of each is given in Chapter 3, and full account in Chapter 7.

Informative inquiry skills involve radical perception, with its two components of being fully present and imaginally open. This is supported by bracketing: attending fully to what is going on in the process of perceiving while making explicit in awareness and holding in suspension the various sets of presuppositions which might otherwise obscure it. At the same time, there is reframing skill: the ability to generate and hold in mind alternative conceptual frameworks and try them out for their fit.

The complementary skills, to do with researching practice in a transformative inquiry, involve radical action, or dynamic congruence. This means attending to all facets of an action and reshaping any of them in the interests of greater mutual impact and reduced dissonance. This is where action inquiry as developed by Torbert (1991) is applicable. It is supported by emotional competence in identifying and managing emotional states, by nonattachment to the form of the action, and by having alternative action frameworks available for use.

Issues of recording data

Generating data by the exercise of these interweaving skills, each inquirer will take time out every once in a while to record them by whatever means he or she has already chosen in stage 1. Given that the length of the action phase as a whole has already been decided, there is still an issue about choosing which bits of experience within that span are to be used as a source of data, and when and how frequently to record them.

This issue arises mainly in outside inquiries, in which each person is out there in the world on their own in a long action phase, which will consist of many mini-cycles of doing–recording, doing–recording.

> In the whole person medicine inquiry, each action phase lasted for six weeks, during which time each doctor explored innovation in a chosen area of practice, trying things out in action, recording data about this, and repeating this cycle many times over during the six weeks (Heron and Reason, 1985; Reason, 1988c).

When to try something out and for how long? When and how often to record data about it? The answers depend on the chosen task, the situations within which it is to be undertaken, and on what it is realistic and practicable for a busy person to undertake and to be able to sustain. There is a lot of rough grain texture to an outside inquiry in this area. Every member will have a different self-directed schedule of doing and recording. Some schedules will be more stringent, regular and systematic, others more variable and irregular in their format. Each person has to strike their own balance between the rigorous, the realistic and their own level of motivation and commitment.

In a long action phase, lasting for days or weeks of application in daily life, and including many mini-cycles of doing and recording the doing, each of these mini-cycles is a piece of one-person experiential research moving between selected action and reflecting on it in order to record it. It is also in the doing as such that action inquiry as defined by Torbert (1991) – with its emphasis on the conscious discrimination and command during action of its essential components – becomes an integral part of a co-operative inquiry.

On inside inquiries, where there is interaction between two or more co-subjects in the action phases, then data generation and recording can go two ways. First and foremost, each person generates and records data on his or her own experience; but also each can generate and record data on what the others involved appear to be undergoing and doing.

> In the co-counselling inquiry on client states, after each client session the client made a record of their states, then the counsellor gave their own account of what seemed to be going on for the client (Heron and Reason, 1981).

On outside inquiries, where each person is not interacting with other inquirers during the action phase, non-inquirers who are present at the open boundary can be asked to record their relevant perceptions of the subject, to supplement the primary self-report. I have referred already to the ethical and epistemological issue here about those who provide the data

having no say in the use to which it is put, since they are not members of
the inquiry group. It may be also possible on some outside inquiries for co-
subjects to make occasional visits to each other's inquiry context, to spend
time there and to record their impressions of the visited one busy in a part
of their action phase.

On inside inquiries, where the group remains together in a special place
for several whole research cycles, each action phase will be from half an
hour to an hour or so, and will consist entirely of generating experiential
data and recording it, so the issue of what and when to record does not arise.

Stage 3   Experiential immersion

Stage 3 can be seen as a state of mind and being at the heart of stage 2. It
is the state of deep immersion in the action phase, a full engagement with
the relevant experience or practice, a great openness of encounter with the
chosen domain. This stage is the bedrock, the touchstone of the inquiry
process. It is the consummation of paying heed in a radical way to the
processes of perception and action, and of the family of skills supportive of
these two deep kinds of attentiveness.

The inquirers may develop a degree of openness to the experience or the
practice so free of preconceptions that they see it and engage with it in a new
way. They may deepen into the experience or the practice so that the
launching frameworks for it appear superficial and are seen to be in need of
elaboration and development. Or immersion in this stage may lead them
away from the original ideas and proposals into new ones, that yield
ground-breaking insights or unpredicted personal and social transformation.

Falling asleep

It is also possible that they may get so involved in what they are doing that
for a time they lose their radical attentiveness. They may also lose the
awareness that they are part of an inquiry group. There may be a practical
crisis, they may become enthralled, they may simply forget. Bracketing off
preconceptions with great openness to what is going on is a threshold state
of mind. It can either lead to new awareness or relapse into nescience and
forgetfulness. It is similar to the practitioner of meditation who, on the
threshold of the meditative state, may either enter its enhanced awareness
or simply fall asleep. So just as inquirers are getting deeply into their
experiential immersion and are starting to succeed in bracketing off their
defining assumptions, they may 'fall asleep' and revert to ordinary consciousness with its conventional beliefs and practices.

Threshold oscillation

There may well, indeed, be periods of oscillation between ordinary states
and the extraordinary states of radical paying heed with their supporting

skills. This seems to be the inescapable occupational hazard of a person being their own instrument for researching the human condition. There is no guarantee that it is possible, at any rate at the beginning, to 'stay awake' in extraordinary states. The transparent body-mind may suddenly glaze over and go dull. Hence the data generated may have gaps and omissions and be low in content redundancy. It may be like the flickering scenes of early films where only a small number of frames are transmitted per unit of time.

Celebration, inquiry and creativity

When people are their own instruments, inquiring into their realities through participation in them, they are not just busy with inquiry. Participative inquiry, in both the epistemic sense of being experientially resonant with the inquiry domain, indwelling it, and in the political sense of being engaged with others in co-operative decision-making, is not just inquiry without anything else going on. It cannot subsist on its own. It partakes of an embrace with other central features of human experience. It is fed and sustained in its engagement with its world by being part of a wider whole.

For any expressive person, this whole consists, perhaps, of three things. First, there is the inquiry itself; second, a celebration of lived experience; and third, creativity in refashioning our world. The inquiry is inter-dependent with the celebration and the creativity: it can reflect something of these two, but cannot entirely encompass or contain them. For inquiry to be living inquiry, it needs to be vitalized by the celebration and the creativity which flow into it from beyond it. If it could include them both without remainder, they would all become impoverished. Inquiry, therefore, cannot accomplish a complete account of the human condition, since it is always joined by these friends whose dance extends beyond its range.

Transformative inquiries which focus on creative practice might seem to offer the most complete account. And in one sense they do, since such practice is also joined by much celebration. But it is also continuously self-transcending. The creative practice I inquire into today is surmounted by a new wave of its forward-moving passion tomorrow. The practical knowing how, which is the focus of a transformative inquiry, because it transfigures its world, opens up new vistas on ways of moving beyond itself. It seems to include its colleagues, creativity and celebration, but they continually leap forward to further horizons, beyond those it is currently mapping out.

Informative inquiries seek to attend to the properties and patterning of our realities. In this they are joined closely by the celebration of lived experience. Paying radical heed to the whole perceptual process unites us with our inherent appreciation of what there is, of our participation in its coming into being, and of our coming into being within it. This kind of appreciation is like birdsong, which lauds the emergence of the singer within a world of sun and wind and leaf. The propositional and presentational outcomes of an informative inquiry tell us about our realities. In this they are a kind of testament, bearing witness to our appreciation of being a presence arising with and among other presences. But this pointing to our appreciation is forever surmounted by the eternal suchness of that appreciation, its very nowness in the permanent surge of being.

This rhetoric is a way of saying that in stage 3, the stage of deep and aware immersion in the experiential focus of the inquiry, the inquirer may not only 'fall asleep' and drop out of the state of paying radical heed, not only oscillate between 'sleeping' and heeding, but may also become so fully awake, that he or she jumps into a kind of celebration or creativity that is right outside the inquiry format. Is the inquiry then rejigged to take account of this forward jump? Or is the jump a transcending sign that the inquiry is on the right track by virtue of leading beyond itself to celebration of the values of being? Thus of the final and sixth experiential phase of an inquiry into altered states of consciousness, I wrote:

> This cycle was co-operatively planned by several group members. It was much more like a concluding ceremony – a celebration and an affirmation – than a formal part of our inquiry ... Unless, of course, you choose to see the celebration itself as a special kind of conclusion drawn from the inquiry. (Heron, 1988c: 190–1)

Stage 4 (1)   The second reflection phase: making sense

I cover a lot of epistemological ground in this section on making sense, because it is at the heart of the method as a method of inquiry. So it seems appropriate to raise some of the main issues involved, without deferring them to later chapters. The first two subsections are of immediate practical relevance. Not all the other issues discussed will be relevant to any particular instance of the reflection phase. In practice this phase can be brief or lengthy, lightly covered or comprehensive, depending on what has gone on in the prior action phase and on the sort of data it has generated.

Reporting, collating and reviewing

Stage 4 is the second reflection phase when the co-researchers come together to make sense of their experiences in the first action phase. Inside inquiries will probably take an hour or two for this: they only have short periods of data generation to consider. Outside inquiries will take several hours, from half a day to two days. They have days or weeks of experience to mull over.

The first thing the inquirers need to do is find some way of sharing their data with each other. This can be done by a series of individual reports, each person in turn giving their findings to the group, with supporting records, numerical, verbal, presentational. The group then together collate the individual findings, sort them into categories and look at patterns of relationship among them (P. Hawkins, 1986). Another approach, which may or may not be preceded by individual sharing before the group, is for one person, or a very small subgroup of at most three people, to do the collating, sorting and pattern-finding. They then bring all this to the group for members to check, amend and approve (P.J. Hawkins, 1986).

> Fundamentally, the making-sense process requires time, energy, patience, and resources. It helps to have plenty of space, lots of large sheets of paper and coloured pens, and a willingness to experiment. The group needs to develop a tolerance for the irritation that comes from thinking too much, and to keep a careful eye out for when members are getting exhausted with the process, and a change of activity is called for to help people relax. (Reason, 1988b: 36)

What the co-researchers are sharing here are their experientially generated data on some aspect or aspects of the inquiry topic. When they have collated and made further sense of the data, this may lead them to modify, extend or radically reframe their original account of the aspect or aspects. Then, in the light of these changes, they can review the overall launching statement of the inquiry, the one that embraces all its aspects, and likewise modify, extend or reframe it. The nature of the changes at these two levels will depend on whether the group has diverged over many aspects or converged on just one or two. Also on whether each individual has been holistic in combining several aspects or partitive in attending to only one or two.

In practice this kind of reframing, of the immediate aspect just explored and of the overall inquiry topic, is likely to be much less formalized, more approximate and inchoate, if not downright messy and unfocused at times. Dionysian inquiries will make a virtue of this and adopt a tacit approach in which the reframing is left implicit in the members' minds during their sharing of experiences.

Making sense and reaching agreement

There are four steps in making sense of experiential data:

- Radical memory and framing at the point of perception and action. This is the grounding step: paying heed to the patterning of elements, and their appropriate framing, in our perceiving and doing.
- Recording this, either in presentational or propositional form or both. Here radical memory and framing are processed and symbolized by the record. Both this and the previous step occur during the action phase.
- Each individual presenting and reporting his or her records to the group in the reflection phase. Here the records are processed and symbolized by a summary of their content.
- The final step is the collation of all the individual accounts of what is significant. This means identifying similarities and differences among them, and meaningful patterns among those similarities and differences.

In the first three steps the individual is progressively identifying significant categories within personal experience, and significant patterning of these categories. In the fourth step of collation, group members are seeking agreement, the supposition being that if they *agree* about what is significant, then it carries more weight and is better grounded. What is 'significant' and 'illuminating' depends on individual and group intuition, on how divergent or convergent the action phase has been, on the focus of the inquiry and where it stands in relation to the informative–transformative polarity, and on its social and cultural context.

Now even if the group has been highly convergent in the action phase, the agreement sought is not an agreement solely about how the individual accounts of experience are identical. It is an agreement about how they do and do not overlap, and about how this identity-in-difference, these diverse perspectives, illumine the inquiry area. The overlap is not an agreement about what is objective. The inquirers are exploring their subjective-objective realities, each person with an idiosyncratic standpoint and viewpoint. Their corporate truth is enriched both by significant differences and significant identities in their accounts of personal experience. Some differences are complementaries, some are disagreements. With regard to the latter, the group's intersubjective agreement may contain a paradoxical element about the relevance of their disagreements. It can celebrate incompatible as well as compatible diversity in the unity.

A total overlap of views is suspect, suggesting collusion or conformity and lack of full individual engagement with experience and with the requisite inquiry skills. No overlap of any sort is unlikely, but would indicate some chaotic disintegration of the co-operative process. For a given group of people, a given inquiry focus, a given degree of divergence or convergence, a given stage in the inquiry, there is likely to be some fitting, well-grounded degree of overlap, of identity in difference, that gives a rich illuminating corporate perspective on the topic.

> The first co-counselling inquiry on client states of mind produced as its final outcome a set of nine different maps of these states: three static state maps, two dynamic state maps and four process maps. They were all interestingly different from each other, each having been originated by one or more group members. We reached agreement about their overlap by the whole group refining each one.

> > To refine the maps, we first of all drew them all out on a large piece of paper on the floor in the middle of the room . . . We then went over each map in turn, comparing it to our experience of counselling, criticising it, categorising it, discussing its uses and limitations, until we were clear about what it represented, and had modified it and developed it to accommodate criticisms made. Thus all the maps of experience described in this paper were derived and refined through a collaborative process. (Heron and Reason, 1981: 20)

Presentational and propositional meaning

The second, third and fourth steps I have just outlined could all be taken by the use of presentational methods: drawings, paintings, photos, sculptures, musical forms, mime, dance, ritual, thick multi-sensory descriptions, poetry, story, allegory, drama, demonstrations. I don't know of any inquiry where this has been done, because of the potent Aristotelian prejudice, in old and new paradigm research cultures alike, in favour of the propositional. But somewhere the opportunity beckons.

For example, take an outside inquiry. During the action phase of days or weeks each person does a series of drawings of their relevant experiences. This is step 2, individual recording. Then in step 3, at the next reflection meeting, each one presents to the group a higher level drawing, which symbolizes the significant pattern of similarities and differences in the drawings of step two. In step 4 each one draws what they see as the significant pattern of similarities and differences in all the individual drawings of step three.

Another presentational approach would be to use story-telling. In step 2, each person writes up story-teller's notes in their diary of relevant experiences. In step 3, each one tells the whole group the composite story of these experiences. In step 4, when all the individual stories have been told, people can tell their story about the telling of all the personal stories. Here they use the resonance of metaphor in the step 4 story-line to bring out significant patterns of similarity and difference in the step 3 stories. Much more informally, group members can simply share their stories of what went on in the last action phase, as a precursor to more general discussion of underlying themes and issues.

This was the case with the health visitors reporting on their work with families (Traylen, 1994), and the women staff reporting on their recent experience of sex and gender issues in the workplace (Treleaven, 1994).

Reason and Hawkins (1988) give a useful classification of stories that are a response to other stories: replies, echoes, re-creations and reflections:

- A *reply* is the story-teller's reaction to other stories, expressing the emotions and associations to which they give rise.
- An *echo* is the story-teller's personal story on the same theme or themes heard in the other stories.
- A *re-creation* is the story-teller's own remoulded version of the other stories: 'This could be a poem, a fairy tale, or some other kind of story; it may be at the same "level" as the original, or move toward the archetypal level' (1988: 92).
- A *reflection* is a story that ponders the other stories: it is about them, standing further back from them.

I believe there is an important future for inquiries which sustain their sense-making, cycle after cycle, primarily within the presentational mode, with a secondary and subordinate interpretation of the presentations in propositional form. This discipline could lead to a rigour of expressive form, and a mastery of radical imaginal meaning. The inquiry group becomes an artists' collective, demonstrating art as a mode of knowledge, giving powerful access to the pre-predicative, extralinguistic world which phenomenologists tend to *write* about too much in analytic mode. The method affirms the metaphorical nature of our understanding (Reason, 1988d).

Denzin also makes a plea for the wider use of what I call presentational forms in interpretative studies:

> Alternative ways of presenting interpretation must be experimented with, including film, novels, drama and plays, song, music, poetry, dance, paintings, photography, sculpture, pottery, toolmaking and architecture. Each of these representational forms speak to the problem of presenting and doing interpretation. By experimenting with them, the interpreter enlarges his or her interpretive horizon. (Denzin, 1989: 138)

Presentational and propositional ways of making sense, of highlighting significant patterns of similarity and difference in experience and action, can be used alone or in a few basic combinations. By presentational forms I mean all nonverbal art forms, plus verbal forms used for expressive, evocative-descriptive and metaphorical effect. By propositional forms I mean verbal forms used exclusively to categorize, analyse and theorize. A simple spectrum looks something like this:

- Exclusive presentational forms with no propositional interpretations and explanations.
- Primary presentational forms supported by secondary propositional interpretations and explanations.
- Balanced dialectical interplay between presentational and propositional forms.
- Primary propositional forms supported by secondary presentational forms.
- Exclusive propositional forms with no presentational forms.

Reason and Hawkins refer to the propositional and the presentational as explanation and expression. They argue that:

> Any complete model of inquiry must eventually show how these two complement each other . . . Thus we create between them a space for dialogue and for dialectical development, so that a theory may be illuminated by a story, or a theory may clarify a myth. (1988: 83–5)

Since presentational forms are manifold – including drawings, paintings, photos, sculptures, musical forms, mime, dance, ritual, thick multi-sensory descriptions, poetry, story, allegory, drama – there is also the possibility of dialectical interplay among these forms themselves. Drawings can be complemented by stories, dances by poems, ritual by music. The complementarity can extend to many different multiple combinations. So the above spectrum is enriched by the possibilities of including presentational forms singly, in combination or in varied clusters.

Informative meaning in propositional form

An informative inquiry is descriptive of some domain of experience, yielding information and explanation about it. Its propositional outcomes will tell us about the inquirers' lived experience of the *natural* world in which they participate, and/or of the *cultural* world in which they participate.

Lived experience of any entity in the *natural* world has two aspects. There is participation in its modes of appearing, in its perceived patterns of form and process. And there is participation in its inner life, in its experience of its world, its way of regarding and being affected by what is going on in its environment.

The first of these aspects requires something like Goethean science. In his scientific work on plants and animals, Goethe practised what he called concrete vision and exact sensorial imagination. This simply meant a deep, intuitive and intensive participation in the imaginal form and development of what he was perceiving. It was an imaginative reconstruction of, say, a plant's whole way of coming into being, and of the archetypal principles informing it, as these are known in and through consciously deepening and extending the transactional process of perceiving it (Bortoft, 1986).

The second of these aspects, participation in the inner experience of an entity, calls for empathic resonance, intuitively feeling into the mode of apprehension or awareness of the other, whether atom, rock, microbe, fish or bird. It involves interior harmonic attunement, a felt inner sense of what the other is undergoing.

These complementary kinds of participative knowing engage us with the primary meaning of lived experience. Such primary meaning is the meaning the world has as constituted by our co-creation of it, our transactional generation of it. It is the meaning inherent in the process of perceiving and feeling the presences in our world. It is nonlinguistic and is grasped by actively, alertly and awarely deepening our intuitive-imaginal, and empathic-resonant, participation in our world.

Secondary meaning is linguistic and conceptual, arising from the ascription of class-names and general terms to the content of our lived experience. It is grounded on primary meaning. The use of language presupposes an agreement about how to use it; and this agreement rests on a shared tacit grasp of primary meaning. Secondary, linguistic meaning is a partial and incomplete transformation into conceptual terms of the primary meaning inherent in our imaginal and empathic participation in our world. So propositional outcomes of an inquiry are to do with revising our conceptual transformation of our lived experience of the natural world, and with elaborating explanatory theory on the basis of this revision.

Such outcomes articulate what in Chapter 10 I call the postconceptual world. This a world in which linguistically charged thought withdraws to allow the transparent body-mind, with its full range of sensibilities, to open to its radical transaction with the given cosmos, and then returns to clothe the intuitions of this openness with revisionary language. Less rhetorically, it is a world we describe by words that transform into concepts our non-linguistic experience of primary meaning. At the same time, we remain very open to that experience, and thus open to reframe our conceptual account.

And we remember that when any conceptual account of imaginal intuition and empathic communion is stated, that account is inescapably relative to its linguistic and cultural context. Its validity can always be called into question when a relevant wider context is invoked.

Conceptual systems obscure the world of primary meaning when they build elaborate superstructures of 'knowledge' on the linguistic transformation, the categorization, of a limited set of primary meanings; and when they get preoccupied with refining the superstructure while forgetting, and failing to extend, its imaginal and empathic foundations. Years ago, Zener (1958) argued that psychology has too narrow a formal conceptual base of phenomenal categories. He said it needs phenomenally sensitive observers to extend this base, in order to provide a more adequate foundation for the superstructure of theorizing and experiment.

The propositional outcomes of an informative inquiry may also tell us about the inquirers' lived experience of the *cultural* world in which they participate. This also has two, but more familiar, aspects. There is participation in the social structure and function of the inquirers' local culture, its pattern of social roles and behavioural functions. And there is participation in its intersubjective experience of shared meaning, in its shared values, guiding norms and belief-systems. These complementary aspects, the structural-functional and the hermeneutic, as reported in the inquiry outcomes, will tell us about the outside and the inside of the culture which the inquirers are exploring through their own experience.

Transformative meaning: portrayals and propositions

Transformative inquiries explore practice within some domain, changing the inquirers' behaviour and the arena within which it is applied. They are involved in developing some measure of a new skill. I make the point in Chapter 6 that the primary outcome of such an inquiry is the skill, the practical knowledge, acquired, and that the essence of a skill – whether physical, technical, emotional, interpersonal, managerial, transpersonal – is the knack required to execute it and that this necessarily transcends language.

Propositions *about* practice are therefore secondary to demonstrations *of* practice. Practical knowledge, knowing how to do something, first and foremost calls for showing the skill in action. In bringing their data about practice to the reflection phase, the researchers can reconstruct and portray some critical aspect of it through role-plays. They can present video excerpts. They can tell the story of their deeds, evoking the impact and quality of their practice in their narrative.

The knack of a skill is its internal practical meaning. We grasp the meaning of the knack only in and through the mastery of it. But we can get a feel for this internal meaning-of-doing by seeing someone display or picture their mastery of it. Hence the importance of demonstrations and portrayals and the imaginative reconstruction of story-telling.

Practice also has external meaning for those who perceive it, and this at two levels, the imaginal and the cultural. Human behaviour has a pattern-ing of sounds, postures, spatial relationships, and relative movements, which has a primary, imaginal meaning about how people are being in their world, which is wider and deeper than the local cultural meaning of what they are about. And when it comes to understanding that cultural meaning, this is intimately bound up in special ways with these wider imaginal features of behaviour. So whether we look at practice as pure morphology, or as social purpose, its external imaginal meaning is relevant and can, like its internal meaning, only be conveyed by demonstrations, portrayals and stories.

Analytic propositional accounts provide the back-up, the programme notes, for practical portrayals or story-telling evocations. As such they can:

- Describe the practice in terms of its several components, and how it evolved and changed. These components are described in Chapter 7.
- Describe the effects of the practice on the situation in which it occurs.
- Evaluate the practice and its effects in terms of relevant criteria. These are presented in Chapter 9.
- Report informative redefinitions of its domain that the practice has engendered.

Stage 4 (2)   Planning the second action phase

After making sense of the data from the first action phase and, in the light of this, reframing its guiding idea, the inquirers plan the second action phase. Here they have a choice between doing the same kind of thing, creatively enhanced by what has been learnt from the first phase, or going on to explore some different aspect of the inquiry focus. If individuals or subgroups were divergent in their choice of aspects for the first action phase, will they continue on with those aspects in the second action phase and develop them further, or will they diverge yet again into other aspects?

Divergent subgroups will often get deeply interested in their special projects. Each subgroup will want to converge on its particular focus over a few cycles, taking it deeper, restructuring it in the light of previous application phases in order to learn more about it.

In an altered states of consciousness (ASC) inquiry (Heron, 1995), four divergent subgroups formed for the first action phase, each with a different focus: and each sustained its focus, with creative variations, over several action phases, before the whole group converged on a common focus for a final phase.

In the whole person medicine inquiry (Heron and Reason, 1985; Reason, 1988c), the doctors individually diverged for the first action phase, and again for the second, then felt too separated and formed into two divergent subgroups, each converging on its own project, which was sustained for the next four action phases.

Imagination, motivation and the logic of method

The logic of method allows for a huge variety of patterns in interweaving divergence and convergence, and this interweaving starts in earnest with choices made for the second action phase. Diverge to the edge of chaos then converge into a higher order complex unity of purpose and project: this might be one methodological exhortation derived from complexity theory (Lewin, 1993).

I suggested earlier that there may be a case for moving from divergence in the opening cycles, through an intermediate model balancing divergence and convergence in the middle cycles, to convergence in the closing cycles. I also proposed that it would be a great mistake to turn this into a procedural rule. A very different procedure would be for the early action phases to converge on a holistic approach to the inquiry topic, the middle phases to diverge to articulate and clarify the parts and details, and the closing phases to converge again on the whole at a more developed level of synthesis.

To be more comprehensive about the logic of cyclic method, there are at least six bipolar dimensions to consider: divergent–convergent, within–between phases, individual–group, partitive–holistic, heterogeneous–homogeneous, informative–transformative. I have so far touched on all of these. They are presented and defined together in Chapter 8, with a figure for considering the manifold ways in which they can interact.

Formulae derived from the figure can be suggestive and illumine issues of validity through interweaving, in sound ways, the several parameters. The six dimensions can generate a vast number of logically promising patterns played out over different numbers of cycles. The topic of the inquiry, the type of inquiry, the social situation within which it is embedded, will delimit the range of relevant patterns. Only the most rigorous, and probably misguided, Apollonian inquiry culture would seek to devise a pattern within and between all its research cycles entirely based analytically on the logic of method.

There are also psychological factors to be taken into account, as well as the logical and the situational, when making a choice of pattern. There is the emotional arousal of the inquirers, their level of engagement with, and motivation within, the inquiry process. And there is also the exercise of their creative imagination, what arises within the productive play of the mind in devising the next step forward.

Experience suggests that it is primarily the interaction between emotional arousal and creative imagination that keeps co-operative inquiries alive and afloat. The logic of method, with its six bipolar dimensions, comes in only as a secondary technology to provide both effective power-steering for motivation and imagination, and, at times, a corrective discipline to their occasional excesses. Apollonian inquiry cultures will wisely bear this in mind in their intentional use of the logic of method for forward planning of research cycles. Dionysian cultures will let the logic of method play itself out in purely tacit mode, using it explicitly only for retrospective analysis, or when crisis or imagination require.

When the project for the second action phase has been chosen, divergent or convergent, the researchers will want to refine the details of it and decide on its duration, if this is not already fixed.

Stage 4 (3)   Review of inquiry procedures

Finally, they will need to review the ways of generating and recording data used in the first action phase and see whether changes in these ways are called for. When this is all done the inquirers are ready to go off into the second action phase, which is stage 5. They have completed one cycle of reflection–action–reflection, including the reflection phase that starts off the second cycle.

Subsequent stages

The inquiry is now launched into a series of cycles. As I said earlier, for any given topic and group of inquirers, there may be an optimum ratio for the lengths of the reflection and action phases of any one cycle, which makes them each as fruitful as possible. Also an optimum total of inquiry cycles to create a rounded inquiry. Both these optima will be tailored to fit into the inquirers' other commitments and priorities. Three is a working minimum for the total number of inquiry cycles. Experience suggests that between five and eight full cycles of reflection and action give enough room for useful outcomes, without being too demanding on time and motivation. This would mean between six and nine reflection meetings, including one to open the first cycle and one to close the last.

Dionysian and Apollonian cultures

The polarity involved in the shaping of subsequent action phases is between the Dionysian and the Apollonian, between emergence and preplanning. A Dionysian culture does not plan the action phase in advance at the prior reflection phase, but lets the reflection gestate and bear fruit spontaneously, so that what each person actually does emerges in creative response to what is going on in their situation during the action phase.

This will only suit certain kinds of inquiry, mainly those to do with practice. Even here, the broad category of practice will be clear in advance, since it is the focus of the inquiry, and it is only the individual version of it that is left to emerge. An Apollonian culture will use, more or less explicitly, the realizations and reframings of each reflection phase to plan the structure and content of the next action phase.

I think any inquiry includes elements of both cultures, even if inclining strongly to one pole. Dionysian cultures will have some Apollonian structure in their reflection phases.

> Reason points out that the women's staff development inquiry which allowed for emergence, creative expression and synchronicity in the action phases, was not without structure in the reflection phases. There was an emphasis on equal time and space for all members, on story-telling, on listening circles, and on a structured process for debriefing and analysing the stories told in the circles (Reason, 1994a: 195; Treleaven, 1994).

Likewise Apollonian cultures will usually only plan one action phase at a time, allowing what emerges in reflection from that action phase to shape the next one. In this sense, the whole line of an Apollonian inquiry has a partial Dionysian thrust. Each cycle of *reflection–action–reflection* arises unpredicted and unplanned from its immediately prior cycle of reflection–action–reflection. It is only each cycle of *action–reflection–action* that is planned on the basis of its prior cycle of action–reflection–action.

A very rigorous Apollonian inquiry culture could plan two or three whole cycles in advance, then let some Dionysian thrust in, but I don't know of any group that has tried this. There is clearly the old positivist danger here of constraining experience too much within some preordained methodological mould. Enthusiastic Dionysians, of course, would hold that this danger is present in just one preplanned action phase.

I don't agree with this last view. There clearly is a logic of cyclic method, and to suppose that it is always misguided to use it intentionally masks the real error, which is never to use it intentionally.

Reflection meeting format

Every inquiry culture will develop its own preferred format for its reflection meetings.

> In the whole person medicine inquiry, each reflection meeting was a weekend after a six-week action phase. In the report we wrote that a typical meeting would include most of the following:
>
> - Sharing experience of application in the last cycle, sometimes in small groups and sometimes in the whole group.
> - Conceptual discussion reviewing and revising the five-part model of holistic medicine in the light of the shared experience of application.
> - Sessions on the theory and practice of validity procedures.
> - Group discussions to devise new strategies for the next cycle of application.

- Time spent sometimes alone, sometimes in small groups, writing individual contracts listing strategies each person would use in the next cycle
  of action.
- Group process meetings to deal with interpersonal tensions and diffi-
  culties, and personal emotional distress. These were included in every
  meeting, and were at least two hours long. Occasional co-counselling
  sessions were used for similar purposes.
- Improvised rituals for opening and closing meetings.
- Meditative and transpersonal exercises.
- Role play to practise strategic interventions.
- When residential, jogging, dream analysis, and other extra-curricular
  activities.
- Sharing food together.
- A general climate during and between sessions that permitted warmth,
  hugs, openness, and support. This in turn enabled the group to accom-
  modate and resolve episodes of quite severe confrontation and disagree-
  ment. (Heron and Reason, 1985: 19)

Reflection meetings which do not cover a whole weekend and which may
only last for a few hours, will need to be more selective, including only
those items which seem to be especially relevant to deal with the emerging
needs of the meeting.

Validity: procedures and skills

The number of inquiry cycles, the balance between reflection and action,
the structure of the cycles, with divergence and convergence and the other
parameters interwoven with them – all these have an important bearing on
the validity or *soundness* of the inquiry process and therefore of its outcomes. There are several other procedures which also enhance the soundness of the process and outcomes. I outlined them in Chapter 3 and cover
them in detail in Chapter 8 (see also Heron, 1988b). They include: reflection and action; aspects of reflection; challenging uncritical subjectivity;
chaos and order; managing unaware projections; authentic collaboration.

In several inquiry reports some of these procedures are not mentioned at
all and this seems to me a major deficit. I suspect this is because it is easy for
inquiry groups to get very achievement- and action-oriented and impatient
with what they choose to see as distracting aspects of research method. It is
a major challenge for initiating researchers to create a research culture in
which validity issues are grasped, applied and established early on. One
initiating researcher reports:

> When I started to mention validity procedures I could see that individuals were
> looking a bit lost; one or two people looked puzzled. When I checked this out, one
> of the group confirmed she felt confused. The group, I felt, were not all that
> interested in the process of inquiry; rather they were much more keen on 'doing
> something', never mind the processes involved. This experience was to be repeated
> several times in the course of the co-operative inquiry. (Traylen, 1994: 64)

There is not a lot of point in group members being busy with an inquiry if
they are not also busy with its soundness. It just becomes another round of

restless, unmonitored activism. This, of course, is a typically Apollonian stricture. It can be countered with the view that there is an element of Dionysian validity in the inherent soundness of a co-operative group engaging spontaneously in cycles of reflection and action.

There is one aspect of valid process that every inquiry report mentions: the question of ownership, dependency, authentic collaboration. This is understandably an issue about which initiating researchers will feel particularly sensitive and exposed. If there is no real co-operation and no relatively independent ownership of the inquiry process, they have failed in their task of initiation.

Reason (1988b: 37–8) exhorts every inquiry group to reflect on and develop its own agreed criteria of validity (at most five or six), expressed in its own terms, together with procedures for assessing the performance of the group against the criteria, and to apply these procedures systematically at each cycle of inquiry, and especially at the end.

The soundness of an inquiry depends not only on the validity procedures applied in the reflection phases, but even more so on the special skills involved in being attentive to experience in the action phases. I discuss these in detail in Chapter 7. They are all about critical subjectivity, about each co-subject being their own well-honed instrument of inquiry. They involve paying heed to one's own experience in an extraordinary way, and are the very bedrock of validity. They constitute a major challenge to both Eastern and Western notions of inquiry. They launch a new paradigm of extraordinary living which transcends the illuminated quietism of the East and the rational activism of the West.

These skills, however, do not have to be acquired by some laborious and elitist training before doing an inquiry. The process of engaging in a co-operative inquiry is itself a discipline for developing the extraordinariness it requires.

Final reflection

A Dionysian inquiry may simply choose to end with a final round of story-telling by its members about its total process, and with its final outcomes still gestating within the hearts, minds and choices of its members. These gestating outcomes will burst forth upon the world after the inquiry is concluded, and in their own good time.

An Apollonian inquiry will need at its end at least one major reflection phase to bring its informative and/or transformative threads together as they have been woven in and out of the several inquiry cycles, and to make sense of the inquiry as a whole. The whole group is involved in reviewing, distilling, collating and refining the cumulative data from all the cycles.

> In the concluding making-sense weekend of the youth workers' inquiry into their own learning processes, small groups met in which each person distilled out from all the prior cycles what he or she had learned about their own effective learning. Each group listed items true

for all its members. Then the whole group met to identify, from the small group lists, 'only that which proved to be true for all of us'. These final convergent items were presented as the group's 'discoveries' (De Venney-Tiernan et al., 1994).

In the first co-counselling inquiry (Heron and Reason, 1981), in the last group reflection phase, we took the most coherent maps that different individuals had refined through their own cycles, and all of us took a part in amending each map until all, including its originator, were satisfied with it and with its relative coherence with the other maps thus treated.

In these early days of such a highly participative method, arriving at a satisfactory point of completion is a very relative matter. Different inquiries, depending on their overall length, topic and membership, will achieve different degrees of it. But an impressive amount of solid work has come forth, of which I only give some examples:

The youth workers winnowed out a well-rounded account of practices and principles of their own effective learning (De Venney-Tiernan et al., 1994).

The women's staff development inquiry generated substantial transformations of personal and professional identity and decision-making, and initiated diffuse organizational change (Treleaven, 1994).

The organizational culture inquiry came up with a full portrait of the culture as 'a web of interconnecting themes' (Marshall and McLean, 1988: 219).

The first co-counselling inquiry generated a comprehensive set of well-formulated maps of client-states; and the second inquiry a wide range of tactics and strategies for dealing with restimulated distress in everyday life (Heron and Reason, 1981, 1982).

The whole person medicine inquiry refined the practice of power-sharing with patients, the use of spiritual interventions with patients, and the skills of 'self-gardening'. Other aspects of its initial five-part model of holistic medicine were only minimally explored (Heron and Reason, 1985; Reason, 1988c).

The altered states inquiry winnowed out a tentative set of criteria for distinguishing between genuine and spurious impressions of the other reality (Heron, 1988c).

The health visitors' inquiry clarified a number of effective strategies for working with families. It had a breakthrough to the concept of well-being in its penultimate reflection meeting and decided to explore this in the last action phase. But in the final reflection phase, there was no time to review this exploration, because discussion was entirely taken up with a first draft of a report on the inquiry (Traylen, 1994).

This last story brings out the importance of clearly separating the final reflection meeting, where the business is to make sense of the whole inquiry, from working on the final report. After final sense-making, and at the same meeting, the main headings and key issues to be included in any report may be agreed, with allocations of authorship and editorship, and plans to circulate and redraft. But the writing, circulating, commenting and redrafting are best done after the inquiry cycles have been finished.

Endings, outcomes and reports

Co-operative inquiries generate much shared passion of commitment among those who have sustained the adventure. The inquirers have broken out of the ancient mould, still upheld by the majority of researchers today, that only the expert elite know how to acquire real knowledge, and how to apply it. The primary outcome of such mould-breaking is a way of being in the world that sacralizes it with a participative awareness shared with others.

This awareness re-affirms and completes the values launched at the Renaissance but side-tracked in the seventeenth century by the gathering momentum of the Cartesian–Newtonian worldview (Skolimowski, 1994). The artists of the Renaissance showed through their own achievements that the human being is a co-creator of the world as imaginal reality. It was not just the person as the measure of all things, but the person as the measure of a sacral reality, of a world that is the spiritual artefact of the depths of the imaginal mind. What the contemporary re-affirmation adds to the highly individual accomplishments of the Renaissance in forms of art, is the collaborative accomplishment of lived inquiry as an art-form.

The outcomes of such inquiry combine a way of being present in the world, a revisioning of its patterning, propositions that articulate it, practices that transform it. I discuss these kinds of outcome in Chapter 6. The middle two of these can be expressed in forms apart from the inquirer, in artistic portrayals and reports. But the first and last are inseparable from the inquirer, and since they have been forged in collaboration with others, this creates a deep bonding. Hence the ending of any inquiry is a celebration of this bonding and a mourning that the active welding of it has come to an end. So there needs to be some full acknowledgement of all this:

> Inevitably some will leave pleased and stimulated by the work while others will be dissatisfied; some will have made lifelong friendships, others may be lonely and hurt. The hopes and aspirations of the beginning have to meet the realities of achievement.

> Time must be taken here to acknowledge all the experiences of the members of the group; for members to express their delights and their resentments, and maybe their hopes for the future. And if the group has been any kind of a success, its explorations will live on, not only in dissertations and papers, but also in the lives and work of its members. (Reason, 1988b: 39)

I am opposed to the idea that the proper outcome of research with people is a written report. Whether the inquiry is informative and describes the inquirers' world, or transformative to do with practices that change their world, the proper outcome is not something on paper, but something within persons. Where people are their own instruments of inquiry into a topic using their own experience, and undergo transformations of being, perception, thinking and behaviour in order to conduct it, then it is clear that the proper outcome is the transformed instrument. The instrument is the evidence is the outcome. Anything written down is secondary and subsidiary.

Reports have important secondary status as communicating something about a co-operative inquiry, both its internal structure and process as well as its outcomes, in the absence of the inquirers. This is especially the case with regard to the outcomes of an informative, descriptive inquiry. But the notion of an informative report must be widened to include audio-visual and artistic portrayals of all kinds, both verbal and nonverbal, as well as the familiar analytic-conceptual prose of academia.

In the case of transformative inquiries, where the outcomes are new forms of practice among the inquirers, portrayals or evocations of the practice become primary; also training others in the practice. Prose reports of the practice, its outcomes and its context, are supporting programme notes. Reports of both informative and transformative inquiries may also have the important political purpose of empowering others to revision their experience and practice.

Reports and presentational portrayals of a co-operative inquiry themselves clearly need to be co-operatively produced or subject to systematic co-operative editing and revision. Here is one way of proceeding with respect to a written report:

- The outline and main content headings of the report, together with any key issues to be included under any heading, are brainstormed, discussed and refined in the whole group.
- Agreements are made about who will write up which parts, and who will be the co-ordinating editors (who may also be authors of one or more parts).
- Drafts of the parts are sent to the co-ordinating editors, who produce a complete first draft of the whole report.
- This is sent to the part-authors and every other member of the inquiry for their comments and suggested amendments, which the editors incorporate as appropriate in a second draft, which is sent round for a final set of comments.
- The editors take account of the final comments and produce a third and final version of the report, which is then available for publication.

Variations of this format were adopted by the youth workers' inquiry (De Venney-Tiernan et al., 1994), and the holistic medicine inquiry (Heron and Reason, 1985; Reason, 1988c). In each case, the initiating researchers were both co-ordinating editors and authors of some parts of the reports.

In other reports, the initiating researchers were the sole authors of the first draft and of subsequent redrafts in the light of feedback from group members (Heron and Reason, 1981; Marshall and McLean, 1988; Cosier and Glennie, 1994; Traylen, 1994; Treleaven, 1994).

Other reports appear to be written exclusively by the initiating researchers without recourse to feedback from inquiry group members and without any acknowledgement that this is the case (Archer and Whitaker, 1994; Whitmore, 1994). This suggests that group members are not regarded as equal co-researchers with the authors. All the inquiries with which I have been associated have always had an agreement that any member of the group is free to write their own personal account of the inquiry without submitting a draft to other members, as long as this is made fully explicit in the report, with an acknowledgement of its limitations, as follows:

> This report has not been written collaboratively with the group, but exclusively by myself. And this is clearly a limitation on any claim that the findings of the inquiry are based on authentic collaboration. (Heron, 1988c)

The notion that there is one proper way to write up a co-operative inquiry is as offensive to its ethos as the idea that there is only one proper way to do it. But since inquiry reports can illuminate the process of inquiry for others, can be politically empowering for others, can have outcomes which others can adopt, and can call for metamorphosed replication or for related but quite different further inquiries, there are various items which it is both interesting and useful to find in them. Here is my current, highly Apollonian, list of what I would find of great interest, although I would be astonished, if not dismayed, to discover all of it in any one report:

- Relevant information about the initiating researcher, including their prior experience or knowledge of co-operative inquiry; and the same about the group members.
- A brief account of the background to the inquiry, how and why it has come into being; including something about the inquiry topic, where it came from, and how it was stated before the inquiry opened.
- Details about methods of recruiting group members, about the induction meeting and responses to it, about the nature of the entry contract, and about the number and gender and ages of contracting members.
- Details of the time-structure: the total number of inquiry cycles, the length of the reflection phases and of the action phases.
- Information about the type of inquiry: full and internally initiated, or partial and externally initiated, inside or outside, open or closed boundary, same/reciprocal/counterpartal/mixed role, Apollonian and/or Dionysian, informative and/or transformative:
  - If externally initiated, how do the initiating researchers deal with their lack of full participation in the action phases?

- If an open boundary in the action phases, do the inquirers elicit any data from the noninquirers with whom they interact at the boundary?
- If an open boundary in the reflection phases, who is invited to visit them and what impact do the visits have?
- An account of how the inquiry topic was processed at the first reflection meeting, and how it was shaped up into a launching focus for the whole inquiry.
- A summary story of all the research cycles with some résumé of what went on at each reflection meeting, what was done in each action phase and of the ongoing fate of the launching proposal.
  - Were presentational as well as propositional forms of recording in the action phases and of making sense in the reflection phases used, and with what effect?
- Information about the overall pattern within and between research cycles in relation to divergence and convergence, and in relation to parts, subwholes or the whole of the inquiry topic.
- The story of inquiry initiation, of the move from dependency on the initiating researchers to:
- Genuine co-ownership of the method.
- Authentic collaboration in applying it.
- Emotional and interpersonal competence in dealing with the underlying anxieties to which it gives rise. With respect to these three items, were different roles allocated to group members, and in what manner?
- An account of the validity or soundness of the inquiry (which includes the previous item):
  - When and how was the validity of the inquiry process self and peer assessed and by what methods and criteria?
  - An overall assessment of the validity of the inquiry process.
  - In an Apollonian inquiry, did making sense in the reflection phases rise from description to evaluation or even explanation? Was there any intentional explicit transfer of learning from the last action phase to planning the next?
  - In a Dionysian inquiry, were richly expressive forms of making sense used in the reflection phases? Was there strong intentionality about tacit transfer of learning from the last action phase to the next?
- An account of the outcomes of the inquiry, whether experiential, presentational, propositional or practical. And an evaluation of the strength of their claim to be warranted belief or knowledge in the light of criteria internal to them, of their grounding in other forms of knowing, and of assessments of the validity of the inquiry process.
- Some sampling of group members' stories about the kinds of inquiry skills they developed in the action phases, and about their overall experience of the project.

6
Inquiry Outcomes

The outcomes of a co-operative inquiry are to do with how its findings are to be expressed, in what forms of knowledge they are to be conveyed. As presented in Chapter 3, and to simplify and summarize in advance, I believe co-operative inquiries can have four interrelated sorts of outcome:

- Transformations of personal being through engagement with the focus and process of the inquiry.
- Presentations of insight about the focus of the inquiry, through dance, drawing, drama, and all other expressive modes: these provide imaginal symbols of the significant patterns in our realities.
- Propositional reports which (1) are informative about the inquiry domain, that is, they describe and explain what has been explored, (2) provide commentary on the other kinds of outcome, and (3) describe the inquiry method.
- Practical skills which are (1) skills to do with transformative action within the inquiry domain, and (2) skills to do with various kinds of participative knowing and collaboration used in the inquiry process.

For informative inquiries, propositional reports (1), supported by presentations, will be primary outcomes. For transformative inquiries, practical skills (1) will be primary, supported by presentations, propositional reports (2) and maybe also by some propositional reports (1). As between propositional and practical outcomes I take the view that practical outcomes have primacy and are the consummation of the inquiry process. For any inquiry, transformations of personal being are foundation outcomes.

Holistic epistemology and the primacy of the practical

On the systemic, multi-dimensional account of knowledge introduced in Chapter 2 and elaborated in Chapter 3, the kinds of knowing that can be developed within the domain of a co-operative inquiry are fourfold, corresponding to the four kinds of outcome given above:

- Experiential knowing: through direct encounter feeling the presence and perceptually imaging the form of beings in their domain.
- Presentational knowing: an intuitive, imaginal ability to express significant patterns of form and process within the domain.

- Propositional knowing: formulating propositions which conceptualize, categorize, and theorize about, the domain.
- Practical knowing; knowing how to practise relevant skills to transform the domain.

The inquiry domain is not an objective world independent of, and the same for, all observers for all time. It is a subjective-objective reality, a world as experienced and interacted with. It is a world in which there is a distinction but no separation between personal being and presented being, the imaginer and the imagined, the conceiver and the conceived, the doer and the done within. In each of these modes and in all of them together, reality is mind-moulded and perspectival. It always bears the great signature of the given. It is always inseparable from how each individual in the group and how the intersubjective culture of the group choose to be, image, conceive and act within it.

In my view those modes of knowing are grounded in each other and emerge from each other. Being fully present in radical perception is the ground for an imaginal expression of significant form and pattern, which is the ground for good conceptual construing, which is the ground for excellence of skill and action (Heron, 1992). Each mode that emerges consummates and affirms at a new level of relative autonomy and value the ground from which it emerges. The excellences of human skill have as their necessary ground conceptual knowledge, but go beyond it and consummate it with an autonomous form which also reveals it, makes it more explicit, extends and transforms it, gives it moral point and purpose and makes it value-charged.

Macmurray (1957), in his Gifford Lectures of 1953, arguing in a different yet related way, makes a strong case for the primacy of the practical in relation to the conceptual. He affirms that 'I do' instead of 'I think' is the starting point and centre of reference for grasping the form of the personal: the self is an agent and exists only as an agent. The self as thinking subject cannot exist as subject; it is in and for the self as agent. Knowing in its fullness is consummated in and through agency; and pure thought divorced from action, the attempt to consummate agency entirely through knowing, leads to a lesser kind of knowing, which is secondary, derivative, abstract and negative (Macmurray, 1957). I shall return to this theme of the primacy of the practical in the final sections of this chapter, and again in Chapter 9.

Four kinds of outcome

How can the four kinds of knowing be communicated as inquiry outcomes? The inquirers' experiential gains, transformations of inner being, can only be conveyed, at their own level, through personal meeting, through being with the inquirers, in their presence. We need to meet them face to face and experience through intimate fellowship, resonant attunement, how their being has been transformed through encounter with the presences and qualities of the inquiry domain, and of the group inquiry process.

Imaginal grasp of significant pattern can be symbolized and expressed, in its own terms, through presentational forms as in the graphic arts, plastic arts, moving and musical arts, and through the use of metaphor evoked by story, myth, allegory, poesy, drama. Such presentational and metaphorical findings can be a precursor to, and complement of, conceptual findings communicated in propositional form as descriptions, explanations and theoretical constructs.

Reason and Hawkins (1988) make out a strong case for this kind of complementarity in what they call the 'dialectic between expression and explanation', between telling stories and conceptual theorizing, between depth and clarity (Ihde, 1971). I discussed this more fully in Chapter 5. Qualitative researchers make a related point in recommending that 'thick descriptions' derived from using all the senses are included in the research report as a ground for the conceptual findings (Lincoln and Guba, 1985; Erlandson et al., 1993).

Finally, practical knowing, acquired skills and competencies, can be conveyed through:

- Application on the job.
- Live demonstrations.
- Audio-visual recordings.
- Dramatic reconstructions.
- Stories which evoke the impact of them.
- Training sessions.

These can be supported in a secondary way by written reports, as outlined in the section below on propositional outcomes. But a report about practical outcomes, while it may be necessary, is not sufficient. On its own it is not enough, since a skill transcends any written account of it.

For sophisticated skills, combining physical, psychosocial and transpersonal elements, it is best if we can be in the presence of those who have acquired the relevant knacks and can show them at work. And for this demonstrated know-how to be truly communicated, we need to begin to acquire the skill ourselves. In this way we can start to get a sense through doing of what the knack is all about, its own internal signature of excellence. Only then can we properly evaluate the written account.

For conveying a skill is more than simply demonstrating it, showing a video recording of it, or telling a story to evoke the impact of it. If you have communicated a proposition to me, this means I have understood it, I can intelligently replicate it in my own discourse. Similarly, if you have communicated your knowing how to do something to me, it means that I can replicate it, so that I too know how to do it, and can put that practical knowledge to use in my own way. It means that you not only show it to me, it also means you start to train me, helping and empowering me to acquire it.

In this sense, practical outcomes are only fully revealed within a whole body of practice, or culture of competence, a concept which I discuss toward the end of this chapter. I think it is important to acknowledge this, while at the same time agreeing that for purposes of general communication, live demonstrations, recorded portrayals, dramatic reconstructions, stories and descriptive reports, will have a vital role to play.

Inseparable and separable outcomes

For convenience I will call the four kinds of outcome presence outcomes, pattern outcomes, propositional outcomes and practical outcomes. Presence outcomes and practical outcomes *per se* are inseparable from the researcher: qualities of being and skills are resident within the person who has them. Moreover, skills are grounded in, and manifest, qualities of being: what a person does is revelatory of their presence, their way of being. Thus in affirming the primacy of the practical, we are at the same time affirming this revelatory role.

Pattern and propositional outcomes are separable from the person: they don't properly exist until they are symbolized in some external medium – graphics, painting, sculpture, choreographic or musical notation, imaginative writing, or scientific report. For purposes of communication they are highly convenient. Patterns of many kinds and propositions of all kinds can be represented on paper or computer screens and moved rapidly anywhere in the world.

The written word itself can represent both pattern and propositional outcomes: the former by the evocation of metaphor in poetry, story, parable, allegory, myth; the latter by the interlinking of concepts in classificatory and theoretical statements. So while the living presence and manifest deeds of inquirers are root and flower outcomes that have limited mobility, the written leaves that carry on the wind to faraway places provide the main loam for the universal spread and growth of knowledge.

If, however, we affirm the primacy of practical outcomes, with their revelation of personal presence, then we have the anomaly that, for a transformative inquiry, any written report, circulating around the world, is only secondary and supportive of the skills which transcend it and which are inseparable from the inquirers who manifest them.

Transformative, illuminative and informative outcomes

Presence and practical outcomes, qualities of being and skills, inseparable from the inquirers, are *transformative* of them. Such personal transformation, by virtue of the inquirers' presence in and interaction with the research domain, extends into social and environmental transformation.

Treleaven initiated a collaborative inquiry involving a women's staff development group in a university. Reporting on individual outcomes for the women, she refers to 'a transformed position with respect to their identities', and to the inquiry process as one that 'can enable an ontological shift – a change in the way of being of a person'. This in turn generates actions that contribute to organizational change (Treleaven, 1994). So here presence outcomes empower practical outcomes, by means of which personal leads over into social transformation.

Pattern outcomes, which represent significant form within the structure and process of the inquiry domain, are *illuminative*. By means of visual, auditory or kinaesthetic images in graphics, sound or movement, or of images evoked by the use of analogy and metaphor in poesy, story or drama, pattern outcomes illumine the domain, throwing into relief the inherent meaning of its perceptual imagery, of its appearing in consciousness. They are 'analogical and symbolic; they do not point out meaning directly; they demonstrate it by re-creating pattern in metaphorical shape and form' (Reason and Hawkins, 1988: 81).

In the inquiry referred to above, Treleaven (1994) used story-telling in listening circles as a prime way of throwing into relief the patterning of gender dynamics in the workplace, and includes some of the stories in her report.

The co-counselling inquiry report on the states clients enter in co-counselling sessions represented these states by a variety of graphic representations with verbal labels attached. There were supplementary descriptions in the text, but the graphics were primary (Heron and Reason, 1981).

In an unreported co-operative inquiry into the application of trans-personal activities in everyday life, which I launched in New Zealand in 1994, a primary outcome, on the day of its final meeting, was a large painting collectively created by all the members of the inquiry group making their individual contributions to it at the same time.

Pattern ways of representing experience can also be used in reflection phases throughout the inquiry as illuminative data about what goes on in the action phases, and as a ground for verbal, descriptive data.

This, too, was used in the co-counselling inquiry just cited: in the reflection phases, the data from each client's just completed session was presented as a drawing, which was the basis for a verbal account.

Reason and Hawkins (1988), in their exploration of story-telling as inquiry, suggest that stories can be used in several ways in co-operative inquiry: to generate data, to make further sense of data, to communicate findings in a marriage of 'explanation and expression'. Pattern ways can further be used to illumine the methods of an inquiry and its meta-outcomes which evaluate those methods.

Propositional outcomes are *informative* and I consider them in the next section.

The range of propositional outcomes

Since a commitment to propositional outcomes is likely to remain strong for some time to come in the world of research, it seems sensible to consider their range. I will first discuss statements that deal with the main findings in transformative and informative inquiries, and then look briefly at reporting the inquiry process.

In transformative inquiries, where practical skills are the primary outcome, propositional outcomes are reports related to practice, are secondary to it and no substitute for it. These reports on practice can:

- Describe the practice, and how it evolved and changed, in terms of some of its several components: the overt behaviour, its strategy and guiding norms, its purpose or end and underlying values, its motives, its external context and supporting beliefs, and its actual outcomes. These components are reviewed in Chapter 7.
- Describe the social and environmental changes the practice has brought about in the local situation and beyond it.
- Evaluate the practice and its effects in terms of relevant criteria, which are reviewed in Chapter 9.
- Report informative descriptions and redefinitions of its domain which the practice has engendered and which support it.

The last of these is where the transformative generates the informative, and where the action paradox, discussed later in this chapter, comes in. Here significant statements about the domain are the consequence of a primary intent to cultivate practice and bring about change within it.

In the whole person medicine project, a subgroup of doctors explored the use of spiritual interventions with their NHS patients. Reflections on these practices led to a basic set of phenomenal distinctions which mapped out the domain of the spiritual (Heron and Reason, 1985; Reason, 1988c).

In informative inquiries, propositional outcomes are directly about the domain of inquiry. They can:

- Describe the domain in terms of its phenomenal categories, its basic patterns, the modes of awareness of its entities; and give a grounding explanation in terms of higher-order connecting patterns; and in terms of ontological significance, that is, the kinds of being involved and their relations.

- Evaluate these accounts as to their adequacy, quality, validity, grounded-ness, trustworthiness, or whatever other term of evaluation the co-researchers choose to use.
- Further explain the domain in terms of more elaborate typologies, theoretical constructs and ontological paradigms. Forms of thinking involved here are reviewed in Chapter 8.

Propositions descriptive of the inquiry process can deal with several different aspects of it. I give a full account of these at the end of Chapter 5. Here is a simplified version of what these propositions can relate:

- The background and origin of the inquiry, its focal topic and intended outcomes, its membership, contracting in.
- The type of inquiry, its methodology and a summary history of its use and of the development of the research topic.
- Procedures chosen to enhance the validity of the inquiry, an account of their use and of the validity of the inquiry in the light of them.
- An account of the outcomes of the inquiry, whether experiential, presentational, propositional or practical.
- An evaluation of these outcomes in the light of relevant criteria and of assessments of the validity of the inquiry process.

Outcomes and meta-outcomes

At this point it is important to note that co-operative inquirers are engaged in two simultaneous inquiries. There is the first-order inquiry that focuses on the chosen topic, and there is the second-order inquiry that is about the whole business of doing a co-operative inquiry. When a group uses at intervals throughout its history any one or more of a range of different validity procedures as discussed in Chapter 8, it is conducting a meta-inquiry into the adequacy of its inquiry.

Thus many inquiry reports contain not only outcomes that relate to the chosen topic, suitably prefaced by an account of the inquiry process. They also discuss meta-outcomes to do with an evaluation of the various elements of this process: their adequacy, use and relevance, possible modifications, future applications. In some reports, these three things can be run together in a confusing fashion:

- The story of the inquiry process.
- Information on meta-outcomes that evaluate it.
- Information on outcomes that relate to the focus of the inquiry.

It certainly helps the accessibility of a report if these three components are clearly distinguished, if only to show how deeply they interweave. Also in some reports there seems to be more about meta-outcomes than about basic outcomes, and this I find frustrating.

Transcendent practice

I return now to the primacy of the practical, and discuss how practice is ineffable, how it generates the ethos of a culture of competence, and how it brings to light the action paradox.

The ineffability of knacks

Skills are not reducible without remainder to any set of verbal statements reporting the skill. As Ryle (1949) put it, knowing how cannot be reduced to knowing that. Practical knowledge, having a skill, transcends propositional knowledge and has its own relative autonomy. At the core of any skill is a knack, an inner key to effective action. The knack is the fulcrum of the skill, its point of leverage on behaviour. You can describe a skill in words up to a point, but the inner core of the action, the knack, defies verbal description. This is so whether the knack is to do with a physical, technical, emotional, interpersonal, managerial, transpersonal skill, their combinations, or any other kind of skill.

Having the knack is the essence of a skill: it is at the heart of knowing how. And at the heart of the knack is a knowing of the excellence of its doing, which is what makes it a knack. This is a criterion of practical validity which is intrinsic to action and which is ineffable. For each specific knack it is beyond language and conceptual formulation. Knacks are things you cannot fully report. They transcend all propositional utterance and take you into the autonomous sublimity of action. So any published paper descriptive of a skill or skills is going to be partial, an incomplete and ghostly cipher. It is beset by its own inherent limitations. It needs to be aware of this and point beyond itself to what it cannot contain.

A culture of competence

I have so far written as if the skills of the individual person constitute the whole of the domain of practice. They certainly manifest the active, cutting edge of it. A taxonomy of them includes a wide array of items which can combine in action in innumerable ways. There are motor skills, perceptual skills, technical skills, verbal skills, cognitive skills, emotional skills, decision-making skills, interpersonal skills, managerial skills, political skills, organizational skills, transpersonal skills, aesthetic skills, to name but a few. However, the realm of the practical includes, correlative to an individual dimension, a social one. There is not only skill manifest in personal action; there is also a body of practice.

A body of practice, which I also call a culture of competence, is manifest in a profession, a community of practitioner colleagues. It is a social repository of skill, a form of practical social order. It cannot be reduced to an aggregate of the individual skills of those who are active in the profession at any given time. Like any form of social order it is a systemic whole which necessarily includes the individuals who are its manifest parts.

But the elements of that order, those features which make the whole a *system*, are a dimension of social reality in their own right.

When fully established, these elements comprise a set of shared beliefs, norms and values which, whether tacit or explicit:

- Delimit the profession or community of colleagues in terms of social positions and roles.
- Prescribe appropriate skilled actions within those roles.
- Prescribe the standards of competence that are relevant to such behaviour.
- Are crowned by an indefinable ethos, a shared valuing of the practical excellence for which the culture stands.

These defining beliefs, norms and values can be stated as a set of propositions and declarations, and it is useful so to state them. But because they define a body of practice which is only manifest when individuals are exercising the relevant skills, and because the core of each skill is an ineffable knack, any verbal account of this culture of competence falls short. The culture as a systemic whole has an *ethos* which transcends any linguistic description of its values, norms and beliefs.

The ethos of a body of practice can be felt; it can be grasped imaginally and intuitively. It can be invoked through metaphor, demonstrated through literal and symbolic presentations, and honoured by the use of ritual. Like a knack, it cannot be expresssed without remainder through language.

The domain of the practical, then, has interdependent and complementary poles: individual skill and a culture of competence. At the heart of the former is an indefinable knack, and the essence of the latter is a felt ethos, *a collective knowing how to value a whole body of practice*, which also transcends verbal description. This knowing how to value shared competence is not an autonomous, individual knowing how in the way that a knack is. It is intersubjective, communal, the consequence of participating in a shared culture of practical excellence. The guilds of medieval craftsmen were, I believe, a focus for the affirmation, celebration and strengthening of this conjoint practical ethos.

Traditionally there has been a fundamental asymmetry between an individual skill and a culture of competence, which represented the established status quo within its profession. Any radical agenda of transforming practice rested exclusively with the individual pioneer. Even where cultures of competence have promoted research and development, the breakthrough has come through the efforts of one or two individuals, sometimes vying with each other.

With the advent of co-operative inquiry and related forms of participative research, cultures of competence can become self-transforming *as collectives*. A co-operative inquiry group that is busy with transforming practice within a profession, is a local culture of competence that has two tiers. As a group of practitioners within a given field, there is a shared ethos in knowing how to value the newly acquired skills. And as a group of collaborating researchers, there is a shared ethos in knowing how to value the inquiry skills involved in acquiring the new professional skills. Torbert (1991) also writes of a community of inquiry within a community of practice.

It follows that when people set up a transformative inquiry with individual practical skills as their primary intended outcomes, this now needs complementing with the correlative intention to regenerate the body of practice, the culture of competence, within which those skills have their social home.

This in turn leads to a distinction between two kinds of inquiry of this sort. There is one that seeks to regenerate a culture of competence by altering the skills internal to it, the skills which differentiate it from other professions. For example, changing medical culture by transforming medical skills. And there is another which intends to transform a culture of competence not by transforming its distinguishing skills, but by importing into it skills from some other profession. So a medical group may want to acquire educational skills to regenerate the ways in which medical culture educates itself, thus to improve the accessibility of its medical skills without changing those skills as such.

Finally, once the interdependent nature of individual skills and a culture of competence becomes clear, co-operative inquiry uniquely offers the possibility, not only of regenerating a culture of competence through working on individual skills, but also of transforming skills through a direct inquiry into transformations of the culture *per se*. Thus an inquiry group could, as a quorum of practitioners within a body of practice, explore the effects on individual practice of working together to clarify and enhance the systemic elements of its professional culture.

At one level this means refining explicit statements of the beliefs, norms and values of the culture, by taking successive versions through several cycles of shared reflection and individual action. More fundamentally it means going beyond propositional clarification to celebrate the transcendent ethos of the culture through shared ritual and other presentational forms of communal expression, and noting what subsequent effect this may have on individual practice.

The action paradox

In the account of propositional outcomes earlier in this chapter, I said that reports on practice can give information about its domain which the practice has engendered, and that this points to the action paradox. The paradox asserts that the most significant statements about a domain are not the fruit of an informative inquiry but of a transformative one.

The relation between mapping statements about a domain and actions within it can go two ways. If I choose statements about a domain as my primary outcome, then what actions I perform within it are secondary to what information I want to generate about it. If I choose skills that transform a domain as my primary outcome, then what information I get about the domain is secondary to what actions I perform within it.

After trying it both ways, and some ambiguous ways, I now believe we get deeper information about the nature of our realities when our prime concern is to develop practical skills which change these realities, than when our prime concern is to get information about them through the exercise of appropriate skills. Information about our realities, like happiness, is something which is better realized when it is not pursued directly, and is a consequence of an anterior choice to transform them.

I don't think this rules out the validity of direct information-gathering, which is a complementary approach; and there are clearly occasions when this is the method of choice. It's just that there is a deeper and more satisfying way to go: into the action paradox that we learn more profoundly about our worlds when we are more interested in enhancing them with excellence of action than in learning about them.

This action paradox is linked with the old adage that 'he who doeth the will shall know of the doctrine', which could be construed to mean that realities reveal themselves more fully to those who have a prior commitment to excellence of action. Since our realities are subjective-objective, the point about true excellence of action is that it is reality-transformative for the person who acquires that excellence. And the transformation brings into conscious relief both what that reality was and what it has become.

A subtle, though limited, form of the paradox asserts that we find out more about our worlds when we seek to develop our skills in finding out more about them, than when we seek simply to find out more about them.

An unreported inquiry into altered states of consciousness which I initiated in New Zealand in 1994 focused on the *knacks* involved in entering such states, rather than attending directly to a mapping of the states themselves. This seemed to develop a more fruitful, but incidental, phenomenology about the states, than if it had been pursued head-on.

7

Radical Memory and Inquiry Skills

In this chapter I take a look at two kinds of radical memory which are the seat of data generation in co-operative inquiry, and then elaborate these as a range of skills for conducting informative and transformative inquiries. At the end I relate the extraordinary consciousness involved in the exercise of these skills to a revised account of multi-level mind.

These skills, together with the several procedures I review in Chapter 8, have a direct bearing on the validity of the inquiry process and its outcomes. They are the skills which engage human subjectivity with the experiential focus of the inquiry, and at the same time enable it to become more open and more critical.

May I suggest to the reader who gets well into the heart of this chapter and starts to find the account of all these skills daunting and disheartening, that the discipline of engaging in a co-operative inquiry and its cyclic process is itself a means of developing them. Furthermore, while the description of them can appear immaculate, the occurrence of them is maculate, fractal, earthy, irregular and granular. We are all beginners.

Informative memory and paying heed

Since the inquirers are their own subjects, their data about their own perceptions and actions is necessarily recorded retrospectively, anything from minutes to hours to a day or more after the event. Hence any record is actually a secondary form of data generation. The primary form, which indeed is at the very point of generation, is memory.

Perception and memory are born together: to perceive is to remember, at least for a bit. The critical bridge between the two is noticing, or, to use the old English term, paying heed to. 'Heed' means careful attention. To perceive anything, in everyday understanding, is simply to register its presence as a certain kind of thing: it is basic acquaintance and identification. It is not the same as paying heed to it, giving it careful attention, noticing something about it. This involves an extra, intentional directing of awareness.

By and large, we don't remember well or for long what we don't pay heed to. But there is paying heed to in an ordinary way, and there is paying heed to in an extraordinary way. To clarify this I need to go more deeply into the nature of perception.

In terms of the relativist ontology presented in this book, reality is a subjective-objective transaction, the fruit of the active participation and construing of the mind in what is given. In terms of perceiving, the perceiver is inseparable from, but not identical with, the perceptual process of imaging in visual, auditory, tactile and kinaesthetic terms. This imaging process is inseparable from, but not identical with, the given which it images and enacts. Thus through perceptual imaging, the perceiver participates in the given, or, to put it crudely, in the world ('crudely' because strictly speaking the world is not the given but how the perceiver participates in the given).

The routinization of perception

But while a person participates in the world through perceiving it and this participation is an active construing process, its nature gets marred by a combination of two things. Firstly, the use of language – the ascription of class names such as 'house', 'tree', 'cat' – has the strong tendency to obscure the unitive, participatory nature of the subject–object transaction. It is prone to create the illusion that subject and object are separate, the object being out there quite independent of the subject in here. Instead of the image being part and parcel of the active process of the perceiver's imaging, it becomes reified as a named thing, separated from the perceiver who is looking at it. Secondly, and consequently, the perceiving process becomes routinized by language. Its active participation sleep-walks inside the clothing of linguistic categories. Then people do not really pay heed to what is going on in the perceiving process.

There are, in fact, two levels at which people can pay perceptual heed. Within sleep-walking, routinized perception, they can pay heed, in terms of linguistic categories, to objects out there and their features. They are simply noticing more about an external object in terms of already existing classifications. This is the ordinary, everyday sense of paying heed. It is elaborated in terms of physical science and technology. It is certainly not to be underrated.

Extraordinary perceptual heed

At another level they can wake up from the categorial dream of language and pay heed, in an extraordinary way, to the participative process of perceiving itself. They can notice how the mind through perceptual imaging is engaged in creative enactment and shaping of the world and its beings. They can sense how this is inseparable from empathic communion with these beings: this means a felt harmonic resonance with their inner presence, with their mode of consciousness, the way they are affected by their world. And thus people can discern features of their subjective-objective reality which the use of language has not so far accommodated, or which lurk obscurely amidst the ambiguities of everyday speech, or which language uses as its base while regarding it as insignificant. What this kind of paying heed can do, together with the memory which it generates, is to intuit something about the patterning of the different entities in our world, the significant form of their interconnections, and about their modes of awareness. Thus it can extend the range of the basic phenomenal categories in terms of which we describe our realities.

The public use of language itself presupposes a mutual awareness, a tacit shared understanding and immersion in meaning of unknown depth, which is not itself mediated by language, and which is the context for agreement about the use of language. This tacit intersubjective realm of primary meaning, inherent in our participative transaction with our world, is both prelinguistic, and also currently extralinguistic. The conceptual meanings of language are a continuous transformation of it, however fixed, rigid and distorting this transformation becomes. This primary meaning is a profound nonlinguistic substrate, the unnoticed context, of all secondary meaning conveyed by dialogue and exchange within a culture. And it is this we can bring to the fore and access through the process of extraordinary heed.

For co-subjects in an informative inquiry the prime way of generating data is through memory, by paying heed moment by moment to our continuous participatory, creative, ever-changing empathic and unrestricted perceptual transaction with the world. This is the most fundamental kind of data generation which inquirers can get ready for when thinking ahead to the first, and every subsequent, action phase.

> Sometimes, when we perceive the world, we perceive without language. We perceive spontaneously, with a pre-language system. But sometimes when we view the world, first we think a word and then we perceive. In other words, the first instance is directly feeling or perceiving the universe; the second is talking ourselves into seeing our universe. So you either look and see beyond language – as first perception – or you see the world through the filter of your thoughts, by talking to yourself. (Trungpa, 1986: 30)

The notion of extraordinary heed is another way of talking about mindfulness, wakefulness, or self-remembering. These are basic disciplines of enhanced high-quality awareness commended in many ancient and modern schools of spiritual practice. Their purpose is to arouse us from the trance of ordinary consciousness, in which we are so hypnotized by the content of experience, that we lose deep awareness of how we generate it. Both Torbert (1983) and Reason (1988d) have drawn attention to the relevance of these teachings for valid inquiry. They relate also to the classical phenomenologist's notion of the second epoché, in which we contemplate how phenomena are coming into being within our consciousness (Husserl, 1964).

Varela et al. propose an enactive paradigm of perception in which perceiving 'is not simply embedded within and constrained by the surrounding world; it also contributes to the enactment of this surrounding world' (1993: 174). They then commend mindfulness and awareness training as a way of directly paying heed to enactive experience.

Learning Resources Centre

Transformative memory and paying heed

This radical perceptual memory generates data for *informative* statements about an inquiry domain. There is a complementary and interrelated kind of memory that generates data on *transformative* practice within a domain. For action and memory are also born together. To act is to remember, at least for a bit. And again, the critical bridge between the two is noticing, paying heed to. Many ordinary, everyday actions are unreflective, born of habit, convention and expediency. We do not pay much heed to them, they are part of routinized behaviour. We can't recall readily or at all actions that we don't pay heed to. They are difficult to remember, even at the end of their day.

As with perceiving, there is paying heed to actions in an ordinary way, and there is paying heed to them in an extraordinary way. Paying the everyday sort of heed to an action means executing it carefully, attending to what one is doing, and using negative feedback efficiently. The last of these means immediately spotting when the action deviates from its 'line' and rapidly getting it back on line.

Extraordinary practical heed

Paying heed to an action in an extraordinary way is at a more visionary and inclusive level of awareness. It involves comprehending the action as a whole, noticing the total configuration of the meaning of what one is doing while one is doing it.

An action as a whole is not just a set of physical movements, nor a set of movements classified by a simple verb such as walks, signals, talks. It is a transactional manifold of meaning, relating a person intentionally to their world. This intentionality includes being aware, while acting, of: the motives of the action, the end of the action and its values, the strategy adopted and its norms, the actual behaviour, the context of action and beliefs about it, and the effects of the action.

Paying heed to an action as a whole is also a dynamic process. It not only attends to all these aspects of the manifold, it also notices whether they are compatible. It modifies any one or more of them where there is incongruence between them. This is what Torbert (1991) has called action inquiry. It is an integral part of the action phase of any transformative inquiry.

For those involved in such an inquiry, where the focus is on practice, the data of memory generated by this paying heed holistically to actions will be primary. It will be more fundamental than the data of memory generated simply by executing actions carefully and effectively.

Informative inquiry skills

In this section I outline four main inquiry skills pertinent to informative inquiries: being present, imaginal openness, bracketing of several kinds and reframing. In the section after this one, I discuss four further skills required in transformative inquiries, where the focus is on practice. However, since informative research is supported by information-gathering practice, and transformative research by information about the context of practice, any inquiry is going to involve all eight to a greater or lesser degree, quite apart from other skills I haven't identified here.

Radical perception: being present and imaginally open

Radical perception means paying heed in an extraordinary way to the process of perceiving as described above. It is the ability to open up fully to our participation in reality through our empathic communion with it, and our unrestricted perceptual patterning of it. It means owning our creative transaction with what is given. We find this behind the screen of language in the immediacy of felt attunement and unrestricted perception (Wahl, 1953). This immediacy takes us into the lived world of primary meaning: the deep tacit experiential pre-understanding that is beneath language, and of which the conceptual meaning of language is a continuous, partial and limited transformation.

This kind of holistic awareness of how our world is being and how it is patterned through our creative minding of it, is a central inquiry skill. It involves the two complementary components of radical perception: being present and imaginal openness.

- *Being present* Through empathic communion, harmonic resonance, attunement, I feel the presence of people and other entities. I participate in their inner experience, their modes of awareness, their ways of giving meaning and being affected. I indwell the unique inner declaration of the being of the other.

  > We cannot claim valid inquiry unless we can be fully present with the persons and things with whom we inquire. (Reason, 1988d: 218)

- *Imaginal openness* Through being open to the total process of enacting the forms of people and other entities by imaging them, I participate in their manifest patterns and intuit their meaning. This is unrestricted perceiving simultaneously on all levels, sensory and subtle.

Together, being present and imaginal openness involve feeling attuned to the inner awareness of a presence while finding meaning in shaping its sensory and subtle perceptual form. This is radical meeting and unrestricted perception: participative empathy as the foundation of the creative shaping of a world in all its modalities and states.

This combination practises the radical empiricism which phenomenologists have long since commended: a pristine acquaintance with phenomena unadulterated by preconceptions (Spiegelberg, 1960). It attends to the pre-objective, pre-predicative world presupposed by all language and propositional knowledge, and which is their continuous nonlinguistic substrate.

This world of primary meaning is unrestricted perception, consciousness– world union, which is anterior to every distinction including that of consciousness and nature (Merleau-Ponty, 1962). It is apprehended by a fearlessness which

> means being able to respond accurately to the phenomenal world altogether. It simply means being accurate and absolutely direct in relating with the phenom- enal world by means of your sense perceptions, your mind and your sense of vision. (Trungpa, 1986: 31)

Attunement with the other, empathy, harmonic resonance, is the way of communion, of participating in the interior world of the other. It grounds and complements and is inseparable from everything I have to say about imaginal openness.

Imaginal openness attends to the processes of what I have called presen- tational construing in perception, Trungpa's 'first perception'. It involves seeing the world with a system of meaning that is inherent in perceptual, and other kinds of, imagery as such, and is the ground of all explicit predication and language-use. I call this primary meaning, or empathic- imaginal meaning, or just imaginal meaning, and distinguish it from secondary meaning, or conceptual meaning, which is born with language and the use of class names. Primary meaning is inherent in the patterning of our perceptual imaging of being in a world, and in the harmonic resonance with which we indwell the presences of our world.

I explore more fully this primary meaning inherent in perceiving a world in Chapter 10. It is important to note that opening to this first perception is not a backward-turning attempt to be in the world like a prelinguistic child. Even if one could do it, this would yield primitive and undifferentiated participation. Rather, it is owning the current, tacit worldspace of under- standing, the deep intersubjective nonlinguistic meaning, which language presupposes, and of which language right now is a continuous trans- formation.

It is an opening to what Skolimowski calls Mind II, more extensive than the logical, discursive, co-ordinating Mind I. Mind II includes 'all the sensitivities that evolution has developed in us . . . the countless windows through which we commune with reality' (Skolimowski, 1994: 9). This opening launches a forward movement to a postconceptual world, where the perceiver by means of the skills I shall now describe, revisions the world in depth and regenerates the way language is used to reveal it.

Varieties of bracketing

A skill necessary to support radical perception is the ability to bracket off the ever-present tacit conceptualization of the world, the unspoken verbal transformation of imaginal meaning, that comes from language-use. This means disidentifying from the belief-system that is built into perception and derived from the common language and worldview of our culture. This implicit belief-system conditions us to see and hear things as trees, houses, fields and cars, interrelated in terms of simple causal laws and embedded in a mechanical universe. We see and hear people in terms of the beliefs, norms, values and social structures of our culture. So we need to bring these implicit everyday epistemic frameworks into clear relief and become fully aware of them. Then we can become relatively independent of them, peer over the edge of them, and regenerate our vision.

A related skill is the ability to divest these conventional belief-systems of the effects of early childhood trauma, which may distort and fixate them with dark emotional loading and projected pathology. When this takes place, the conceptual frameworks of everyday perception become charged with threat, negative expectation and disempowerment. This kind of ingrained doom-laden colouring needs to be cleansed from the human instrument, if self-reflective inquiry is to proceed with any grace.

Thirdly, there is the ability to bracket off the framework made explicit in the launching statement that guides the inquiry. This framework is a revisionary belief-system, present in outline only, which may challenge conventional views, and which characterizes in a special way the domain you are going to inquire into. So this skill means two things. First, you wear innovative lenses to enable you to enter and see the domain in a special light. Second, at the same time you wear them lightly, and are able to take them off and put them back on every once in a while. This is so you can participate in the subtlety of experience and pay heed to how it does and does not conform to the lens-view.

Reframing

These three bracketing skills are consummated by the skill of reframing. This is the ability while busy with experience not only to bracket off conventional, pathological and launching frameworks and so be imaginally open to radical perception. It also means conjuring up alternative frameworks, different ones again, and trying them on and off for imaginal size and fit.

The skills of bracketing and reframing combine in what Torbert calls 'a reframing mind' which 'continually overcomes itself, divesting itself of its own presuppositions', a process which he likens to an 'ongoing jousting, at one and the same time, with one's attention and with the outside world' (Torbert, 1987: 211–13). It is the competence of Bateson's Learning III, in which the mind can choose its premises of understanding and action: it can detach itself from any framework, and peer beyond and reflect upon its presuppositions. It can move with agility between different conceptual structures (Bateson, 1972). It is the skill of the 'self-reflective' mind which has learnt 'to attend to its own processes' and is no longer trapped in its own frames (Reason, 1994a: 37).

It is also the outlook of Gebser's integral-aperspectival mind. The aperspectival mind grasps that no perspective is final. It is transparent to the context of its own operation, is open to the context of that context and so on. Gebser sees this as a newly emerging structure of consciousness, and with it there are emerging the 'aperspective world' and a rising global or planetary culture (Gebser, 1985; Feuerstein, 1987). Wilber (1995) endorses this with his notion of vision-logic, an integral awareness that is grounded in the transparent body-mind, in feeling through the lived body.

The relevance of Buddhist practices

There is an analogy in all this with the Tibetan Buddhist practice of the 'turning about in the deepest seat of consciousness' of *manas*, intuitive mind (Govinda, 1960: 77). On Govinda's account of Tibetan doctrine, *manas* is an emanation of and continuous with universal mind, *alaya-vijnana*, also called store-consciousness, in which the archetypes of all things are stored. *Manas* also takes part in everyday thought-consciousness, *mano-vijnana*, which co-ordinates perception. So *manas* mediates between the everyday mind and universal mind. In doing so it becomes a source of error if its power feeds the egoic splitting of subject from object in everyday mind. It becomes a source of liberation if it turns about to attend to the universal store-consciousness whence it emanates and which is the archetypal, unitive ground of the perceptual process.

Reason also points out the relevance of mainline Buddhist teaching and practice for developing 'a reflective, reframing mind'. Behind the attachment of the everyday mind to its constricting perspectives, there is 'a mind which is able to see through this attachment and is open to the ways in which we create ourselves and our world moment to moment' and which is available through meditation (Reason, 1994a: 34; Rinpoche, 1992). Co-operative inquiry calls for these meditative skills to be operative in the midst of doing research; and it is itself a discipline which develops these skills.

Transformative inquiry skills

The four skills so far considered are all to do with informative inquiry, which seeks to be descriptive and explanatory of our realities. There are also four complementary skills to do with researching practice, in transformative inquiry. As I have already suggested, because of the interdependence of the two forms of inquiry, all eight skills will have relevance, with differing emphasis, in either kind.

Radical practice: dynamic congruence

Radical practice is the skill of paying heed in an extraordinary way to the process of action, as described earlier in this chapter. It attends to the following aspects of action and their compatibility, and reorganizes them to correct dissonance among them. It is the same as action inquiry (Torbert, 1991).

- The motives involved in the action.
- The guiding end of the action and its underlying values.
- The current strategy adopted to realize that end and its guiding norms.
- The actual behaviour that implements the strategy, its style and competence.
- The context of action and beliefs about that context.
- The effects of the behaviour on the context and beyond it.

To illustrate these various aspects of action, suppose I am a practitioner inquiring into power-sharing with a client, then:

- My motives are some admixture of the self-regarding, the other-regarding, and the overdetermined.
- The overall end or purpose is power-sharing as part of a wider model of whole person practice, the underlying intrinsic values being those of enhanced human well-being, autonomy and co-operation.
- The strategy is role-reversal, inviting the client to become the practitioner for a while, the guiding norm being that of truth-telling within the reversed role.
- The actual behaviour is proposing, explaining and seeking assent to the role-reversal, and moving out of my practitioner chair to make it possible; with some fittingness, sensitivity and clarity.
- The context includes the nature of our role-relationship and our contract, the current issue for the client, the state of mind of the client, our previous history, the arrangement of furniture in the room, and the time available.
- The effects are how the client reacts and participates.

Of all these several components, most of them are variable: I may modify many of them, some being more alterable than others. But my underlying intrinsic values are at any given time in my life non-negotiable. They define the ground on which I stand up to be counted. They provide the principles which determine how I evaluate the other components, an evaluation which may lead to some of them being changed. They give rise to the norms that guide the use of strategies, and to criteria for the actual behaviour such as elegance, appropriateness, sensitivity and executive efficiency.

The purpose of paying heed to action at the ordinary level is to keep it on line by noticing how it deviates off its line. This is simply attending to doing it well, to excellence of execution. Ordinary paying heed looks at the actual behaviour, how it is being put together, and what its effects are. It corrects behaviour by noting how it deviates from standards of elegance and efficiency internal to it and by taking account of its immediate outcomes. So it has a close-up executive focus on the relation between strategy, behaviour and outcomes.

The purpose of paying heed at the extraordinary level is to notice a much more inclusive congruence. It attends to all the components of an action, to the fittingness of their patterning as a whole, their practical compatibility;

and it reshapes them to enhance congruence and reduce dissonance. It is a dynamic process with a wide focus, comprehensive view.

Does the purpose of power-sharing seem, in the doing of it, to be a valid part of whole person practice? Does its seem, in action, to have been well-conceived? Does it seem, in action, to need integration with some other part? Is the purpose of power-sharing at ease with this particular strategy for realizing it? Is this particular strategy suited to this kind of client? Is the underlying motive congruent with the overall purpose? Does the purpose, or the strategy or the behaviour exemplify the guiding values? These are some of the wider issues that now become relevant, as well as the ordinary close-up focus on the relation between strategy, behaviour and outcomes.

This kind of radical paying heed to action is at the interface between the conceptual, reflective mind and the intuitive, imaginal mind. It is more than reflection-within-action, it is reflection-within-action itself subsumed and enlivened by an intuitive, imaginal grasp of the whole pattern of the action in its intentional, behavioural, social and environmental dimensions. This grasp is not some strenuous labour of the ordinary mind. It does require some preparation and training of the ordinary mind to lay hold of the conceptual geography of holistic action. Thereafter, it falls as radical grace from the dynamic powers of a pre-existent, extraordinary level of mind. I discuss this idea in a later section in this chapter.

Emotional competence

Emotional competence is a term I have used for several years (Heron, 1982a, 1990, 1992) to cover the field recently labelled emotional intelligence (Goleman, 1995). It means the ability to identify and manage emotions. In an emotionally repressive culture such as ours, the first challenge is for people to recognize what they are feeling. This is the skill of so-called meta-mood, being aware of one's current emotional state. Identifying, owning and accepting a state, through self-awareness, is the basis for managing it – by expression, control, transmutation, catharsis.

- The expression of love, regard, affection, delight, to other people is a central skill. More generally every authentic choice is a form of emotional expression. It proceeds from a personal preference, and a preference is an option to which an emotional value is assigned (Damasio, 1995). Autonomous action presupposes the agent is in touch with the emotional value of his or her preference among the options available.
- Aware emotional control is free of self-assault: it honours what it deals with. It means choosing not to act on certain emotions, and does this by switching attention off them without at the same time repressing them. This may be done by changing the arousal level. You can switch out of low arousal states of being sad or depressed by triggering high arousal through going for a run; or out of high arousal states of anger

and anxiety by lowering arousal through deep relaxation. Or it can be done by cognitive restructuring, that is, seeing the situation in a different light, so that this changed appraisal generates a different emotion.

- Transmutation and catharsis are complementary ways of managing cumulative distress emotions of grief, fear and anger. Transmutation involves restructuring consciousness at deep levels thereby transforming emotional pain into calmness; whereas catharsis means releasing and unloading distress from the psychosomatic system (Heron, 1990).

Radical practice presupposes the agent is not fixated on performance, driven by pathological motives. Distress-driven, maladaptive conduct blots out the possibility of acting with awareness and intentionality. The very process of inquiring into the human condition may stir up in the researchers defensive behaviour which can distort the inquiry process and the radical practice at its focus. This defensivenes is about aspects of themselves which they have had to repress and deny in order to survive and be accepted when growing up in an emotionally alienated society.

To take charge of this, the inquiring person and group need the skills of identifying and managing the emotions involved. These skills include being able:

- To process the painful emotion repressed in earlier years as a consequence of hurtful events. This healing of the memories involves recovering them and restructuring them with liberating insight, a process which may also entail the cathartic release of the distress – the anger, fear or grief – that is congealed within them.
- To spot and interrupt the tendency of residual painful emotion to distort current behaviour with a symbolic re-enactment of old traumas.
- To maintain or regenerate creative, intentional action when this kind of distorting tendency is activated by events.
- To spot this kind of tendency at work in others, and confront it supportively, in ways that are enabling to them.

Less radically, emotional competence also means the ability to identify in oneself and others the effects of social conditioning of a nontraumatic kind. This is at times when unreflective, purely conventional norms take over behaviour and obscure what could have been its deeper purpose and more telling strategy.

To these several components, Reason (1988d) adds an awareness of the existential choices and perspectives we bring to our work, and of the archetypal, mythic patterns which are expressed through our lives.

Non-attachment

Another skill within radical practice is analogous to bracketing in radical perception. It involves intentionality that is clear in line, but is not over-identified with the situation of action. This means one can be fully open to what is going on in the situation without being too caught up in one's current view of it. It also requires an ability to wear lightly and without fixation the purpose, strategy, behaviour and motive which have been chosen as the form of the action. This is the knack of not being attached to the main parameters of an action, of not investing one's emotional identity in it, while remaining fully committed to it. Non-attachment means flexibility of intent, so that the agent allows the situation to breathe freely and suggest other options.

Self-transcending intentionality

Alongside non-attachment is the ability to have in mind, during action, a range of alternative purposes, strategies, forms of behaviour, motives; to consider their possible relevance and applicability to the situation; and to have an adaptive willingness to adopt any of these to reshape the action as circumstances and one's overall principles suggest.

While dynamic congruence operates within the current parameters of action, self-transcending intentionality is the concurrent ability to entertain different sets of parameters, to envisage comprehensive practical sub-stitutes. This is analogous to reframing in radical perception.

Skill in articulating values

Axiology is the study of value in general, embracing ethics, but also aesthetics, economics and other fields. In ethics, value is about what is good in itself, what is desirable as an end in itself. The basic question relates to what states of affairs, for human beings, are intrinsically worthwhile, not as a means to anything else. Such states are the ultimate ends of action. I suggested earlier that each person's intrinsic values are the non-negotiable ground on which they stand up to be counted.

Intrinsic values provide the ultimate *human* ratio, or guiding reason, of action. They are autonomous; they stand on their own epistemological ground, not to be justified by theological assertion or statements of fact. They are also subjective-objective, relative-universal in their formulations. On the one hand they are relative to the personal and cultural context out of which they have emerged. On the other hand they have reference to the needs and interest of our common humanity within shared features of the human condition. No statement about what is good in itself is ever final, but every such statement that is thoughtfully put together claims general relevance.

Axiological skill means that the researchers, whether busy with informa-tive or transformative inquiries, are able to articulate a set of shared values, as a basis for making judgments of relevance about what they are doing and how they are doing it.

Values and principles

For my part, the state of affairs I take to be desirable as an end in itself is human flourishing, which I conceive as a mutually enabling balance between autonomy, co-operation and hierarchy:

- By autonomy I mean a state of being in which each person can in liberty determine and fulfil their own true needs and interests.
- By co-operation I mean mutual aid and support between autonomous persons, including negotiation, participative decision-making and conflict resolution.
- By hierarchy I mean a state of being in which someone appropriately takes responsibility for doing things to or for other persons for the sake of their future autonomy and co-operation. This is part of parenthood, education and many professions. The challenge of hierarchy is to get it right: neither overdo it, nor underdo it.

What follows, at any rate on a teleological view of ethics, from this assertion of what is good as an end in itself, are guiding norms of high generality, moral principles of wide relevance. For me, these are:

- A principle of flourishing, defined as a commitment to provide conditions within which people can in liberty and co-operation, and with appropriate degrees of hierarchy, determine and fulfil their own true needs and interests.
    - Included in this is a principle of respect for personal autonomy, which honours the right of every person in any situation to make autonomous choices about what they do or do not do, and to be given adequate information about any proposed activity so as to be able to make an informed choice about it.
- A principle of impartiality, or justice, defined as giving everyone in any situation equality of consideration. This does not mean that each one gets the same treatment. It means that differences of treatment can be justified by relevant differences between the people concerned. It is these relevant differences that get equality of consideration. Each person's special needs and interests are considered equally. As a result everyone is treated appropriately, differently and fairly.

The point about all this is that any inquiry with people about the human condition ideally presupposes they have articulated their shared values and guiding norms. These provide standards for the selection of inquiry topics and the conduct of the research, and, in transformative inquiries, for evaluating the practice which is the focus of the inquiry.

Inquiry skills and critical subjectivity

All the nine skills so far mentioned will have a claim on any inquiry group, with differing emphasis among the first eight, depending on whether it is

more informative or more transformative. This all sounds rather formid-
able and in one sense it is. The call is to a radical kind of participative
awareness in which the researcher is his or her own instrument for
inquiring, through perception and action, into the human condition.

This is inquiry not just into what is given, but into how the inquiring
human instrument is engaged in shaping the given. Reason and Rowan
wrestled with this and said such inquiry is 'objectively subjective' and that
to be valid it required 'critical subjectivity', preceded by 'cleansing the
instrument', dismantling the warped rigidities of behaviour, belief and
emotional response that can infect human subjectivity (Reason and Rowan,
1981b, 1981c). When the instrument is relatively clean, there is this rigorous
array of skills to be acquired for keeping its subjectivity critical. Then it can
manage with rigour its own consciousness on the hoof, as it shapes its
realities in transaction with the given.

I have already suggested that the discipline of co-operative inquiry is a
means of developing these skills. To practise its cyclic process is to acquire
them.

Extraordinary consciousness and multi-level mind

Furthermore, the array of skills does not have to be heroically erected as a
totally new structure of mind. This is where oriental paradigms, such as the
Buddhist one mentioned above, are relevant. The classic and prevailing
paradigm of mind in Western culture sees it as tripartite, involving thinking, feeling and willing. It also tends to regard mind as a one-storey affair,
a bungalow of awareness whose windows look out on the physical world
only.

Of course, there is the modern addition of the unconscious mind. But in
the popular imagination this is largely a Freudian affair, a basement into
which is repressed the seething cauldron of the id. Hence the nine skills
I have outlined seem as though they are to be some new construction,
laboriously erected as a second storey once the low bungalow roof has been
removed.

The oriental paradigm suggests that the mind is already multi-storey. It
has no low-level one-storey roof. It is just that the occupant of the ground
floor is so busy looking out the windows, he or she has failed to notice the
lift installed in the central core of the house. It is not that the nine skills
have to be built up as an added second floor. This floor already exists, fully
arrayed with the equipment for managing enhanced consciousness. There
is, in fact, a tacit, pre-existent level of mind into which we can expand our
limited, everyday awareness. Its vantage points already generate the
enriched perspectives which provide the framework for the inquiry skills we
need.

However, the oriental paradigm of multi-level mind is limited, in my
view, in one fundamental respect. In its application to human development

it is basically quietist. The transformation of consciousness it generates through the disciplines of meditation is essentially for those whose being is passive and quiet, withdrawn from concern with the world and social life. It is exclusively an informative inquiry, and one, moreover, that jumps to an absolute level of description.

For the information it yields about the human condition is that beyond the restrictive subject–object dualism of the everyday mind there is the vast, 'open, unconditioned space of mind itself'. This is not your mind or my mind but 'the self-existing wisdom and power of the cosmic mirror that are reflected both in us and in our world of perception' (Trungpa, 1986: 78). A person in touch with this certainly has social impact, the paradigm claims, but it is the impact of one whose presence evokes the same kind of experience in others.

What I am suggesting in this book is a more comprehensive paradigm. It certainly sees extraordinary consciousness as informative at an absolute level of description. But also as informative at a whole range of inter-mediate extrasensory levels of description that are of interest and relevance to individual and social development. Furthermore, it regards extra-ordinary consciousness not simply as that which fills the attuned and passive recipient, but also as transformative, as that which moves the agent of change. There are thus pre-existent levels of mind that illumine and empower the enlightened planetary citizen with a commitment to environmental and social transformation.

This view now seems to be espoused by Wilber (1995), in contrast to his previous work. In earlier writings (Wilber, 1983), he strongly asserts a transcendental reduction of the Many to the One: all persons and forms of culture are nothing but a deviation from and an illusory substitute for absolute Spirit, so that meditation on Spirit is the only real moral imperative (1983: 321). While there are still anomalies in his account of Spirit, he now asserts that it is:

> not just how to contact the higher Self, but how to see it embraced in culture, embodied in nature and embedded in social institutions. (Wilber, 1995: 497)

Training for inquiry

Reason (1988d) gives an interesting account of the ways he and his colleagues and their postgraduate research group at the University of Bath have been developing high-quality awareness as a preparation for various kinds of participative research.

- They meet as a circle for silent attunement and mutual resonance; and sometimes for circle dancing, intentionally to 'evoke the archetype of the circle, of human equality and presence'.
- They meet as a support group and an encounter group, to attend to their interpersonal relationships.

- They confront their distress, using a variety of experiential psycho-therapies to deal with the defensiveness and old hurts that the business of inquiry stirs up.
- They develop mindfulness through disciplines such as T'ai Chi and Buddhist meditation.
- They explore participative knowing by using psychodrama to recreate aspects of the research situation.
- They explore participative knowing using Skolimowski's yoga of participation (Skolimowski, 1994). This involves approaching with reverence some natural phenomenon, such as a tree, rock, water; communing with it in silence; and identifying with its form of consciousness and way of experiencing its world.

This represents a breakthrough in normal postgraduate practice in an English university, and commends itself widely.

8

Validity Procedures

I now describe in more detail a set of interdependent procedures, outlined in Chapter 3, whose effects taken together can enhance the validity of the inquiry process, and thus its outcomes. They are relevant whether the inquiry is primarily concerned with acquiring knowledge about a domain or with transforming it through practice. Each of them needs to be planned, and either wholly or partially applied, within the reflection phases of the inquiry.

They seek to free the various forms of knowing involved from some of the distortions of uncritical subjectivity. These distortions mean there is a lack of soundness with which a form of knowing, whether experiential, presentational, propositional or practical, is being managed. This may relate to its relatively autonomous use and development; or to its inter-dependence with one or more of the other forms of knowing.

These procedures need supplementing with the inquiry skills, reviewed in Chapter 7, which have particular application at the heart of the action phase of an inquiry. It is the procedures and skills together which may resolve uncritical subjectivity.

Research cycling

As I said in Chapter 3, the assumption of research cycling is that the research outcomes are well-grounded if the focus of the inquiry, both in its parts and as a whole, is taken through as many cycles as possible by as many group members as possible, with as much individual diversity and collective unity of approach as possible. Once the research cycling gets under way, it establishes a feedback loop that has negative and positive gains in both directions, from action to reflection and from reflection to action. This is illustrated in Figure 8.1. In negative feedback, engagement with experience generates data which prunes the research proposals of what is ungrounded, irrelevant, beside the point. And the developing research proposals strip this engagement of want of discrimination, of needless vagueness, ambiguity, illusion and confusion.

In positive feedback, the experiential data amplifies, deepens, diversifies, extends and renders more interdependent, the research proposals. And they in turn alert the inquirers to wider, deeper, more subtle or more obvious, aspects of their experiential commitment.

This notion of two-way negative and positive feedback is not at all to be confused with checking one's ideas against some independent external

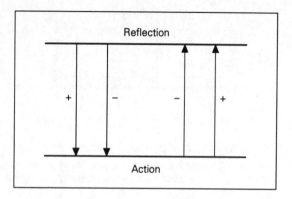

Figure 8.1   *Two-way positive and negative feedback*

reality. On the contrary, it is a dialectical engagement between two forms of knowing, propositional and experiential, between conceptual map-making and participative engagement. These are two different and comple-mentary ways of articulating reality, of shaping what is given. Propositional knowing shapes reality in terms of concepts, experiential knowing in terms of empathic attunement and unrestricted perceptual enactment. By virtue of their very different kinds of leverage, they have a lot to offer each other, both by pruning and by fostering growth. Research cycling can be individual, collective and combined.

Individual research cycling

Each inquirer is exclusively their own control on a serial basis: the two-way feedback loops between reflection and action operate for each person separate from every other. Of course, if there is no interaction during the inquiry between people using this kind of individual cycling, then there is no co-operation at all. For an inquiry that uses individual cycling to be co-operative, there must be some interaction: the first, last, and at least one intermediate, reflection phases need to be shared.

Collective research cycling

Here the inquirers function as a group at every phase. They always reflect together; and they always experience together, either interacting as a group, or doing individual things side-by-side in the same energy field. This is the group process or group-based inside inquiry which I discussed in Chapter 3. In the action phase, their respective experiences may modify each other. This is obvious in a group process inquiry, which is about group inter-action. It also applies in a group-based inquiry where individuals may be exploring the same experience side by side in the same energy field, but without interacting. Individual experience is empowered and enhanced by being group-based in this way.

In the reflection phase, all individual data from the action phase is shared in the whole group. Each person reflects on their own data, also on the data and personal reflections of everyone else; and this is carried over into collective planning of the next action phase. There is thus a lot of interactive influence among the inquirers, both within the reflection and the action phase, and in the two-way feedback loops, positive and negative, between them.

> In the group process inquiry I launched in Dublin into 'the energy of the group' (1982, unreported), all the experience phases were collective and interactive. Then each individual would have a solo reflection phase expressing in writing and/or graphics their account of the group interaction that had just occurred. These were shared and discussed in a collective reflection phase, leading to some broad consensus about what had gone on. On this basis the next phase of group interaction was collectively planned.

> In the altered states group-based inquiry (Heron, 1988c) all the cycles were collective. Experiences were always either interactive or side-by-side. And personal outcomes were always formulated and shared directly in the group.

What is essential in such inside inquiries is that each person has a say in the reflection phase, and is fully involved in the action phase. This is to ensure that co-operation is based on comprehensive individual participation, not undermined by some dominant subgroup.

Combined research cycling

A balance is sought between some individual research cycling and some aspects of collective research cycling. This balance can be struck in many different ways. One or more separate individual cycles of action and reflection can be followed by collective reflection, in which individual findings are shared and discussed, and in which the content and method of the next one or more individual cycles are planned collectively.

> A version of this was adopted in the first co-counselling inquiry (Heron and Reason, 1981): people worked in pairs taking it in turn to do one action and recording-with-reflection cycle each, then took the data from this to share with the whole group for collective reflection.

> In the holistic medicine inquiry (Heron and Reason, 1985; Reason, 1988c), there were individual action phases lasting six weeks, which included many minor solo reflection phases when recording data. And there were several weekend-long major collective reflection phases to process all the individual data. In these two inquiries, the action phases, together with minor reflection phases for recording data, were always individual, and the major reflection phases were collective.

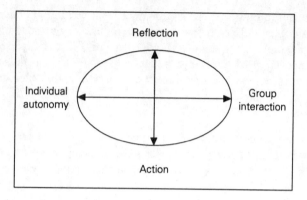

Figure 8.2   *Fourfold interaction*

Youth workers researching their own learning processes used sub-groups, and less frequently the whole group, for both action and reflection phases, with individuals having solitary reflection phases during the meetings for recording, which was then shared in both the small and large groups (De Venney-Tiernan et al., 1994).

Fourfold interaction

Research cycling is thus concerned not only with how reflection and action can enhance each other, but also with the way in which individual autonomy and group interaction can empower one another. An inquiry is most potent and effective, if it can maximize this fourfold interaction: both the distinct individual effect and the collective reciprocal effect of the mutual influence between reflection and action. This is symbolized in Figure 8.2.

Of course, this is all a counsel of perfection. For any given inquiry, one adopts that form of cycling, usually some version of combined cycling, that seems best suited to the subject matter of the inquiry, and that offers an accessible and manageable balance between individual and collective effects.

The balance of divergence and convergence

Divergence and convergence, together with several other parameters, are about the basic logic of cyclic method. I will enlarge here the introductory account given in Chapter 5.

Within and between phases

- Divergence *within* an action phase means that individuals or subgroups each explore different aspects of the inquiry topic, and the differences are internal to that phase.

- Convergence *within* an action phase means that individuals or sub-groups each explore the same aspect of the inquiry topic, and the sameness is internal to that phase.
- Divergence *between* action phases means that individuals or subgroups each explore on the next action phase something different to what they explored on the previous one.
- Convergence *between* action phases means that individuals or sub-groups each explore on the next action phase the same thing they explored on the previous one.

So group members can diverge within each of several action phases, but converge between them. Within any phase everyone is doing something different to everyone else, but each person continues to explore the same thing on each successive phase. Conversely, group members can converge within each of several action phases, but diverge between them. In any phase everyone is doing the same thing as everyone else, but on each successive phase they explore something different.

The many within and between combinations of divergence and convergence, involving all group members or subgroups, and applied to parts, subwholes or the whole of the inquiry topic, make for a vast array of possible research designs.

Total divergence

Applied over several research cycles, total divergence means that everyone does something different in every action phase, and no-one repeats anything they have done in a previous action phase. So if there were ten inquirers and six research cycles, then sixty different aspects would be explored, ten of them on each action phase. This generates data that gives the maximum overview of the disparate elements of a topic, but one that is entirely impressionistic. Every part has only been attended to once by one person. And no one part has been taken round a research cycle more than once by anyone. The outcomes are also low in coherence, since no-one has attended to how the parts of the whole work together.

Total convergence

Applied over several cycles, total convergence means that everyone does the same kind of thing in every action phase. So, again, if there were ten inquirers and six research cycles, then the same aspect would be explored sixty times – six times by each person. This generates data that gives a progressively refined and in-depth account of one part of the topic. This account, however, becomes suspect because there is no complementary view of how that part integrates with, and is influenced by, any other part and the whole. So this one aspect may become falsely revised because it is considered in complete isolation from everything else.

Total convergence could also be applied over several action phases to a holistic account of the inquiry topic. But the final holistic version would also be suspect: its component parts remain undifferentiated and undeveloped. There have been no phases of partitive divergence to bring them separately into relief. The holism may therefore be spurious.

Intermediate model

The intermediate model aims at some kind of balance between divergence and convergence, maximizing their benefits and minimizing their deficits. There is enough divergence of experience to get a good grasp of the various parts of the whole with which our inquiry is concerned. And there is enough convergence on each part, or subset of parts, taking it through two or more research cycles, so that it is more fully grounded. We also need holistic convergence, in which all the parts are taken together, as a whole, round the research cycle more than once, in order to articulate more directly their interplay.

There are innumerable possible versions of an intermediate model. Here is one that runs from divergence to convergence via an intermediate stage of balance between them

- Group members diverge over the early action phases, each person exploring a different part of the inquiry topic. Each individual, with respect to their chosen part, has to decide whether to stay convergent with that part over the several phases, or whether to diverge over two or more different parts.

  In the holistic medicine inquiry (Heron and Reason, 1985; Reason, 1988c), early action phases were highly divergent, each individual choosing to explore any aspect of any part of the initial five-part model which took their fancy. Some doctors kept diverging phase to phase. This let each person get up a good head of creative steam and become involved. It also brought out the multi-faceted nature of the inquiry area.

- In the middle action phases, group members balance divergence and convergence. There are several divergent subgroups: each chooses a different subwhole from the others; and each converges on its chosen subwhole over a few cycles. The members of one subgroup may (or may not) diverge among the different parts of the subwhole on which they are converging.

  In middle action phases of the holistic medicine inquiry, one subgroup of doctors converged, phase to phase, on power-sharing with patients, and another subgroup converged on spiritual interventions within the NHS surgery. Within each of these aspects there was some divergence over sub-aspects: subgroup members tried out different kinds of power-sharing, and different sorts of spiritual intervention, on successive phases.

- In the final action phases, group members converge, everyone exploring over successive cycles the whole that is a composite of the subwholes.

  The holistic medicine inquiry had no final holistic action phases, the two subgroups continuing with their different themes up to the end. Holistic integration was only dealt with in the final reflection phase. In my view, this was a weakness of the emergent design.

  The second co-counselling inquiry (Heron and Reason, 1982), on how people handle restimulated distress in everyday life, turned this model on its head. There were four week-long action phases, and weekly half-day reflection phases. In the first two action phases we all converged on coping strategies, and in the last two we diverged into three different subgroups only one of which continued on with coping strategies, the other two looking at different complementary issues. The final reflection phase had the task of pulling all this together. This was an inquiry in which the need to diverge broke out dramatically halfway through, and caused a good deal of interesting disruption and chaos.

Another sequence moves from convergence on the less coherent, through divergence, to convergence on the more coherent. I don't know of any example of this.

- Group members converge in the early phases on a whole of inchoate composition in order to bring it into focus.
- They diverge over the middle phases to differentiate the parts of the whole and to clarify the relative autonomy of the parts.
- They converge through the final phases to explore the whole at a higher order of definition as a systemic composite of parts.

In a fourth sequence, used in the ASC inquiry (Heron, 1988c) what goes on within each action phase is convergent, with everyone exploring the same kind of content, but the content of each successive action phase diverges into something different. This model generates a lot of impressionistic data over a wide field. There is a lot of cross-checking between individuals about each kind of content, since everyone is converging within each action phase. However, it still errs on the side of divergence: nothing is taken round a cycle by anyone more than once.

These various models are just illustrations to suggest the many possibilities. An inquiry group, whether Apollonian or Dionysian, needs to get a feel for the logic of cyclic method and the range of design options. The Apollonian group will make a co-operative decision about which option fits their situation and excites their creative imagination. This decision-making needs to be piecemeal, applied to just the next action phase, so that the overall design emerges progressively as the inquiry advances and insights unfold. The Dionysian group will find it fruitful intentionally not to plan action phases in advance, but to let the action arise in creative response to the situation. After several such cycles, the group can apply the logic of research cycling retrospectively to see what form the sequence has taken.

Polarities of method

Getting a feel for the logic of cyclic method means taking conscious account of its main defining parameters. There are six polarities which interact to outline this logic with regard to the action phases. I define them altogether here for the first time, and illustrate them in Figure 8.3. The first four are the immediate nuts and bolts of the matter.

- The divergence–convergence polarity: whether group members are inquiring into different aspects or the same aspect of the inquiry topic.
- The within-phase–between-phases polarity: whether the divergence or convergence is within an action phase (doing different or the same things in this phase), or between action phases (doing in the next phase things that are different to or the same as things done in the previous phase).
- The individual–group polarity: whether an individual, or a subgroup, or the whole group is diverging or converging.
- The part–whole polarity: whether what the group members are inquiring into is a discrete part, or a subwhole or the whole of the inquiry topic.
- The heterogeneity–homogeneity polarity: whether group members are framing or evaluating an aspect of the inquiry topic in the light of different or the same paradigms, principles, assumptions, belief-systems.
- The informative–transformative polarity: whether the group members are busy with an inquiry topic that is descriptive of some domain, being informative about it; or with one that explores practice within some domain, being transformative of it.

I suggested in Chapter 5 that any excessive attention to the use of logical formula in research cycling is misguided. It is primarily the interaction between emotional arousal and creative imagination that keeps co-operative inquiries in being. The logic of method, with its six bipolar dimensions, is a secondary support for imagination and motivation, not the prime analytic mover. But until the logic of method is mastered, creative imagination may be impoverished in what it can deliver.

   In order to aid this mastery, Figure 8.3 maps out the six polarities in schematic form. Some positions on the grid logically determine others and exclude others. Thus if a group *within* an action phase is divergent about the inquiry topic as a whole, this can only be so if group members are heterogeneous in the way they frame that whole. For example, each one might see it hierarchically ordered in a different way. The divergence is found only in the heterogeneity. If a group within an action phase is convergent about the inquiry topic as a whole, this can only be so if group members are homogeneous in the way they frame that whole.

P = Part S = Subwhole W = Whole			Informative						Transformative					
			Heterogeneous			Homogeneous			Heterogeneous			Homogeneous		
			P	S	W	P	S	W	P	S	W	P	S	W
Divergent	Within phase	Indiv.												
		Subgr.												
		Group												
	Between phases	Indiv.												
		Subgr.												
		Group												
Convergent	Within phase	Indiv.												
		Subgr.												
		Group												
	Between phases	Indiv.												
		Subgr.												
		Group												

Figure 8.3   *Polarities of method*

Figure 8.3 separates individual, subgroup and group, both within phase and between phases. One reason is to do with subgroups and subwholes. So if several subgroups are diverging among different subwholes within an action phase, which means that each subgroup is converging on its own subwhole within that phase, then it may be the case that the individuals in a subgroup are diverging among the different parts of the subwhole on which they are converging.

Once again, it is important to acknowledge that Dionysian inquirers will find this kind of analysis irrelevant when they are living out the dynamic, emerging process of deeply felt inquiry.

The reflection phase

I have so far spoken of divergence and convergence in relation to the focus of the action phase. But they also apply, of course, to the imaginal or conceptual maps of the reflection phase. And these two applications are somewhat independent of each other. For the inquirers can all converge on the same sort of content in the action phase, yet have widely divergent maps of that content in the following reflection phase.

Some sort of balance between divergence and convergence is required at the conceptual level, at any rate over the whole series of reflection phases. Divergence of conceptual mapping establishes a wide range of differing perspectives on the same topic. This is essential to honour a subjective-objective reality. But equally, to honour such a reality, it needs to be shown how these diverse conceptual views overlap to illumine their common topic.

In the early reflection phases inquiries are enriched by divergent conceptual mapping. When individual maps are presented to everyone else, the elements of overlap among them will be noted. But it is unwise to press for conceptual convergence between individual maps early on; otherwise you may get premature intellectual closure round the experiential data, thus distorting rather than disclosing it.

In the later shared reflection phases, if there are too many idiosyncratic individual maps piling up, then it will be wise to work collectively on conceptual convergence.

In the ASC inquiry (Heron, 1988c), conceptual convergence started to be developed after the fourth cycle, in the devil's advocate procedure. What then emerged in replies to the advocates' attacks on the diverse individual impressions of the other reality, was a set of criteria for distinguishing between genuine impressions and subjective illusions.

In the first co-counselling inquiry (Heron and Reason, 1981), in the last shared reflection phase, we took the most coherent maps that different individuals had refined through their own cycles, and all of us took a part in amending each map until all, including its originator, were satisfied with it and with its relative coherence with the other maps thus treated.

What aids both divergence and convergence in the reflection phase of the group, are sharing and feedback. Each person shares recent past experience and how he or she has made sense of it. The resultant comparisons and contrasts between individuals' accounts will bring out both divergent and convergent aspects of these accounts. Similarly my comment on your account, and my feedback on your recent experience (if I was there at the time), will also throw into relief both different and similar perspectives. All this is essential for valid reflection, for holistic inquiry and learning. The truth for any group is surely found where different individual perspectives converge to illuminate common ground. Unless you get enough divergence, you will not get illuminating convergence.

The balance between reflection and action

If validity is enhanced by research cycling, moving to and fro between reflection and action, then it also depends on getting a right balance between these two phases. If the inquirers have prolonged action phases with only minimal time out for reflection, then their findings have low

validity. The inquiry has become supersaturated with experience: no adequate, coherent findings can be distilled out of it, or refined in it.

Conversely, if the inquirers reflect a great deal about a few brief episodes
of minimal action, this too will result in conclusions with low validity. The
inquiry suffers from intellectual excess: its findings have inadequate experiential support.

What constitutes a good ratio between reflection and action, one that
enhances validity through positive and negative feedback loops, is surely
inquiry-specific, depending upon the sort of experience involved. There is
no general formula. Long hours of contemplative reflection may be needed
to clarify the content of a few seconds' experience of a beatific state.
Whereas a few minutes reflection may be sufficient to describe what
happened during many hours in an immersion tank. Or, more prosaically,
it may need a lot of consideration to get clear what was going in a brief but
elliptical conversation. And only a little thought may illuminate a lengthy
period of straightforward co-operative action. It is also true that as well as
the sort of experience involved, there is the quality and intensity of the
reflection to take into account.

In the ASC inquiry (Heron, 1988c), the action phases ranged between
half an hour and well over an hour, with the reflection phases tending
to be not less than an hour.

In the holistic medicine inquiry (Heron and Reason, 1985; Reason,
1988c), each reflection phase covered many hours over one weekend,
while each action phase covered six weeks of daily professional work,
with, of course, intermittent times of recording the data from such work.

In the first co-counselling inquiry (Heron and Reason, 1981), each
person spent 20 to 30 minutes in the action phase, 15 minutes in a
private reflection phase, then over an hour in a collective reflection
phase.

In the second co-counselling inquiry (Heron and Reason, 1982), the
action phase was a whole week of daily life (with intermittent recording of data), and the collective reflection phase was five hours in a
block once a week. All these different ratios seemed reasonably
appropriate to their different subject matters.

The only guideline I can think of for this procedure is that the inquirers
monitor the ratio and discuss it from time to time. They have to judge from
within the parameters of their particular inquiry what a good ratio is.
Maybe they will have to try out several different ratios before getting a
sense of the right one. Maybe a variety of different ratios will be fitting; for
example if each cycle requires its own ratio. Maybe it becomes obvious
quite quickly, as a matter of common sense, what a good balance is.

The inquirers will usually have time constraints from their other commitments, and these too have to be taken realistically into account. This

raises the inescapable problem of programming priorities and prior engage-
ments, with the result that the ideal ratio may not be practicable, in which
case group members strike the best possible deal with their respective
agendas.

Aspects of reflection

In Chapter 5, I looked at issues of making sense and reaching agreement,
of presentational and propositional meaning, and of informative and
transformative meaning. I want to say something more here about the use
of reflection in informative inquiries. This is a highly Apollonian section, so
readers in Dionysian mood may want to hop over it, and return to it when
it is needed.

After an action phase in an informative inquiry, there are at least four
major forms of thought for the following reflection phase: the descriptive,
the evaluative, the explanatory, and the applied. It is important to remember
that presentational construing and meaning, as discussed in Chapter 5, can
be brought to bear on the development of all of these.

Description

When describing, the inquirers are busy with pure phenomenology, seeking
to convey to themselves and each other, as fully, coherently and evocatively
as possible the content of the action phase. They are open to empathic-
imaginal meaning, mapping what went on, framing lucid descriptions,
articulating in conceptual terms the basic phenomenal categories of experience. I introduced this form of thought in Chapter 5, and described
empathic-imaginal meaning in Chapter 7.

Evaluation

When evaluating, the inquirers are judging how sound their descriptions
are, that is, how well they are grounded in the recollected experience of
the action phase. This means refining and extending what was done when
thinking on one's feet in the midst of that phase. The inquirers are
rehearsing again, after the event, the same skills needed to discriminate
awarely during the experience. I described these in Chapter 7. They include
bracketing off three frameworks: the tacit conceptual constructs built into
perception; the projected templates from childhood trauma; and the inquiry
propositions which launched the action phase now being reviewed.

At the same time as rehearsing this openness to recollected experience,
there is the skill of sifting through alternative conceptual frameworks and
trying them out for fit and relevance. In this whole process, experiential,
presentational and propositional forms of knowing are being tested for
their mutual coherence, and the propositional form is being modified to

increase that coherence. Findings from previous reflection phases will be included.

> Sometimes the presented content is ambiguous. Thus in the ASC inquiry (Heron, 1988c) impressions that seemed to be of some other reality could have been the articulation of some not very clear but ordinary state in this world. So judging whether a description of these impressions was well-founded involved finding criteria to distinguish between real and illusory impressions of the other world. Certainly, in early reflection phases of that inquiry, collective reflection got too preoccupied with describing ostensibly occult impressions, and fell far short of finding criteria with which to evaluate them.

The evaluative question for all our articulations of subjective-objective experience is whether our subjectivity is uncritical, unfocused and unrefined. Does it distort the objective pole of the experience? While the objective pole, the cosmic given, can only be known through the articulations of the subjective pole, it is clearly not the case that any old articulation will do. What there is may be protean and metamorphic in its accessibility through diverse forms of human sensibility, but it demands not only creative and imaginative subjectivity, but also critical, rigorous and disciplined subjectivity.

Explanation

Explanatory reflection is a higher-order form of thought which builds theory on the basis of the phenomenal categories which are descriptively derived. Such theorizing may involve one or more different sorts of thinking, as follows:

- *Holistic thinking* Explanation in terms of a pattern of organization and interaction, of the relative autonomy and interdependence of parts within a whole, of simultaneous dynamic mutual influence, of a comprehensive analogical connecting pattern, of dynamic sequences of emerging order, of interacting grades and levels of being, of modes of awareness/prehension/ways of giving meaning, of ways of integrating the within and the without, none of which can be reduced to explanations in terms of linear cause and effect.
- *Bipolar thinking* Explanation that takes account of the interdependence of polar opposites and avoids unipolar reductionism.
- *Hermeneutic thinking* Explanation of phenomena that acknowledges their relation to, and emergence out of, a dialogical, cultural and historical context with past and prevailing values, norms and belief-systems. Explanation of human behaviour in terms of values, norms and beliefs held at the level of autonomous intentionality, or of social convention, or of psychosocial pathology.
- *Aperspectival thinking* Explanation which acknowledges that no perspective is final, that each view is relative to its context, that each

context is relative to its context and so on, and *also* that there are relative merits among different perspectives.

- *Subtle thinking* Explanation in terms of subtle level dynamics: immanent entelechy and transcendent archetype, discarnate influence, powers and presences.
- *Mystical thinking* Explanation in terms of divine reality.
- *Deterministic thinking* Explanation in terms of linear cause and effect sequence, of causal laws within a framework of relative determinism (which is the same as relative indeterminism).

None of these seven sorts of thinking is incompatible with any of the others; rather they complement each other. Deterministic thinking is only incompatible if it is set within a metaphysical framework of absolute determinism.

Some aids to developing explanatory reflection are:

- *Loose construing* Making sense of past experience with a light and loosely fitting set of concepts that lets the experience breathe. Tolerating obscurities and ambiguities, and avoiding premature intellectual closure. In early reflection phases it is better to be vaguely right than precisely wrong.
- *Divergent thinking* Considering diverse aspects and perspectives of the past experience, and in different ways. This too is particularly important in early stages of the inquiry, as I have discussed in some detail above.
- *Presentational construing* Making sense of past experience by the use of presentational methods: drawings, paintings, photos, sculptures, musical forms, mime and movement, ritual, thick multi-sensory descriptions, poetry, story, allegory, drama, demonstrations. This can be done as sense-making in its own right, and also to loosen up creative, conceptual thinking.

    In the first co-counselling inquiry (Heron and Reason, 1981), members used a lot of graphics in making sense of their individual client sessions, and with good effect.

- *Free or directed association* Making sense of past experience may be facilitated by associating freely or directly to it.
- *Firm construing* Working for greater coherence and density in the conceptual framework that makes sense of the experience phases. This is relevant in the later reflection phases.
- *Convergent thinking* Reflecting on divergent aspects and perspectives, refining each and bringing out the common ground they illuminate. This is central in the later reflection phases.

Application

In the fourth part of the reflection phase, the inquirers are proposing what sort of content to explore in the next action phase, how to explore it and how to record this exploration. An important part of this planning will be application: some transfer of the learning that has been distilled from previous action phases.

One thing I have learned from co-operative inquiries so far is that there is a good deal of informal transfer of learning from one cycle to another. So some sort of cyclic processing of ideas is going on. But it is quite difficult for a co-operative group to be fully intentional about the discipline of rigorous refining of strategic ideas through several cycles. The difficulty is in drawing the learning out of the previous action phase with sufficient acuity for it to be used to shape up clear intention for the next action phase.

The learning sometimes (but by no means always) seems to overflow tacitly from one action phase to the next, with people in the intervening reflection phase having a strong intuitive feel for what is going on, but only a partial or limited intellectual grasp of the transfer process. Dionysian inquirers will, of course, consider such tacit overflow a virtue to be encouraged, not a deficit to be resolved.

In the holistic medicine inquiry (Heron and Reason, 1985; Reason, 1988c) this transfer, in the earlier cycles, was at best tacit only. We did not consciously and intentionally use prior findings to influence subsequent planning. We think the transfer happened subliminally and unconsciously. It only became more conscious, explicit and intentional when each of the subgroups converged on its chosen theme over a series of later cycles.

In the ASC inquiry (Heron, 1988c) it seemed that almost all the transfer was tacit, or at best the result of some rather vague and unfocused associative or imaginative process. We plunged in Dionysian mode from one bizarre cycle of action to another, generating more and more impressionistic data, with only a minimal conscious grasp of how prior findings affected current planning. Alarmed at this, we set up the devil's advocate procedure after several cycles, and in this way we confronted each other to make explicit the tacit transfer and the tacit learning.

What seems important about reflection in an Apollonian inquiry, is that it is never merely descriptive, but also evaluative and explanatory in the ways mentioned above. As the cycles unfold, there is increasingly conscious application of these three forms of reflection in planning the content and method of the next action phase.

In a Dionysian inquiry, it is the intention not to be reflective in this way, that is important: a clear choosing to make sense of prior experience in intuitive, expressive ways. The work of the next action phase is born out of this spontaneously after appropriate gestation.

Challenging uncritical subjectivity

The basic point about co-operative inquiry is that the inquirers are taking proposals from the reflection phase to restructure them in the light of

experience in the action phase. But to take an idea down into some experiential domain, whether the idea relates to information about that
domain, or to transformative practice within it, is a tricky business.

Firstly, the inquirers are likely to have a strong prior commitment to the
idea. It must seem in advance to be sufficiently plausible for them to be
willing to make a commitment of the whole person to explore it in action.
So for this reason they may be somewhat resistant to noticing inadequacies
in the idea that the experiential grounding reveals.

Secondly, making the experiential test involves them in a change of
being. They become different: the idea is no longer just grasped by them
intellectually. They have lived through it, they know it on the pulse,
connaturally as the philosophers say. They have worn it as the garment of
their doing, and so it becomes warming and endearing to them. For this
reason too they have a vested interest in not noticing its shortcomings in
the face of experience.

Thirdly, and most crucially, they have to entertain the idea in order to
have the appropriate experience or engage in the relevant practice. The idea
defines what they have to do in order to ground it. So they have to go
along with the idea, believe in it sufficiently in order to get into the
pertinent kind of encounter or practice. And this is the most critical reason
why they may fail to notice any corrective content of experience.

So an important aspect of the procedure for challenging uncritical
subjectivity is vigilance in spotting how ideas fall short when taken into the
action phase. The inquirers need to believe in an idea enough to get
experientially involved in it, and at the same time they need to be
unattached to it, watchful for shortcomings, noticing more than belief in it
entails, and having alternative ideas readily available.

This is an individual task for each inquirer in each action phase, and
when recollecting experience in the reflection phase. But there is not only
individual nescience to take into account. There is also collective or consensus collusion, uncritical intersubjectivity. When this occurs the inquirers
are all tacitly agreeing to articulate a pseudo-reality. They collude in not
noticing, or if they notice, in not mentioning, aspects of their experience
that show up the limitations of their conceptual model or programme of
action.

As well as colluding in not noticing corrective aspects of their experience,
they can collude in many other ways: in obscuring the false assumptions
implicit in their leading ideas and/or in their ways of taking these ideas into
action; in unaware projections distorting the inquiry process; in lack of
rigour in their inquiry methods and in applying vigorously the various
validity procedures.

It seems wise to have a special procedure to counter any tendency to
collusion of these various kinds. A formal devil's advocate practice works
well. When a group decides to adopt this method, then any member can
indicate, during a group reflection phase, that they wish to speak as devil's
advocate. This means that the person is concerned about validity, and

wants the freedom to confront fully some possible collusion. This allows anyone to press hard a rigorous challenge, while merely wondering whether, rather than necessarily believing that, something has gone wrong. And it encourages members to seek out doubts even when the group is most sanguine about its work.

The method can be applied in two complementary ways: on a spontaneous individual basis, and in a full group formal session. It may be wise to use both in the same inquiry. But in the two examples that follow, each inquiry only used one to the exclusion of the other.

In the holistic medicine inquiry (Heron and Reason, 1985; Reason, 1988c) any member could at any time take up 'the mace', a staff, to indicate that they were temporarily adopting the role of radical critic, in order to challenge some possible hidden collusion. This worked well in a piecemeal, impromptu, individualistic way. But it was *en passant*, a spontaneous interlude in some other business. And it sometimes degenerated into mere prankishness, and mischievous boat rocking. The inquiry as a whole lacked a more systematic use of devil's advocacy, in which a full session involved everyone in a critical review of possible collusion.

In the ASC inquiry (Heron, 1988c) we did hold such a full session, driven to it by the mass of divergent, impressionistic data, fraught with ambiguity, which we had generated. Each inquirer in turn sat in the 'hot seat' and had read out, from records kept over four cycles, their impressions of the other reality. Any other inquirer could then come forward as devil's advocate, and sceptically analyse these impressions, reducing them to some purely naturalistic explanation.

The defendant then had three choices: to give a reasoned defence of the impressions as valid impressions of the other reality; to yield to the advocate's reductionist explanation as being the most reasonable; or to stick to their intuitive feel, even though unable to argue the case. This procedure, sustained over some time, did sharpen our awareness of possible criteria for differentiating between extrasensory and naturalistic impressions.

The report on the youth workers' inquiry into their own learning processes gives the following account of their use of the procedure:

When an individual or small group was sharing their learning, another small group acted as Devil's Advocate, asking probing questions which assumed the contribution(s) to be 'wrong', 'illusory', 'colluding', 'confusing', 'dishonest', 'inaccurate', or 'contradictory'. Another individual or small group acted as supporter(s) to the contributor(s), ensuring all parties heard each other, sharing an understanding of both questions and answers. They also ensured the contributors were not overwhelmed by the pressure of the process and that the Devil's Advocacy procedure's purpose as a method of falsification was to ensure that what was being researched and learned, was real and relevant for individuals, the group and our work together. It aimed to prevent us from stating something to be true simply because we wanted to believe it to be so. As a result of this, our findings are only those things we *all* came to know to be true and could provide evidence for.

The Devil's Advocacy process was also helpful in enabling us to differentiate between the various *aspects of reflection*. It helped us describe our experience more clearly – what had happened for me, for you, for us; and also to evaluate our experience – what it meant for me, for you, for us. Furthermore, it increased our efficiency and effectiveness in practical reflection – deciding how the next phase of our work could, would, or should be influenced by these reflections. (De Venney-Tiernan et al., 1994: 126)

Chaos and order

If the inquirers are really going to be open, adventurous and innovative, they may put all at risk to reach out to their truth beyond fear and collusion. The result can be, especially in the earlier stages of the inquiry, that divergence of thought and expression collapse into confusion, uncertainty, ambiguity, disorder and chaos. Then most or all the inquirers will feel lost to a greater or lesser degree. About the first co-counselling inquiry, we wrote:

> Accepting chaos facilitates the emergence of order. Experiential researchers need to have a high tolerance for ambiguity and confusion. New ideas may be found by allowing, celebrating and encouraging, going through, the stages of confusion which the inquiry generates. (Heron and Reason, 1981: 50)

The inquiry process is a bit like a 'dissipative structure' in organic and inorganic chemistry (Prigogine, 1980), in which new order is created by perturbation. Or like the self-organizing dynamic of a complex system that gets itself to the edge of chaos and then emerges at a higher level of complexity, as mooted by complexity theory (Lewin, 1993).

It is paradoxical to call this collapse into confusion and chaos a procedure. The inquirers can't plan for it and programme it in. They can't say: 'Now let's have some chaos.' This is likely to generate only pseudo-chaos. But they can plan to be creatively divergent. If chaos sets in when such creativity and divergence start to get out of hand and overstep the bounds of everyone's conceptual tolerance, then they can learn to recognize the chaos, stay with it and accept it. And this without anxiously trying to clean it up, without getting trapped by fear into premature and restrictive intellectual closure.

The principle of faith here is that if the inquirers hang in with the chaos *awarely*, it will in its own good time, by the principle of the interdependence of opposites, become the seedbed for the emergence of some new, useful and illuminating bit of order. But it is a risky business. There can be no guarantee that order will emerge. The whole inquiry may go down the drain.

Equally, there can be no guarantee that chaos will occur. But there will clearly be some degree of confusion, at least in the early stages. Issues to do with maintaining adequate divergence, with group interaction and peer decision-making will see to that. And whatever the degree of confusion, the challenge is for the inquirers to go with it for a while, not pull out of it anxiously but wait until there is a real sense of creative resolution.

The inquiry of health visitors into their work with families stumbled into chaos in one of their later reflection meetings, after several cycles of deep engagement with their practice. It arose when the group finally faced the challenge of clarifying for themselves the aims of the health visitor role.

> Just when we were feeling so confident the group was thrown into con-
> fusion, uncertainty and depression . . . We were swamped by the enormity
> of the task and scared about whether we would be able to make sense of it
> all . . . The group's pre-occupation with action had, I think, something to
> do with avoiding the key issue of our lack of clarity about the health
> visitor's role, which had always been present hovering in the wings. I had no
> idea how we were going to address this. All I could hang onto at this stage
> was the thought that if the group could hold this chaos for long enough
> perhaps something would emerge. (Traylen, 1994: 76)

In the next reflection meeting, the group spent a lot of time dealing with the uncomfortable feelings engendered by the chaos, then, after further discussion, experienced a breakthrough centred on notions of well-being and family empowerment.

In the holistic medicine inquiry the degree of real chaos was minimal. The inquiry was characterized more by manageable sorts of minor disorder and messiness. In the original monograph we wrote:

> The group and its members would have to go through an almost
> psychotic degeneration into disorder if they were to re-create a genuine
> holistic practice. (Heron and Reason, 1985: 108)

The ASC inquiry (Heron, 1988c) lived with a good deal of conceptual chaos and ambiguity about the status of the many divergent impressions of the other reality accumulating over the first four cycles. Order emerged out of the chaos, mainly through the devil's advocate procedure after the fourth cycle, and this was overdue rather than premature.

The management of unaware projections

The very process of inquiring into human nature, human interactions and the human condition, may stir up fear and defensiveness in the researchers. The fear is of that which is both unknown and very close to psychological home. The defensiveness is about those aspects of themselves which they have had to repress and deny in order to survive and be accepted when growing up in an emotionally alienated society. Such fear and defensiveness, once stirred up, will reinforce each other, and may distort the whole process of psychological research. Devereaux (1967) puts forward a similar view, arguing that this defensive process is akin to therapist counter-transference in psychoanalysis.

Let's look more closely at the structure of defensiveness. If as a child I want to express my real nature, and this urge is repeatedly interfered with, then I feel, depending on the situation, the distress of grief, or fear or anger. If I am also constrained to suppress such valid distress, then I am conditioned a second time to become false to myself. In order to get whatever kind of restrictive support is available from those who oppress me, I deny both my real self and the pain I feel at its interruption. I erect an alienated self with which I identify. I defend myself against the truth about myself (Heron, 1992).

I become addicted to projecting onto the world the anxiety of my denied distress, seeing the world as a threatening place, which thus reinforces my addiction to my false self. I am stuck in an interlocking compulsion not to identify my real nature and not to see what sort of an exciting and challenging world it is possible to construe. Overlapping versions of this sort of view of what happens to people in our sort of society are put forward in the works of Guntrip, Jackins, Janov, Lowen, Perls, Reich, Winnicott and others.

If researchers are stuck unawarely in this kind of defensiveness, then their research is likely to fall foul of it too:

- They may compulsively *not* inquire into persons as persons.
- They may research rats as surrogates for persons.
- They may use conceptual models that reduce personhood to external behaviour observed by others, or to mechanistic stimulus–response reactions.
- They may use research methods that reduce persons to objects and to subpersonal functioning.
- They may research extensively trivial and peripheral bits of behaviour.
- They may manipulate and deceive their experimental subjects.
- They may never ask their subjects how they construe the experimental situation and give meaning to their actions within it.

Their research becomes, in part at any rate, a kind of pathological acting out of their own repressive denial of the truth about themselves. Indeed, some writers have argued that the whole scientific enterprise can be seen as a defensive collusion (Maslow, 1966; Griffin, 1984).

> I wish also to challenge experimentalists to explore the bias within their own approach, which I believe they currently ignore. We have argued before that anxiety plays an important part in any inquiry, and that if it is ignored it will probably be projected into the inquiry itself, thus distorting the method and/or the findings. Good inquiry from a stance of critical subjectivity will take this into account, but I know of no evidence that experimental researchers are even aware of this issue; certainly they do not seem to take it into account in their inquiries. I invite those who use experimental approaches to read our writings on this issue and to comment. (Reason, 1986: 36)

Researchers who are aware of this kind of defensiveness, who have started to dismantle it through some personal growth process, will still need to watch for its distorting effect on the research. For even if the co-operative inquiry model is itself outside this effect, the application of it is likely to stir up disruption from all kinds of unfinished emotional business.

Some candidates for such disruption are:

- The choice of content area.
- The planning and management of the research cycles.
- Lapses in recording.
- Neglect of validity procedures.
- Emotional and intellectual difficulty in noticing and reporting important experiences.
- Becoming disgruntled, resistant, bored, distracted, rebellious about the whole enterprise.
- Interpersonal tensions and disruptions.
- Consensus collusion of all kinds.
- Messy peer decision-making, etc.

Co-operative inquirers will need to take time out during their research to monitor for the distorting effect of their own fear and hidden distress. Sometimes it may be sufficient simply to identify and report on this effect in order to get free of it. At other times it may be necessary to release some of the underlying emotional pain; or to transmute it through some meditative method. This management of unaware projection is just one aspect of the general inquiry skill of emotional competence, which means the ability to identify and manage emotions, and which I discuss in Chapter 7.

> The youth workers' inquiry into their own learning processes included among its formal roles 'distress managers'. The group agreed that every member was available to play this role for any other, and report that everyone was used and equally valued in it.

>> We were all aware of how easily our current experience and perceptions are 'contaminated' and influenced by our subconscious. It was important that these [old agendas] were prevented from distorting or contaminating our research. We did this in two main ways. First, we agreed that each would be available individually to support and help work through any issue which the research had raised and we felt unable to deal with in a grouping. This would be shared with the group, if deemed relevant, whenever the individual felt ready to do so. The second method was our use of a 'Devil's Advocacy' procedure. Its intended use was as a *falsification* mechanism, but it acted simultaneously as a powerful tool in the management of unaware projections. (De Venney-Tiernan et al., 1994: 126)

> Whitmore's inquiry about programme participants becoming evaluators of a prenatal programme for single expectant mothers, ran into serious interpersonal conflict by the third meeting.

>> This issue would haunt us throughout the process. There were days when we simply adjourned to the local coffee shop to talk it out. I remind myself, in

the log, that these times are important: 'I must be flexible and allow time for personal issues to be discussed and to give support when needed. Today we accomplished very little of the 'task' but a lot of process. Works get done intermittently, but personal needs must be attended to.' (Whitmore, 1994: 90)

The health visitors' inquiry regularly took time at reflection meetings to process and share anxieties and other feelings generated by their practice, and by the inquiry itself (Traylen, 1994).

The women's university staff inquiry made space to express emotions of anger, despair, grief, joy and laughter, that accompanied their stories of gender issues in the workplace (Treleaven, 1994).

In the holistic medicine inquiry (Heron and Reason, 1985; Reason, 1988c) from the start we had regular group process sessions to identify interpersonal and intrapsychic material that might distort the research, and to give it space at least to be talked somewhat out of the way. We also used regular pair sessions including co-counselling. Both approaches yielded modest gains, but more deep seated material was rarely reached, there was little catharsis, and a good deal of consensus collusion was unresolved.

In the ASC inquiry (Heron, 1988c) there were three in-depth sessions of emotional house cleaning, involving regression, catharsis and insight. This gave scope for the rigorous use of devil's advocacy. But more house-cleaning was undoubtedly needed. Going into the attic of the psyche calls for a good deal of active sorting out in the basement, combined with a high degree of critical judgement exercised on the ground floor.

Sustaining authentic collaboration

One aspect of validity is the coherence between the perspectives of different individual researchers: the overlap between well-researched, autonomous and interdependent viewpoints. These will not really be authentic unless each person is a fully fledged collaborator, contributing at each stage of the inquiry with a real grasp of what is going on. There are two aspects of authentic collaboration. First, the relationship between group members and the initiating researchers. And second, the relationships among group members themselves. I will deal with these in turn.

When initiating researchers launch an inquiry they choose a research topic, invite a number of interested persons to become co-researchers, and then initiate them into the research method. If real initiation has taken place the co-opted inquirers internalize issues to do with the research method. They make the whole inquiry enterprise their own in a vigorous way.

If the initiation is more apparent than real, then the co-opted inquirers are merely yes-people, being guided and shepherded into appropriate behaviour, without any real grasp of what they are about. They are just followers of the initiating researchers. Any agreement reached is likely to be spurious. Collaboration is unauthentic. The co-opted inquirers simply rubber-stamp what the initiating researchers get up to.

The initiating researchers, while doing the initiation, will quite appropriately have a high profile about method at the outset, and will also, most probably, be the facilitators of the group's decision-making. But it is not appropriate for this high profile to continue indefinitely. If it does, the initiation has failed: there has been no effective delegation of knowledge and skills.

The initiation, then, must include an important element of training and consciousness-raising, in which group members are learning through practice new research skills and the rationale for them. So it helps if the initiating researchers are competent in this kind of training, and know how and when to manage the transition from more directive to more participative forms of decision-making in the group (Heron, 1989, 1993a). I have discussed this in more detail in Chapter 4. In commenting on issues of ownership, power and collaboration in the six inquiries in his book, Peter Reason says:

> The question, 'Whose research is this?' runs centrally through many accounts. What is fascinating is the amount of work and attention the initiators have devoted to developing participatory group relationships. The group first has to be created and established with enough clarity of purpose and method that it has some chance of success, a culture of collaboration developed over time, and then space has to be provided for initiatives from participants to take over and transform the inquiry beyond the original dreams of the initiator. (Reason, 1994a: 201)

Marshall and McLean make a strong and clear statement about the paradox of leading people into freedom. They assert that co-operative inquiry is not about equality, because of the discrepancy between their research expertise and that of the group.

> The fundamental discrepancy in knowledge and research experience represented a risk that all the key decisions and interpretations would come from us. In the event we were gratified that our chosen strategy of acknowledging this expertise at the beginning, and taking a clear initiative early, had resulted in their empowerment later ... The learning for us here is that by acknowledging our paradigmatic power, by being explicit in our use of the cultural metaphor, we provided a framework within which people could operate creatively and relatively independently. (Marshall and McLean, 1988: 219)

There are several signs of successful initiation. The members show by their comments and initiatives their mastery of content and method. They take charge of group decision-making and choose awarely how they make decisions. They rotate the group facilitator role among themselves, taking this role over from the initiating researchers. They keep an eye on contribution rates. They are as vigilant as the initiating researchers about the use of validity procedures such as balancing divergence and convergence, the use of devil's advocacy to challenge uncritical subjectivity, the management of unaware projections, and so on.

In the holistic medicine inquiry (Heron and Reason, 1985; Reason, 1988c) the initiation was adequate but imperfect: all members grasped the broad thrust of the research method, but some remained mystified about its detailed aspects, and one or two were sceptical about its claim to be a genuine alternative to conventional research.

In the ASC inquiry (Heron, 1988c) the initiation was abducted, so to speak. The group took over the method rapidly and enthusiastically, impatient about its finer points, and blocked attempts by me later in the inquiry to push hard on what I considered to be important methodological issues.

The second important aspect of collaboration is that between individual members. Some may be more fully initiated than others. Even when all are fully initiated, some may hang back for reasons to do with their personal and interpersonal process. The question for everyone regularly to ask is whether there are any passengers. These are group members not putting forth their energy and enterprise, whether in shared reflection, collective planning, validity checks, or even in the action phases.

As well as those who hang back, there may be those who push forward, disrupting group process by their own distressed agendas. The youth worker inquiry on how people learn reported on two co-researchers who

> were perceived by other co-researchers to be 'looking out for themselves', without regard for the other co-researchers. One was perceived as trying to grab power, the other as demanding group time and attention. (De Venney-Tiernan et al., 1994: 131)

In group reflection phases, high contributors may habitually and unawarely push aside low contributors. And such an imbalance in contribution rates may become a fixed pathology of the group. This may overlap with a sexist imbalance, in which male views predominate to the exclusion of female views. Also in the reflection phases, verbal skills may be over-valued, to the exclusion of those who could have made an important contribution in terms of non-discursive skills, making sense of their experience in terms of graphics, colour, movement or expressive drama.

And even if all group members contribute fully, influence hierarchies may become established. The views of some may tend to hold more sway than the views of others: everyone speaks but only some are really listened to. It is important to check that views are influential because of their content, not because of some extraneous factors to do with the impact of the speaker; and to ensure that reputation based on past wisdom does not obscure present folly.

Various things can be done by the group to encourage and sustain authentic collaboration among its members. Individual cycles of action and of reflection guarantee a baseline of equal participation from all inquirers. In group sessions – to do with reflection, planning, validity – the use of rounds, in which each person has a verbal turn, helps to sustain full collaboration. And the interplay between verbal and nonverbal ways of making sense of experience can be used. In open discussion the group facilitator can actively manage contribution rates, drawing in low contributors and shutting out persistent high contributors; can keep an eye on sexist imbalance, and on improper influence hierarchies. I have discussed all this in more detail in Chapter 4.

The inquirers may also need to take special time out, in a formal validity session, to review the issue of collaboration: to look at the developing effectiveness of the initiation; to explore psychological reticence, contribution rates, sexist imbalance, the use of verbal and nonverbal skills, and influence hierarchies; to find out whether the outspoken and influential do voice the genuine aspirations of the more retiring; to devise strategies that ensure that all get a piece of the action and a voice in the reflection.

Perhaps most important of all is building trust as a basis for collaboration. Whitmore, initiating an inquiry with an oppressed group, knew she would have to spend time building trust.

Gradually, we built up trust, so that in the end, they felt comfortable about sharing their feelings with each other and with me. (Whitmore, 1994: 94)

But equally, Treleaven, inquiring with her university peers, in commenting about facilitating the transition process into a collaborative inquiry, underlines trust.

In the transition phase there was a need to build trust between the women in the group and trust in the process of inquiry. We did this initially by sharing our hopes and concerns related to the inquiry and its process, examining what commitments we were each willing to offer, and what we would each require of ourselves and other participants in working towards fulfilling our stated interests. We explored our varying understandings of confidentiality and its relationship to trust as it ranged from personal trust to the political complexities of trust in the workplace. Within the inquiry group, we were committed to sharing power (though of course we had people or topics that tended to dominate), and to individually being responsible for creating value from our participation in the collaborative processes (though there were times when we forgot and just felt impatient!).

Our approach was typical of feminist practice with explicit agreements that enabled each woman to have space in which to be heard without interruption (though in practice we had enthusiastic interrupters from time to time), to speak only for herself, and to respect each participant's contributions to the inquiry as confidential . . .

The development of trust and group bonding are conditions which fundamentally influence participation and the extent to which people are willing to explore issues through situations grounded in their experience. (Treleaven, 1994: 152–3)

Open and closed boundaries

In Chapter 3 I introduced, with examples, the distinction between inquiries which have a closed boundary, and those which have an open boundary, during the action phases. Closed boundary inquiries do not include, as part of the action phase, interaction between the researchers and others in the wider world. Open boundary inquiries do include such interaction.

If open boundary inquirers elicit no data from other people with whom they interact in the action phases, a valuable source of relevant feedback is ignored. Of course, the inquirers can report their impressions of how the other people reacted, and this is clearly important. But on its own it is not enough. There needs to be some personal comment or feedback directly from these people themselves.

In the holistic medicine inquiry (Heron and Reason, 1985; Reason, 1988c) the main part of the action phases was the doctors' work with patients. The doctors had much valuable data of their own to report on these patients. But direct feedback from the patients concerned was very limited; and in this respect the data available to the inquiry was limited.

If the data is generated by other people, but they have no say in how it is explained and used, then a norm of co-operative inquiry is infringed. Subjects in an inquiry have a basic right to participate in all decisions about how knowledge based on their experience is gathered and used. One solution to this dilemma, for groups of professionals, is to include in the inquiry group members of the client group they serve. Then the co-operative inquiry process involves, for example, doctors *and* their patients, health visitors *and* members of the families they visit. So far within the culture of co-operative inquiry, the issue of important data at the open boundary has not been well-addressed.

Variegated replication

If a crudely articulated subjective-objective reality is to be developed further, to the point at which concerted action can thoroughly articulate it, then the design and outcomes of any inquiry which focuses on that world must be portrayed and stated with sufficient clarity and thoroughness so that future inquirers can both reconstitute it, and extend their grasp of it and their action within it. The same argument applies to a developed subjective-objective reality, for there will always be more extended forms of concerted action to take within it, and more to construe within it.

So a co-operative inquiry needs to be replicable, not in any crude sense of literal repetition, but in the more imaginative sense of being available for creative metamorphosis. The original study will be done over again, but in a significantly different way. The initial perspective, research design and practical content will be recognizable and thoroughly reworked. Yet there will be enough overlap for the follow-up to be a legitimate development of the original.

Literal and exact replication is inconsistent with the nature of a subjective-objective reality. If the present inquirers are truly going to construe the reality of the previous inquirers, then they must do so, and plan to do so, in their own autonomous and idiosyncratic way. They can only see their version of it, and they can only properly see this through their own constructs not the constructs of their predecessors – which are a launch pad not a terminus.

Concerted action

The question here is this: do the outcomes of the inquiry enable the inquirers to *act* in a coherent and concerted way within the inquiry domain? Do their various actions dovetail and interweave so that they agree they have practical knowledge which manifests value in a sustainable way?

In a transformative inquiry, which is directly concerned with practice, this question can be asked and to some degree answered within the history of the inquiry. The question is important because of the idea, discussed in Chapter 9, of practice as consummating the other forms of knowing – propositional, presentational and experiential – on which it is grounded. It consummates them by showing that the subjective-objective reality which they articulate has value, manifests worthwhile concerted action. 'Concerted' means people acting together and interacting. It is agreement in deed, in active use and application of beliefs.

The claim to validity made for the propositional outcomes of an informative inquiry may be well-grounded, but is still in a sense incomplete. Their truth-value awaits consummation by that which is its complement and also lies beyond it, the celebration of being-value. The completion occurs when they are taken into a further inquiry to explore their implications for practice. In the next chapter I explore this idea that practice consummates the inquiry process with the celebration of being-values.

9

Validity and Beyond

Let me recapitulate the points about validity which I have already made in previous chapters, and then proceed to develop them further in this chapter, after looking at validity in quantitative and qualitative research.

- 'Validity' is a healthy term in ordinary discourse, and is not to be abandoned in social science because of its abuse by positivism and its politics. Epistemological validity has no inherent connection with either objectivism or power: it is a precondition of rational discourse, and other ways of knowing, in any domain. The poststructural rejection of it is suicidal and nihilistic. The challenge after positivism is to redefine it in ways that honour the generative, creative role of the human mind in all forms of knowing (Chapter 1).
- Co-operative inquiry rests on a paradigm of participative, subjective-objective reality, which holds that there is a given cosmos in which the mind actively participates, with which it communes and from which it is not separate, and which it can only know in terms of its constructions, involving all our mental sensibilities (Chapter 1).
- The outcomes of a co-operative inquiry are valid if they are well-grounded in the forms of knowing – practical, propositional, presentational, experiential – which support them. The basic grounding form is experiential knowing. The forms of knowing are valid if they are well-grounded in the procedures adopted to free them from distortion, and in the special skills involved in the knowing process. The validity of the outcomes also depends on the application of autonomous criteria at their own level. And validity itself, concern with the justification of truth-values, is interdependent with that which transcends it, the celebration of being-values (Chapter 3).
- Where practice is the primary outcome, it is validated by being grounded on criteria of sound practice: executive, technical, psycho-social, intentionality and value criteria (Chapter 3).
- Inherent in experiential knowing, integral lived experience, is a tacit shared substrate of nonlinguistic primary meaning, which is the context for the secondary, conceptual meaning involved in our use of language (Chapter 7).

A statement is 'valid', in ordinary usage of this term, if it is sound or well-grounded, if there are good and relevant reasons for making it. A document is valid if it is drawn up in a legal manner, which may include being appropriately signed and not having reached its expiry date. In research, the term 'validity' carries over both these meanings from everyday usage. The first transfers intact, the second with a shift from the legal to the rational.

Research findings are valid if they are sound or well-grounded, and have been reached by a rational method – one that offers a reasoned way of grounding them. What is important is that researchers are clear about the grounds of validity they are claiming and critical about the extent to which they have reached them.

What researchers mean by the soundness of their findings will depend on their assumptions about the nature of existence, being or reality. Findings that are sound or well-grounded have some sort of wholesome relation to reality, however that reality is construed. The researchers' assumptions about the nature of reality and of how one comes to know it soundly – or truly – will determine what they regard as an acceptable methodology. From a view about reality to a view about knowledge, truth and method: ontology, epistemology and methodology are linked. Guba and Lincoln (1994) develop this point fully in their account of different paradigms in qualitative research.

Validity in quantitative research

Traditional positivist research assumes there is one objective reality, the world perceived by the senses, which is the same for all observers and independent of what they think about it. Research findings are sound if they are accurate, if they match this reality and measure it correctly. This is so-called internal validity and it appeals to a simple correspondence, or dictionary, theory of truth. This holds that truth is 'conformity with facts', as if facts are out there quite apart from us and waiting to be conformed to. Internal validity has been defined as 'the isomorphic relationship between the data of an inquiry and the phenomena those data represent' (Erlandson et al., 1993: 29–30).

This in turn dictates criteria for an acceptable methodology. The research must be designed so that its findings are generalizable – so-called external validity – hence, for example, the importance of randomized sampling. It must be designed so that it can be replicated by others with similar results thus establishing the reliability of its findings, their consistency or stability. And it must be designed so that it is free of researcher bias and distortion, thus ensuring the objectivity of the findings.

The collapse of positivism is basically to do with the collapse of the objective fact. In positivist research, theories are to be tested against the observed facts, which are assumed to be independent, nontheoretical entities out there as the empirical touchstone of truth. The well-established, counter-positivist view is that every statement of fact is itself theory-laden, is necessarily set in a theoretical framework. It is an interpretation of reality based on a range of non-empirical assumptions. In short, there are no exclusively objective facts. So there can be no objective science based on objective data: no observations can be made independent of how I choose to conceptualize them on the basis of prior theory. For an enlargement of this critique, see the first two sections of Chapter 11.

Validity in qualitative inquiry

Classic qualitative research includes all those methods which have in common the study of people *in situ* in their own social setting, and the understanding of them in terms of their own categories and constructs. Generally, these methods accept an interpretivist or constructivist view of reality (Schwandt, 1994) as mind-dependent, especially applied to people's view of their own social situation and social context. There has therefore been a shift in the way validity has been construed, but it has been a bit of a backward-looking struggle.

First of all, Goetz and LeCompte (1984) seemed to need to hold on to positivist notions of validity and reliability and relate them to qualitative procedures. Then Lincoln and Guba (1985), followed by many others (for example Erlandson et al., 1993; Leininger, 1994), took all the positivist criteria and did a parallel conversion of their terminology, meaning and associated procedures. Validity in general became a matter of *quality* or *goodness* or *trustworthiness*. Internal validity was converted to *credibility*, supported by such techniques as triangulation and member checks. External validity became *transferability*, achieved by thick descriptions and purposive sampling. Reliability became *dependability*, fed by an audit trail of different kinds of data, ways of recording it and filing it. Objectivity became *confirmability*, also fed by the audit trail.

This conversion is nostalgic for positivist criteria, and attempts to recreate for qualitative researchers some of the (apparent) security of positivist method. Indeed, Guba and Lincoln have since written (1994: 114) of their converted criteria that 'their parallelism to positivist criteria makes them suspect'. They say that 'the issue of quality criteria in constructivism is . . . not well resolved, and further critique is needed'.

The conversion includes a version of the correspondence theory of truth. Internal validity, remember, in positivist research is about conformity with fact, about whether the findings match objective reality. Lincoln and Guba (1985) convert this into credibility, and insist that the most important technique to establish credibility is member checking, which means asking the people being studied to verify the interpretations made by the researchers. In other words, the essential thing for the researchers to do is to see whether their interpretations correspond with the indigenous perspectives of their informants. 'Credibility', writes Leininger (1994: 105), 'refers to the truth as known, experienced or deeply felt by the people being studied.'

However, constructivists also believe that their investigations are a transaction with the investigated which literally *co-creates* findings: the dialogue between researcher and researched leads to 'a consensus construction that is more informed and sophisticated than any of the predecessor constructions' (Guba and Lincoln, 1994: 111). This effectively puts an end to establishing the credibility of findings by member checking. Findings co-created by researcher and researched members go beyond member-only views, and thus cannot be made credible by trying to appeal to member-only views.

Can member checking still be used in earlier stages of the inquiry, when the researcher wants to make sure he or she has understood the respondents' views prior to formulating a conjoint view? In terms of strict constructivism, member checking in any objective sense is impossible. If I, the researcher, ask you, the member, whether my account of your view is correct, and you say it is, then we have co-created a new construction which is subtly different from and supercedes your original view. When any two people agree, after suitable discussion, that they have grasped the reality of one of them, that reality is changed by the shift from a unilateral to a bilateral perspective.

Repetitive member checking throughout an inquiry is from the very first check a progressive transformation of indigenous views into a consensus construction of researcher and researched, even if the researcher never explicitly puts forward his or her own personal views. Three things work towards this effect: the imprecise form of anyone's social 'reality'; the selective nature of what the researcher chooses to check, and the researcher's way of reframing what is thus selected in order to check it. So the question of validity still remains: what makes for the quality, trustworthiness, credibility of any of these developing consensus constructions?

After their *trustworthiness* criteria of 1985, Guba and Lincoln later proposed (1989: 245–50) some *authenticity* criteria. In the light of this second set of criteria, the research outcomes show that: informants have equal access to the inquiry process, being involved from the outset about the choice of salient questions and how to answer them (fairness); they have enlarged their personal views of their culture (ontological authenticity); they have improved understanding of the views of others in the culture (educative authenticity); they have been stimulated and empowered to act to reshape their culture on the basis of their expanded awareness (catalytic and tactical authenticity).

This change of criteria is a move from a concern with truth to a concern with goodness, from whether the outcomes are credible, to whether they are desirable, from epistemology to axiology. The new criteria are all to do with values, with what human states of affairs are intrinsically worthwhile. There is also a shift from thinking of outcomes not just as a set of consensus propositions, but more relevantly as a set of inward and outward actions and social transformations among the members of the culture being researched.

This shift still leaves the issue of the truth or credibility of consensus constructions unresolved. But it puts practical outcomes (i.e. informants' actions) and their value criteria firmly on the inquiry agenda, and in this respect is in accord with co-operative inquiry. However, there is one deep anomaly.

Guba and Lincoln (1989: 260) state firmly that 'the evaluator must share control' not only with regard to 'the *substance* of constructions but also with respect to the *methodology* of the evaluation itself'. So how can Guba and Lincoln both assert this and at the same time strongly specify the value criteria (their authenticity criteria) for judging the goodness of the action outcomes of future unknown stakeholders and respondents? If members of a researched culture are to collaborate fully on research content and method, the only authentic criteria for the value of their research-influenced actions are those they collaborate in formulating. Indeed, it could be argued that since the practical outcomes are not manifested by the external researchers but only by the members of the researched culture, the members alone should be responsible for formulating the relevant criteria.

Participative reality

Rejecting positivism, the transactional or participative view of reality (Merleau-Ponty, 1962; Bateson, 1979; Reason and Rowan, 1981c; Spretnak, 1991; Heron, 1992; Varela et al., 1993; Skolimowski, 1994; Reason, 1994a) sees it is subjective-objective, an intermarriage between the creative, construing of the human mind and what is cosmically given.

> The cosmos or the universe is a primordial ontological datum, while the 'world' is an epistemological construct, a form of our understanding. (Skolimowski, 1994: 177)

All experience of reality *includes* its articulation by the mind, both at the level of sensory imagery and at the level of concepts and language-use. The mind can only know the cosmos in terms of its constructions.

At the same time because the mind actively engages with the cosmos which it articulates, it is not separated from it. Our mind creatively articulates in percept and concept its felt participation in what is present. It is through this participation of mind that we are in touch with what is other. Worlds and people are what we meet, but the meeting is shaped by our own terms of reference. Hence our realities are always subjective-objective. This ontology calls for a new view about truth and ways of knowing, a new account of acceptable methodology.

I mentioned in Chapter 1 that the constructivism of Guba and Lincoln (1989, 1994; Lincoln and Guba, 1985) is ambiguous as to whether all reality is a mental construct, wholly mind-dependent, or whether it is only partially, though always, mind-dependent. Schwandt (1994: 134) holds that Guba and Lincoln are equivocal as to whether reality is or is not a mental construct. They say that all realities are 'constructed realities', invented by human minds, but also that these constructions are related to 'tangible entities' such as events, persons and objects. This implies that these tangible entities are not wholly created by the mind and are ontically real.

In this case, their constructivism is closer to the transactional or participative view, but without the bridging notion of participation. Participative reality is neither wholly subjective nor wholly objective, neither wholly dependent on my mind nor wholly independent of my mind. It is always subjective-objective, inseparable from the creative, participative, engaged activity of my mind but never reducible to it, always transcending it. This is also, it seems to me, what one of the original constructivists, Goodman, is saying in his account of 'irrealism', which does not hold that everything is irreal 'but sees the world melting into versions and versions making worlds' thus making ontology 'evanescent' (Goodman, 1984).

Truth as the congruent articulation of reality

I have already proposed, in Chapter 1, that it is an unnecessary mistake to abandon concepts of validity and truth just because positivists and established sociopolitical structures have misappropriated and abused them for oppressive purposes. This is to sell the pass to the enemy who blocks it and controls it. Such concepts are too central to the integrity of everyday human life and discourse to be abandoned by the research community in the cause of postmodernism and poststructuralism. They are categorial notions that have no necessary connection with objectivism and politics. Rather, they are necessarily presupposed by any field of intelligible discourse, and cannot be reduced to terms within one particular field without undermining the use and relevance of dialogue within that field.

'Valid' is a perfectly healthy word, and in a generic, overall sense applied to the expression of any form of knowing simply means sound, well-grounded, well-founded. 'True' is a closely related, and also healthy, word as long as it is stripped of any necessary association with objective fact. What is important about it, once the notion of independent fact is taken out of it, is that it implies some validating relationship with reality, other than the mistaken notion of correspondence.

I will use it here in a generic sense to mean 'articulating reality'. By 'articulating' I mean a combination of both revealing and shaping, of finding meaning in and giving meaning to. The force of the term 'reality' is to affirm that, however much we give meaning to our experience, there is something given to give meaning to.

Also I propose that 'true' is applied not just to propositions but to the forms of expression of the other cognitive modes. So we can speak of true encounters, true presentational portrayals, true actions, as well as true statements. Valid knowledge, whether experiential, presentational, propositional or practical, is knowledge whose form of expression is true, in the sense that it articulates reality. We can't call these four modes forms of *knowing*, without at the same time acknowledging their relationship with *truth*.

Furthermore, this use of 'true' in relation to four forms of knowing is in accord with usage in ordinary speech. So we say of an interpersonal encounter (experiential knowing) that there was a true meeting of minds; of a piece of music (presentational knowing) that it is true to heartfelt experience; and of a person's action (practical knowing) that it is true to his or her principles.

My ontological thesis is that reality is subjective-objective, that is, always dependent on personal mind and never exclusively dependent on personal mind because of the presence of the cosmically given in which the mind participates even as it shapes it. Thus a claim to knowledge is valid, and the expression of it is true, if it articulates a subjective-objective reality. And what makes a subjective-objective reality a reality, I suggest, is a congruence between the four ways of knowing, the four forms of knower–known: the experiential knowing of what is present, the presentational knowing of imaginal patterns, the propositional knowing of conceptual constructs, and the practical knowing of skills and competencies.

Furthermore, what establishes such congruence between the four ways of knowing is the process of dialogic inquiry with other people similarly engaged, by means of cycles of inquiry in which the four ways are brought successively and repeatedly to bear upon each other. So people together convert a tentative, loose-fitting and ill-grounded set of fourfold beliefs (see Chapter 3) into a congruent, well-grounded set of fourfold knowings. It is intersubjective concert among the inquirers – with a suitable mix of heterogeneity and homogeneity since their reality is *subjective*-objective – about the emerging fourfold congruence that establishes the validity of their claim to have articulated a subjective-objective reality.

Thus the ontology, epistemology and methodology of the matter are, as always, closely interwoven, interdependent and interdefined. Reality is a subjective-objective business of four modes of knowing. Claims to know this reality, that is, articulate it, are validated by a co-operative method of interweaving the four modes to establish their congruence.

The primacy of the practical

I wish to review here how practice is set within the context of a fourfold epistemology. For experiential knowing, reality is a presence or presences with which we empathically attune and whose forms we enact and shape through unrestricted perceiving (Varela et al., 1993). It is lived experience of the mutual co-determination of person and world. For presentational knowing, reality is significant form and pattern, in perceptual and other imaging, that interconnects analogically and metaphorically in a whole network of other significant forms and patterns. For propositional knowing, reality is the combined sense and reference of concepts. For practical knowing, reality is excellent practice and its effects. Each of these is a component of a subjective-objective reality.

There are two important features of this fourfold epistemology. Firstly, there is a pyramid of support or grounding. Experience of a presence is the ground of having presentational knowledge of its significant patterns of imagery. Both these together are the ground of propositions about it. And all these together are the ground of taking effective action in relation to it. Experiential knowledge as felt resonance and unrestricted perceiving is the ground of fourfold knowing, intentional action is the consummation of it, with presentational and propositional knowing mediating between them. Each kind of knowing both emerges from its ground and has its own relatively autonomous form.

Because of this relatively autonomous form, each of these forms of knowing can function in a limited way without the other three, *except* for practical knowing. There is a fundamental asymmetry in the epistemological pyramid. Thus I can feel a presence immediately behind me with little or no presentational, that is, perceptual, data about it, with no propositional data, and without taking any action in relation to it. I can apprehend presentational data, as with audio-visual images, in the absence of the people or things being filmed, without propositional information about them, and without acting in relation to them. And I can understand statements about something, without meeting it, without any presentational data about it, and again without acting in relation to it. However, I cannot take *intentional action* in direct relation to something without having some conceptual information about it, without having some presentational data, and without meeting it.

Macmurray (1957), to whom I have referred in Chapters 1 and 6, had a limited account of this asymmetry in his view that you can divorce pure thought from action, but you cannot divorce effective action from thought. He went on to argue that while thinking is consummated in and through action, you cannot consummate action in and through pure thought.

Intentional action, at the apex of the supportive pyramid of fourfold knowing, consummates it and brings it to an integrated focal point. Undertaken by a group of co-inquirers, it becomes a concerted and congruent set of behaviours that is honed through cyclic integration of all four modes, and includes that integration as a necessary condition of its continuing practice. It cannot exercise its form of knowing in separation from the other three cognitive modes. It is necessarily active together with them. But while it is grounded in them, includes them, and completes them, it also transcends them with its own autonomous articulation of a subjective-objective reality as manifesting the value of human flourishing. This affirms, in a special way, the primacy of the practical.

Practice as consummation

'Practice as consummation' is a way of saying two things. Firstly, practice as the outcome of an inquiry *fulfils* all the other modes which support it in the pyramid of knowledge. It fulfils them because it involves them all, integrates them, gives them human point and purpose, imbuing them with intentionality, and completes them by manifesting them. Secondly, it *celebrates* them by showing that the subjective-objective reality which they articulate manifests excellence. This celebration is not a proof of them. It shows them forth in and through the values of human flourishing. It is a declaration by concerted doing that goes beyond justification.

What is important here is the word 'concerted': people acting together and interacting through intersubjective consensus. This is agreement in deed, in active use and application of beliefs. Reality is necessarily that which is public and shared, it depends on a consensual account of its status and credentials. That it is *reality* is a consensus to do with the grounding of the forms of knowing in each other. That it is *intrinsically valuable* as a domain of human flourishing is a consensus to do with the consummation of all the forms in excellent doing. The grounding is epistemological, the consummation is axiological.

Grounding and consummation

On the one hand concerted practice consummates the multiple knowings that articulate a subjective-objective reality. On the other hand the practice is validated by its grounding in the other modes of knowing. We have here interdependent, bipolar aspects of their congruence. This is illustrated in the pyramid model of Figure 9.1. This and the next two figures were first introduced in the overview of Chapter 3 as Figures 3.6, 3.7 and 3.3 respectively.

What is below grounds and validates what is above, and what is above consummates, celebrates and shows forth what is below. At one pole it is the congruence between the four modes of knowing as their *grounding* in each other, and ultimately in experiential knowing, unrestricted and integral lived experience, that makes their forms of expression valid. This establishes that they articulate a subjective-objective reality. At the other pole it is their congruence as being *consummated* in and through concerted and excellent practice, the apex of the pyramid, that fulfils them and shows them forth. This crowns their world with the value of human flourishing.

So grounding validation and consummating celebration are interdependent and mutually supporting. But the bipolarity is asymmetrical in terms of the kind of value and the main intensity of the flow. Practice provides the point, purpose and fulfilment of all the groundedness. It goes beyond the truth-values of validation, which are the concern of grounding, to the being-values of manifestation, which are the delight of consummation. Practice as consummation lifts knowing above justification into the dynamic affirmation of persons in relation. Bipolar congruence includes validity and transcends it. Bipolar congruence can also be shown as a dialectical process in which each aspect flows into the other, as in Figure 9.2.

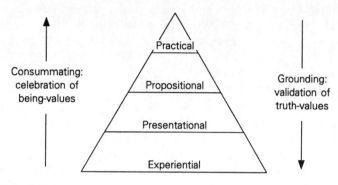

Figure 9.1 *Bipolar congruence*

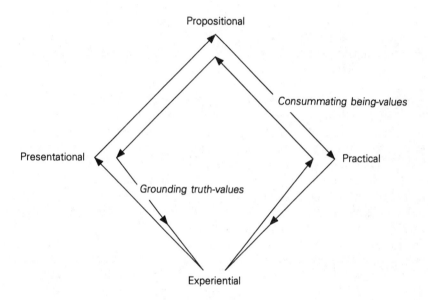

Figure 9.2 *Bipolar congruence as dialectical process*

All forms of knowing are for action. They are:

called upon to make a difference to what is going on in our lives. The grounding mode of feeling is not only a static delight in all kinds of beings through compresence with them, it is also dynamic delight in enhancing their uniqueness. This dynamism of delight moves upward through the hierarchy of knowledge to find its final expression in action, in competence to improve the lot of everything. (Heron, 1992: 173)

The underlying theme in all this is that any research method that is exclusively preoccupied with validity issues is insecure about the values of being. As Goethe observed, being too busy with justification misses the point of life, which is about exuberance. Valid outcomes alone are not enough. They need to be self-transcending and metamorphose into exuberant outcomes. Beyond epistemological validity is the joy of human life.

More on the congruence theory of truth

This all makes for an extended and an integrated theory of truth as the congruent articulation of reality. It is extended because it takes the notion of truth beyond its traditional restriction to propositional knowing and applies it to experiential, presentational and practical knowing also. It is integrated because it is concerned with the congruence of its extended forms, and because it complements congruence as groundedness, with congruence as consummation, the celebration of worthwhile practice.

The theory also affirms that truth, being in subjective-objective form, is thereby relative-universal. It is relative to the subjective and intersubjective multiple perspectives of any given inquiry group set in its linguistic and cultural context. But since these are perspectives on what is cosmically given, what there is, their relativity bears on what is universal. When multiple knowings have been tested for their congruence, they can lay their claim to truth, that is, as having a relation to that which is universal. This is a relation, however, which is necessarily that of subjective and intersubjective construing. Reality is always articulated by human sensibility, always subjective-objective, so truth is always relative and context-bound, but it is still, if sought with appropriate rigour, truth.

Thus to define truth as the congruent articulation of a subjective-objective reality, does not mean that the element of truth lies only in the objective component of the articulation. The objective component is always subjectivized and intersubjectivized: this is in the nature of all forms of knowing. Personal and shared perspectives on what there is: it is the whole of this that gives truth its form. Thus there can be personal, idiosyncratic truth, as well as shared, intersubjective truth; and both are always framed within the context of a particular language and culture (cf. Skolimowski, 1994). This makes truth a variable, changing, unfolding, artefact of creative minds in ever-shifting social contexts, participating in, and shaping, given being.

Beyond pragmatism

Traditional and current discussions of the validity of knowledge claims are all about propositional knowledge. The assumption throughout the literature of qualitative research is that the outcomes of the research will be a set of propositions. The radical constructivism of von Glasersfeld (1991) is still only a re-instatement of the pragmatic view of truth applied to theoretical statements. He follows Dewey's instrumental account of

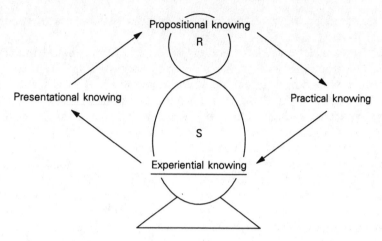

Figure 9.3 *The circuit of fourfold knowing*

pragmatism: propositional knowledge is valid if it is instrumental in attaining one's goals, in achieving effective action.

In an informative inquiry, where propositional outcomes are primary, I reject pragmatism as a theory of truth. I don't believe, with the pragmatists, that the propositions are true because they work. I think they are true, in the sense already defined, because they are grounded in experiential, presentational or other propositional knowing. A proposition, in my view, is not true because it works, rather it works because it is true; its working does not *establish* its truth, it *consummates* it. Action, as practical skill and competence, gives thought moral manifestation, but does not validate it.

What validates thought, as well as internal logical criteria, is its ground in experiential knowing, in the lived-through world of primary meaning, the continuous substrate which language transforms into concepts. This knowing may arise in the context of action, but is not itself action. This is evident in the circuit of knowing, shown in Figure 9.3, where practical knowledge, exercising a skill, leads over into new experiential encounter, and it is this which grounds new propositional knowledge. A careful reading of Macmurray (1957) shows that he held this view, except that he tended to conflate action with experiential knowing. Still, I find Macmurray a better progenitor than Dewey and epistemological pragmatism.

Autonomous forms of validity

Truth is not only about the congruence of the four forms of knowing, their grounding in each other. There is an aspect of truth which is to do with the relative autonomy of each form of knowing, the fact that while it is grounded in and emerges from the prior form, it transcends it with its own independent identity. This means that each form of knowing cannot be fully validated by its grounding in prior forms. It has criteria of validity internal to itself.

Practice cannot be validated entirely by criteria formulated at the conceptual, propositional level. It has a criterion internal to the exercise of a skill, which is the knack of knowing how to perform it. This is a knowing of the excellence of the doing that is within the doing. A knack is a self-validating account of an action at the heart of the knowing how that constitutes it. I elaborated this idea in Chapter 6.

In the same way, propositional knowledge is not all validated by the presentational and experiential knowledge on which it is grounded. Criteria internal to conceptual knowledge include: principles of grammar and linguistic intelligibility; principles of the logically self-evident and of necessary connections between ideas, as applied in logic and mathematics; transcendental or presuppositional arguments for basic principles to do with value and ethics; contextual criteria for clarifying the relationship between this set of propositions and what others state in the same field of inquiry. And so on.

Criteria internal to presentational, imaginal knowing are analogical and metaphorical in nature. While the validating criterion residing within experiential knowing is the immediate declaration of beings and being as such, of the presence of what is there. This self-validation of experiential knowing, that we participate, through shaping and being shaped, in inter-penetrating worlds of declarative presences, is the foundation for the other forms of knowing, and of validity as groundedness.

The validation of practice

Firstly, as I have just said, practice has a self-validating criterion internal to it, which is the knack of knowing how to perform it.

Secondly, on the congruence theory, practical outcomes are also validated by being grounded in prior modes in the pyramid of modes of knowing. What this most immediately means is being grounded in conceptual, propositional knowing. So how do we validate practice by the use of propositions? By using a range of criteria, articulated and validated at the conceptual level, that are special and peculiar to the domain of action; and of these there seem to be at least five kinds. We are here in the domain of practical or normative thinking, reflecting on principles and standards of practice.

Executive criteria

- Can the practitioners execute the practice? Can they actually do what they say they can do, over a significant time span, under all relevant conditions and with an appropriate economy of means?
- Can they do it elegantly, with style and with grace?

Technical criteria

- Does the practice have the effects claimed for it? Do the practitioners demonstrate their own technical imperative that if they do this practice, such and such will be the outcome?
- Is this form of practice the most effective? Is there a more effective way to achieve the same outcome?

Psychosocial criteria

- Is the practice – both the way it is done and its outcomes – relatively free of emotional pathology? In other words, is it free from distortion by unawarely displaced personal distress? Is it psychologically sound?
- Is the practice relatively free of organizational pathology? Is it free from distortion by the restrictive and rigid norms and values of the social structure within which it is exercised? Is it organizationally sound?

Intentionality criteria

- Is the practice intentional, not merely *ad hoc* or reactive? Does it proceed from the inquirers' considered purpose or vision, rather than from adaptive survival in response to the turn of events?
- Do the inquirers give evidence of creatively sustaining congruence among the components of their practice – its motives, its guiding purpose and values, its strategy and norms, its actual behaviour, its context and its effects?

Value criteria

- Does the practice contribute to personal and social transformation according to the inquirers' view of an intrinsically worthwhile way of life for human beings?
- Does the practice support the inquirers' view of basic human rights?

It is highly doubtful whether any transformative inquiry will want to evaluate its practical outcomes in terms of all these criteria. For any given practice some will be more relevant than others. The value, or axiological, criteria, or some version of them, are indispensable for any transformative inquiry. Whatever criteria are selected can be applied by procedures of self and peer assessment (Heron, 1988a).

It follows from the theory I am using that applying these criteria establishes the truth-value of the action, where action is conceived as a way of articulating reality. If I know how to help someone, this is a way of giving meaning to and finding meaning in what there is, a way of articulating reality. This knowing how is either valid to some degree or it is not. In other words, either I really know how to help someone or I don't. To establish which is the case, I need to apply relevant criteria. I think this is perfectly in accord with ordinary usage, where we ask whether a person's action is true to his or her principles. In other words, is the action grounded in what for that person are relevant criteria?

There is a fundamental complementarity of view at work here. When actions are looked at from the point of view of their grounding, we are concerned with their truth-value. When they are regarded as consummation, we are concerned with their being-value, that is to say their affirmation of that which is intrinsically worthwhile as a state of being. The being-value is grounded on the truth-value, the truth-value is consummated by the being-value. And this interdependence is asymmetrical in the flow of value. The being-value transcends in value the truth-value.

The question then arises, is an action right or wrong. In the axiological ethics which I am propounding, the rightness or wrongness of an action follows from the value or disvalue it manifests. The basic question is what states of affairs are intrinsically worthwhile, and so worth realizing. In my view, these are states of being in which humans flourish in an integration of autonomy, co-operation and an appropriate degree of hierarchy, inter-dependent with the flourishing of the planetary ecosystem. If an action manifests such states, then it has intrinsic value, and is therefore a right action.

The validation of propositions

The view of validity so far applies only to transformative inquiries, where the focus is on practice. Throughout this book I have taken the view that going for practical outcomes and going for propositional outcomes are complementary approaches. While the deeper way, the route of primacy, is to choose practical outcomes supported by propositional ones, there are also occasions when there is a case for pursuing propositional outcomes without practical ones, in what I call informative inquiries.

This account of validity in informative inquiries where the primary outcome is a set of propositions, will also be included within a transforma-tive inquiry to deal with any secondary informative propositions it generates alongside the primary practical outcomes.

Propositional findings are valid if they meet relevant criteria at their own autonomous level: these are linguistic criteria to do with grammatical usage and intelligibility, logical criteria to do with internal coherence of meaning, and contextual criteria to do with relations between the findings and relevant propositions made by others within the same field of inquiry. And they are valid if they are *grounded* in relevant presentational and experi-ential knowing. But they await *consummation* in a future transformative inquiry that is elaborated from them.

Hence there is an important sense in which any claim to completion made for the findings of an informative inquiry is unwarranted. They become complete when these propositional outcomes are taken into a further inquiry to fulfil them and celebrate them in practice, and transcend their truth-value in being-values of human flourishing.

Participative knowing

What does it mean to say that propositions are valid if grounded in experiential knowledge? It means that statements are coherent with its participative knowing. In *Feeling and Personhood* (Heron, 1992), I describe experiential knowing as basically mediated by feeling, which I distinguish from emotion and construe as 'the capacity of the psyche . . . to indwell what is present through attunement and resonance'. Through feeling I participate in the distinct presence of a being and its immaterial qualities. This is empathic communion: a harmonic resonance with the inner life of the other, with its mode of awareness, its experience of its world, its way of regarding and being affected by what is going on in its environment. Experiential knowing also involves the imaginal mind: the enactment, the shaping of the world through unrestricted perceptual imaging, sensory and extrasensory. This also is participative. The imaging process of perception is inseparable from both perceiver and perceived.

Experiential knowing, then, combines participative empathy and participative imaging. Through resonance and attunement, I feel, participate in, the presence of a being and its mode of awareness. At the same time I interpenetrate the patterning of its manifest form by perceptually imaging it in an unrestricted way. I feel the unique presence we call a tree, its dignity and receptive communion with its world, while shaping its perceptual form on sensory and subtle levels. This participation is only partial, since both I and the being I call a tree transcend the immediate participative process, and since for my part the depth of the process is a function of my intentionality, of how much I choose to engage awarely with it.

Both forms of participation are subjective-objective, a personal articulation of reality. I feel the presence and inner being of something only through its compresence, its presence in and with my presence. It declares its presence not as it is in itself but as it is in a unitive communion with me. Similarly, I perceive something in an unrestricted way only in terms of my enactment of it: that is, from my standpoint, through my modes of imaging and my range of sensibilities, and with my articulation of significance.

A proposition about the world is well-grounded in experiential knowing when it integrates both empathic communion with the interior presence of what is there, and intuition of significant pattern in its perceptual appearing. We open ourselves to feeling compresent, to a deepening degree of communion and participative attunement. Thereby we let what is there declare its inner being more fully. We use our imagination to retrace, recreate our unrestricted perceptual imaging from within. And so we learn more about the archetypal templates, the homological principles our imaginal mind is pouring into the perceptual process. I referred in Chapter

5 to the analogy here with the Goethean appproach to scientific method (Bortoft, 1986).

Skolimowski has a related view when he itemizes some of the main characteristics of what he calls participatory research:

> The participatory research is the art of *empathy* –
> is the art of *communion* with the object of inquiry –
> is the art of learning to use *its* language –
> is the art of *using* its language –
> is the art of *talking* to the object of our inquiry . . . –
> is the art of penetrating from *within* –
> is the art of *indwelling* in the other –
> is the art of *imaginative hypothesis* which leads to the art of identification –
> is the art of *transformation of one's consciousness* so that it becomes part of the consciousness of the other . . .
>
> Most of these attributes of the participatory research are not alien to us. We know them from our own personal experience – from the experience of loving and being loved . . . from deep experience of great works of art, whereby through empathy and communion we are indwelling in the world the artist has created for us . . .
>
> Empathy is a form of positive identification, a positive participation. To empathize is to become one with another, to beat the same rhythm with another, to understand through compassion and *from within*. (Skolimowski, 1994: 160–3, author's italics)

The question still remains about what it means to say a proposition is coherent with this sort of participative knowing. It certainly does not mean correspond in the literal sense of qualitative or structural likeness. It means symbolize in the sense of a dynamic relation between the proposition and the experience it symbolizes. In terms of Peirce's theory of signs, it is not an icon but an index. The proposition evokes the experience, calls it forth, or, to change the metaphor, refracts it, uncovers and reveals it. It recreates the participative knowing on which it is grounded, by echoing it. It symbolizes the experience by participative resonance. The art of poetry thus becomes relevant to framing it.

What is involved is the fundamental act of transforming into concepts the empathic-imaginal, primary meaning that is both prelinguistic and currently extralinguistic. This is the deep tacit nonlinguistic meaning of the world of integral and unrestricted lived experience, in which we intersubjectively participate because it is a necessary condition of agreeing how to use a language, and of which our use of language is always giving a conceptual transformation.

Agreements about findings

Co-operative inquiry method, based on the assumption of a subjective-objective reality, means that each individual co-researcher will construe or act within the agreed area of inquiry, using agreed procedures, in their own idiosyncratic way, from their own standpoint. Hence the agreement sought and reached about the findings – whether presentational, propositional or practical – by the co-researchers is not an agreement of identical representations or practices. It is one of varied perspectives or behaviours, which illumine a common area of inquiry. It is about how the different experiences do and do not overlap, and about how this mix of diversity and unity articulates more or less fully the inquirers' subjective-objective reality. Their corporate truth about this reality is enriched both by significant differences and significant identities in their personal versions.

As I said in Chapter 5, a total overlap of versions is suspect, suggesting collusion or conformity and lack of full individual involvement in the inquiry process. No overlap of any sort is unlikely, but would indicate disintegration of that process. For a given group of people, a given inquiry focus, a given degree of divergence or convergence, a given stage in the inquiry, there is likely to be some fitting, well-rounded balance of overlap and range of difference that yields a rich illuminating articulation of their reality.

If the agreement is about both the diversity and the unity of the findings, then the articulation of reality is not necessarily clear and unambiguous. For there are two kinds of diversity. There are differences that are compatible, like different photographic views of the same thing, or like variations of the same action that have the same effect. And there are incompatible differences, like contradictory evaluations of what is the most relevant or revealing view, or like variations of the same action that have quite different effects. In any co-operative inquiry some element of incompatibility and hence of ambiguity must be allowed; and what is allowable is a matter of judgement and collective decision. For a piece of participative research generating acceptable ambiguity of agreement see Brown and Kaplan (1981).

Reality-making social contracts

Reality is public, shared, we are all in it. To say something is a reality is to say it is not, in principle, *just* subjective. I may be the only person to have articulated it, but when in articulating it, I declare to myself it is a reality, then I am asserting it is potentially sharable. Strictly speaking, I only *believe* it is a reality. I do not *know* this until there is some well-established intersubjective agreement about it. A reality that is public is one about which we significantly agree. There is enough overlap in our individual views for us to talk in common parlance and to act in effective concert.

Intersubjective agreement, then, is the vital part of a subjective-objective reality, which ought properly to be called a subjective-intersubjective-objective reality. This honours both the idiosyncratic personal perspective and the intersubjective consensus. Our view of reality, then, depends on the forms of our agreement. Reality is the product of a social contract, a contract about how we choose to articulate it.

The first basic form of reality-articulating social contract is nonlinguistic. It is two human beings simultaneously meeting each other through sustained mutual gazing and mutual touching. Two people are looking into each other's eyes and holding hands. It is only through gazing and, in a different modality through touching, that two people meet in the fully reciprocal sense. Simultaneously in the same kind of act each one gives and receives and the other receives and gives. And there are other, subtler modes of empathic communion also involved. This relation of meeting is a social contract that articulates an interpersonal reality, whereby each one participates in each other's presence without loss of personal distinctness. This first reality-articulating social contract is in the mode of experiential knowing.

The second basic form is also nonlinguistic: it is people signalling expressively to each other in terms of significant dynamic patterns. Their signals agree in articulating a shared world of such patterns. This can also apply between a human and some animals: I run, my dog runs, I throw, my dog leaps, and so on. The second reality-articulating social contract is in the mode of presentational knowing.

The third basic form of reality-articulating social contract is a language. Somehow, on the basis of the first two nonlinguistic contracts, we agree about the rules of its syntax, the sense and reference of its terms. This agreement in itself articulates a reality in tacit propositional form. Just to learn a language is to be initiated into an intersubjective articulation of reality. Language-use shapes an implicit propositional world. This third and conceptual reality-articulating social contract is in the domain of propositional knowing.

The fourth basic form of reality-articulating social contract, interwoven with the use of language, is the set of tacit values, beliefs and norms that constitute a culture. Culture is a highly relative term, and different kinds of culture nest within each other with varying degrees and sorts of accommodation. There is the culture or civilization of a whole epoch, the culture or civilization of a more limited age and place within an epoch, the culture of a given society – from a neighbourhood to a group of nation states – and a whole variety of subcultures within a society. The socialization of a child is its acculturation, its initiation into the shared values, beliefs and norms of a particular set of nested cultures. Being socialized and acculturated is basically knowing how to behave in a given social context. The fourth reality-articulating social contract is in the mode of practical knowing.

Within modern, postindustrial civilization, a very important class of subcultures are research subcultures, which for convenience I will simply call research cultures. Each research culture has a social contract, or a research contract, about methodology. This is an agreement among the researchers in the mode of practical knowing. The contract is about how to behave, about how to do research, about what method will properly articulate reality. This means, of course, that they have already articulated a broad, metaphysical view of reality and of how you get knowledge of it, in order to agree as to what constitutes a 'proper' method. Every sort of research necessarily assumes an ontology and an epistemology in order to agree on a methodology.

These paradigm assumptions are rooted in considerations quite other than those formally concerned with rational inquiry. This is because they are preconditions of rational inquiry. To some extent the rational limitations of a paradigm, which become evident when it is overworked, prompt a paradigm shift. And to some extent these limitations will suggest the sort of paradigmatic changes that will transcend them. But no one paradigm can be the sufficient rational cause of another, since by definition they are transrational constructions which provide the framework for rational method. There is a morphological leap motivated by wider and deeper concerns of the soul to do with the whole potentiality of the person.

These concerns are about wholeness of being, fulfilled by a dialectical interplay between complementary, even contradictory, ways of being in a world. So there arises a need strongly to counter a current paradigm because its sustained, widespread use is felt to have become oppressive to the person as a whole. The need may be so strong that it generates a new paradigm with irrational and contradictory features, which the originators of it cannot afford to notice – just because of the strength of their need.

What is more important than its internal consistency is that the new paradigm is radically different from the old, yielding new and counter-balancing kinds of satisfaction. The Cartesian paradigm for Newtonian science assumes an incomprehensible relation between the entirely different realities of mind and body. The positivist paradigm for more recent science assumes an indefensible concept of objective fact. Both were needed to restore the human spirit: the first after too much medieval theocratic rationalism; the second after the enervating effect of nineteenth century idealism and its dissociated account of the coherence theory of truth.

The point about reframing, aperspectival mind – the inquiry skill described in Chapter 7 – is that it is inclusive of its own paradigm assumptions, open to the shifts that underlie them, the shifts that are to come. It is open to the paradigm of paradigms, knowing that any account of that also has a shift underlying it and a shift yet to come.

The participative paradigm invoked in this book is the result of a soul reaction of two kinds. The first is dissatisfaction with the alienated encounter with a separated reality, produced by the positivist paradigm. The second is dissatisfaction with the ambiguity about meeting any reality, produced by the constructivist paradigm. The participative paradigm finds reality, and the soul its satisfaction, in the relation of meeting the given. The meeting tells us it is given, the relation tells us we articulate it through participation. What is the shift to come?

10

A Postconceptual Worldview

The purpose of this chapter is to articulate more fully the radical kind of empiricism on which my account of co-operative inquiry is based. By 'empiricism' I mean an openness to integral lived experience which does not prejudge in a limiting way its content. This lived experience is inclusive, and is not predefined as restricted to the senses or to ideas or to any other kind of one-sided account of reality.

In order to elaborate this view, I wish, first, to restate the distinction, introduced in Chapters 5 and 7, between primary, or empathic-imaginal, meaning and secondary, or linguistic-conceptual, meaning, and to extend the account of these; second, to use this distinction to articulate three different, basic worldviews, the preconceptual, the conceptual and the postconceptual; and third, to give my account of some aspects of a postconceptual worldview.

Primary and secondary meaning

Primary meaning is the meaning inherent in our lived experience, our being in a world, that is both prior to the use of language and continuously underneath and within our use of language. Human sensibilities participate in, and thus articulate and shape, the presented cosmos. In so doing they give and find meaning in the very process of generating our being in a world. I have suggested that this lived experience has the interdependent poles of empathic communion, harmonic resonance with the inner mode of awareness of other beings; and of radical perceiving, the shaping and enactment of being in a world through the process of imaging it, where this imaging includes and is not restricted to sensory imaging. Hence I also call primary meaning empathic-imaginal or simply imaginal meaning. It is the meaning of the 'lived-through world', which Merleau-Ponty insists is misrepresented and distorted by the 'objective thought' of positivist science and 'dogmatic common sense' (Merleau-Ponty, 1962; Hammond et al., 1991).

This primary meaning is thus resident in our transactions with the given cosmos in terms of felt presences and imaged patterns. It has at least seven major properties:

- Because of our basic empathic communion with each other, the lived world of primary meaning is intersubjective, shared. At some deep level we know we have the same sort of experience within the same sort of world, a shared kind of subjective-objective engagement with the given.

- The meaning is tacit, indwelling the exercise of our sensibilities as they participate in and shape the cosmos. This is analogous to the way in which the meaning of a dream is tacit, indwelling the generative process of the dreaming mind.
- It is also unlimited. A fundamental feature of primary meaning is figure–ground hierarchy. When we participate in a manifest pattern, we know experientially its focal figure in relation to its immediate ground. This also means that at some deep subliminal level we are acquainted and engaged with the whole hierarchy of grounds or contexts in which the focal figure is embedded; and deeper still with the ground of this endless hierarchy of grounds. The primary meaning of this particular lived experience here and now entails a deep tacit grasp of a universal and oceanic meaning. This is an inchoate sense, not only of the ground of the ground of the experience and so on, but also of the ground of this expansive sequence itself.
- The lived experience of primary meaning is teleological, purposive. It is moved to realize an ever-progressive end-state of explicit or secondary meaning, in which primary meaning is raised into conscious relief by symbolic rendering in a set of basic expressive forms. The experiential realm of primary meaning is the generative ground of art, language, culture and intentional action. The human project is that of transforming, through all these expressive modes, primary into secondary meaning. This, to mention but a few instances, is evident in the urge of the painter or sculptor to articulate significant forms of sensory experience; of the poet to reveal the metaphorical resonance between widely divergent forms of experience; of the creative thinker to convey in language the pregnant meaning of preconceptual imagery deep in the imaginal mind; of the waking dreamer to formulate in explicit thought the surge of primary meaning in a dream; of the natural scientist to distil into coherent reports the deep meaning inherent in our perceptual generation of our sensory world; of any two or more people to articulate and share through dialogue this or that or the other aspect of their lived experience; of the mystic to sing the praises of the eternal ground of the endless hierarchy of figures that are grounds to other figures and have grounds that are figures to other grounds.
- The lived experience of primary meaning is ontologically inclusive of the sensory and the nonsensory, the physical and the transphysical, the real and the imaginal, the subject and the object, the personal and the transpersonal, internal awareness and external form, individual and collective, the hierarchy of contexts and the ground of the hierarchy. All these bifurcations and complementarities of being are in the domain of secondary meaning. To take any one pole and impose it exclusively on the domain of primary meaning, is to engage in improper rationalism at the expense of a radical openness to integral experience.
- As soon as primary meaning is symbolized by human constructs it ceases to be primary meaning and becomes secondary meaning, which

is always relative to the linguistic and cultural context within which it is formulated. No final account of primary meaning can be transformed into secondary meaning, which is always context-specific and context-bound. So any secondary account of primary meaning presupposes a primary context not as yet identified in that secondary account.

• Primary meaning itself is not absolute, fixed and final. It is a construct that articulates reality in subjective-objective form. It is how at some deep level we choose to shape reality through our manifold sensibilities. It may be variable, changing, and perhaps unfolding. It has its own kind of contextuality to do with the range and nature of our sensibilities and of their setting. Skolimowski, using the term 'sensitivities', characterizes this range as Mind II which is much more extensive than the discursive and co-ordinating Mind I. Mind II is:

> the sum total of all the sensitivities that evolution has developed in us. By sensitivities we mean all the capacities through which we live our lives, thus sensing, seeing, intuition, instinct; the capacity to make love, to make poetry, to dance, to sing, to contemplate stars; as well as the capacity for moral judgment, the aesthetic sense, the sense of empathy, the whole orchestra of different powers through which life is expressed, apprehended, and sculpted into recognizable shapes.
> Life always takes distinctive shapes and forms. These forms are moulded not by the cold intellect but by the variety of sensitivities – which are the sculptors, the transformers, the transmogrifiers of reality; the incredibly accurate registers of the changing seasons of nature and of the changing moods of human beings, of grief and sadness, of joy and ecstasy; the silent witnesses which can hear the stars singing as well as the cries of human hearts. Sensitivities are the artists which receive and transform, which nourish us aesthetically and inform us intellectually; they are the countless windows through which we commune with reality. (Skolimowski, 1994: 9)

Secondary meaning is conveyed in at least four major symbolic forms:

• The nonverbal arts.
• The uses of language.
• The social practices and structures within a culture.
• Individual intentional actions.

The last of these emerges from and is supported by the three prior forms. It also consummates them and has the potential to transform them and move them on to new levels of articulating primary meaning. A transformative co-operative inquiry which has individual practical outcomes within a culture of competence, supported by both presentational and propositional outcomes, exhibits all these four forms of secondary meaning.

Linguistic forms of secondary meaning

Linguistic forms of secondary meaning involve the ascription of class-names and general terms to the content of our lived experience. They are grounded on shared, intersubjective experience of primary meaning.

Language is public; and its use for public discourse depends on a prior tacit agreement among people about the rules of how to use it, rules about the sense and reference of words and about the structure of intelligible sentences. This agreement cannot itself be mediated by language, since it is the use of language about which agreement is being sought.

It can only be mediated, for the first language-users, by nonlinguistic expressive signs, the meaning of which is grasped intersubjectively by direct harmonic resonance of lived experience, immediate empathic communion, between the signmakers, at the level of tacit and oceanic primary meaning. Thereafter, all linguistic discourse continuously presupposes this substrate of tacit, participative, shared pre-understanding, even when language is being used for mutual abuse and recrimination. There is a view that the organism is programmed with linguistic universals. But the very first language users still have to agree about how they are to convert these innate universals into the expressive forms of a particular local language. So the issue of agreement in use still remains.

Linguistic meaning is a partial and incomplete transformation into secondary, conceptual terms of the primary meaning inherent in our imaginal and empathic participation in our world. And we remember that when any conceptual account of imaginal intuition and empathic communion is stated, that account is inescapably relative to its linguistic and cultural context. Its validity can always be called in question when a relevant wider context of primary meaning is invoked.

Conceptual systems do a disservice when they separate subject and object, objectify perceptual images in terms of restrictive definitions, categorize lived experience in limiting reductionist terms, then repress the depth of primary meaning and erect an alienated model of a world on this repression. They are cut off from their radical, nourishing, grounding source. They do a service when they seek in their own terms to reveal, echo and celebrate through symbolic elaboration their unlimited primary ground. Thus the paradox of language is that it can create conceptual frameworks which either obscure primary meaning, or reveal it and deepen our appreciation of it.

Preconceptual, conceptual and postconceptual worlds

The use of language lifts us out of the immediate identification with lived experience that characterizes small children before they can speak, and animals. This primitive identification is without any capacity for reflective openness to primary meaning or any wide-ranging, creative intentional response to it. Being in a world at this unawakened level of participation, I will call, for human beings at any rate, being in a *preconceptual world*.

The individual (or the human race) may, after the acquisition of language, be in thrall to the empathic-imaginal world for some time. But eventually the use of language and the reflection which it makes possible, enable us to disidentify from this primitive participation. We can generate conceptual frameworks which both detach us from lived experience and, by symbolizing aspects of it, enable us to relate to it with more intentionality and depth. These frameworks have high cognitive mobility: they can be fitted over primary meaning, taken off, replaced and moved around. They equip us to have a great diversity of beliefs about the world, to develop autonomous systems of ethics (Bookchin, 1991), politics and science; and to distinguish between appearance and reality, between the aesthetic and the epistemic dimensions of what there is.

If we become too identified with our use of conceptual frameworks, we treat the limited world they depict as the total reality. They then obscure the depth and range of primary meaning which they only very partially articulate; and so we feel separate from reality, with subtle alienation and *angst*. Being in a world whose depth of primary meaning is hidden and dimmed by the alienating and restricted use of language, I will call being in a *conceptual world*. The positive side of a conceptual world is its achievement in science of various kinds, in ethical, political and social thought and practice. Its negative side is its reduction of primary to conceptual meaning, that is, its reduction of the territory to the map; and hence its limited account, which is also a denial, of its base in empathic-imaginal reality, and its repression of the deeper and wider potential of integral lived experience.

However, we can deploy concepts with a grounded awareness of the primary meaning of our being in a world. We can use them while remaining open to their nonlinguistic, empathic-imaginal substrate. They can then throw into relief and deepen our appreciation of this tacit ground. It is surely the point and purpose of the conceptual mastery that comes with language that it should be in a mutually enhancing dialectical inter-play with the primary meaning inherent in our generative participation in the cosmos. The paradox of this interplay is that without conceptual ability, the realm of primary meaning remains relatively undisclosed; and with it, that realm can only be refracted in ever-changing secondary, conceptual maps, that are always relative to the linguistic and cultural context within which they have been framed. Hence any secondary map, bound by its cultural context, also has a wider context of primary meaning which it has not yet identified.

Artists of all kinds are the precursors and point the way towards this interplay. They use language, and nonlinguistic forms of expression, to symbolize their vision of the primary meaning of their world. Poetry, imaginative literature, painting, sculpture, music, song and dance, offer us manifold visions of the inherent significance of living and perceiving our realities. These kinds of presentational knowing give the writer, artist, musician and dancer both disengagement from their lived experience so that they can then enter into deeper participation with it, and the inner freedom to wield their forms of expression with revelatory effect. The imagination, liberated from over-identification with participative reality, can illumine its tacit primary meaning through the symbolism of art, perhaps the most direct and dynamic way of evoking our empathic-imaginal experience of our worlds.

When it comes to scientific, conceptual transformations of the primary meaning of lived experience, we have at least three interpenetrating levels:

- There are descriptive, propositional accounts of its immediate nature. Forays into this field have been made, for example, by phenomenology and Gestalt psychology, both of which have sought to pay attention to, and conceptualize, the significant features inherent in experiential wholes. These endeavours are always on a knife-edge: too much empathic-imaginal immersion and they lose conceptual focus; too much conceptual elaboration and they lose experiential reference and relevance.
- There can be further flung theories, which build up conceptual frameworks grounded in primary meaning, with full acknowledgement of it and openness to it, thereby revealing it more fully in terms of the superstructures it can support. The theories may explore a whole range of part–whole, or figure–ground, hierarchies, within one or more domains of lived experience. Various kinds of generalized holistic and systems theory may be precursors, such as Wilber's twenty tenets about the common features of holons (Wilber, 1995: 35–78).
- There are theories which look not only at part–whole, or figure–ground, hierarchies, within lived experience, but consider the ground of lived experience itself. These theories take us into the domain of divine science, the 'sacred science' of which Reason (1993) has written.

Being in a world in which language and concepts are used to reveal, elaborate and celebrate primary meaning, I will call being in a *postconceptual world*. In *Feeling and Personhood* (1992) I also called this a postlinguistic world. A postconceptual worldview is not one in which concepts are abandoned; it is one in which the use of concepts is continuously self-transcending. It seeks to avoid conceptual closure and alienated contraction, while it retains all the benefits of independent ethical, political and scientific thinking in revised forms. It reaches out expansively to reframe itself, subject to the claims of a wider and deeper vision, elaborating conceptual frameworks which remain continually open to the experiential depths of primary meaning and its limitless hierarchy of contexts or grounds. It is a world born by an ever-expanding intentional re-enactment of the origin of language. As the use of language thus progressively regenerates itself, more and more primary meaning is transformed into secondary, conceptual systems.

The postconceptual world is the world of Torbert's reframing mind, Bateson's Learning III, Reason's self-reflective mind, Gebser's integral-aperspectival mind, and of Wilber's vision-logic grounded in the transparent body-mind, all of which I referred to in Chapter 7. It is also the world of those postmodern poststructuralists who do not deny truth and meaning as such, but hold that all truth and meaning are context-bound, and that context is boundless, infinitely extendable (Culler, 1982).

The purpose of this account of preconceptual, conceptual and post-conceptual worlds is to bring out the main different kinds of relation between primary and secondary, conceptual meaning. In so far as it suggests a developmental sequence, individual or cultural, it has obvious analogies with three-phase accounts of the historical development of human consciousness. Reason (1994a), following Barfield (1957) and others, puts forward his 'myth' of these three phases. First there is 'original partici-pation', in which people are embedded in their world, with undifferentiated consciousness, no separation between subject and object and little reflective-ness. A second phase, reaching a peak in Western industrial societies, is that of 'unconscious participation', when the differentiated ego emerges but becomes alienated and controlling because it not only transcends original participation but represses it. The third stage is one of 'future participation' towards which we are now moving and which involves a dialectical interplay between a re-awakened unitive, and an enlightened differentiated, awareness.

Reason gives an interesting and important sketch of the possible nature of future participation. It is his programme for the kinds of knowing that will usher in our understanding of what I call the postconceptual world. He thinks future participation will: be rooted on concrete experience and a reclaiming of the body; be self-aware and self-reflective with a capacity for continuous reframing of experience, for being independent of any one framework, and for being able to peer over the edge of all frameworks; order experience in terms of patterns of connectedness and circuits of information flow; actively use imagination and metaphor to deepen a multi-faceted way of seeing things; use language to revision our experience in terms of the creative interdependence of mind and world; mean an experience of the self as ecological, distinct but not separate, interdependent with its environment and within co-operative community (Reason, 1994a: 33–9).

The classic problem of phenomenology

It seems relevant here to sketch out a personal account of a postconceptual world, to symbolize as secondary meaning some of the main features of empathic-imaginal meaning inherent in my integral lived experience. The sketch is an attempt to state the radical presuppositions of any inquiry. Each inquiry will seek to articulate – through presentational, propositional or practical forms of knowing – how its particular topic is grounded in the primary meaning inherent in being in a world. The sketch is in principle open to, and needs, review by systematic co-operative inquiry. It is a conjecture; and it is always an open question whether such an account is grounded, and how well it is grounded, in the primary meaning it purportedly transforms into concepts.

This is the classic problem for any phenomenologist like Merleau-Ponty (1962) who is being highly predicative about the pre-predicative world. How can you say things in language about the extralinguistic world? Well, you can't and you can. Presence and imaginal forms are irreducible to any conceptual account of them. Presences are presences and images are images. To interpret them in words and concepts, and then suppose that the interpretation is what really matters, is to miss their point. Hillman (1975) and his followers have affirmed this clearly about the image, which speaks in its own terms. Creation is empathic-imaginal through and through from resonating with and perceiving rocks to sensing subtle winds in interior states of consciousness, and is autonomously declarative of its inherent meaning.

But while words about empathic-imaginal experience cannot be a substitute for it, they can be revelatory of it, in the sense that they can take you back to it, point you towards it, invite you to open to it more fully. The conceptual account can encourage you in new ways to listen to how the image, for example, speaks in and through your own imaging process. Ernst Gombrich in the catalogue notes for an exhibition at the National Gallery in London in 1995 wrote about the presence and absence of shadows in European art in a way that was revelatory for viewers and enabled them to go to the paintings and participate in them in a new way.

Furthermore, the secondary meaning of a postconceptual world is in principle open to revision through deconstruction, by openness to the wider contexts always to be found in the realm of integral lived experience and primary meaning.

A sketch of a postconceptual world

What, then, are some of the main features of a postconceptual world? I offer an account in the subsections below, remembering that they transform primary into secondary meaning, which is therefore immediately within the hermeneutic situation (Heidegger, 1962; Gadamer, 1976), subject to the influence of prevailing preconceptions and interpretations which I translate from my cultural background. So the validity of my account is immediately in question. It is all the time a moot point how much the conceptual maps which follow reveal primary meaning by reflecting it and pointing towards it, and how much they obscure it by irrelevant, imported theorizing. There is, of course, no final account; only one that strikes the best available deal between my lived experience of primary meaning on the one hand, its linguistic and cultural context on the other, and my transformation into secondary meaning, which mediates between them. And any such individual account awaits the more stringent perspectives of future co-operative inquiries.

Participation

Our lived world is participative: the perceiver is part of the perceived and vice versa. They participate in each other in and through the imaging process, a process which while it goes on is inseparable from each. The auditory image of bird song is not separate from the listener or the song, which is not separate from the bird. The perceiver is also distinct from any particular imaging process, is not identical with it, is *in* it but *not* it; and so is distinct from the perceived. The perceived too is distinct from any particular imaging process, is not identical with it, is *in* it but *not* it; and so is distinct from the perceiver.

Perceiving is an ever-changing kaleidoscope of the combined inseparability and distinctness of the perceiver and the perceived, each of whom is both immanent in and transcends the process of perceptual imaging. This mutual distinctness in partial union of the perceiver and the perceived is the hallmark of a perceptual world. The relation of participation between perceiver and perceived is always transient, partial, perspectival, incomplete and changing, capable of expansion and development. It articulates a temporary subjective-objective reality.

Perceiving is not just a participation in external form and forming, it is also participation, through harmonic resonance, empathic communion, in the internal mode of awareness of what is being perceived. To perceive anything is to have a feeling for how it is undergoing its experience of being-in-its-world. This participative feeling, too, is transient, partial, affectively perspectival, incomplete and changing, capable of expansion and development.

Communion

When I perceive you perceiving me and vice versa, there is mutual empathy and participative knowing. We engage in interior communion, a togetherness within, while conjointly re-enacting the form of our appearing without. In mutual gazing, I meet you meeting me and vice versa: four processes seamless, interfused and transforming each other, yet identifiable. In this way we dynamically deepen our interior oneness while remaining entirely distinct without separateness. Our enacted forms of appearing become complementary textures within a shared and inward field of consciousness.

Seamlessness

Our perceptual world is seamless, holistic, multi-modal and with a fourfold distinctness of imagery. We image our being in a world visually, aurally, tactually and kinaesthetically: we see, hear, touch, and sense our movements. Taste and smell are enhancements of localized touch, when we touch food with the inside of the mouth, and when we touch air with the inside of the nostrils. Feeling pleasure or pain and related sensations are fulfilments or disturbances of any one or more of these several modalities.

The four primary ways of imaging the given – seeing, hearing, touching, and sensing movement or posture – constitute the enactment of our world. They are a seamless whole in which each is utterly clear and distinct from the others, yet they all interpenetrate and participate in each other through their inseparability from the perceiver and the perceived. This fourfold distinctness and interfusion is part of the magic of our being in a world.

Imagination is reality

Our perceptual world grounds perspectival and serial perceptual imaging in pure imagination. Imagination is an integral base of our reality. Kant, Coleridge and others have long since distinguished between primary imagination which produces reality, and secondary imagination which phantasizes variations on that produced reality.

We image our worlds from our centre in interaction with the cosmic given, which presents itself at and within our boundaries. This imaging is perspectival and radial with a two-way transaction: a view from the centre also shaped by a flux from and within the periphery. In thus imaging pattern and form, we inextricably interweave perceiving and imagining. The imaging of a form is compounded of perceptual imaging and imaginative imaging, and the latter grounds the former. The perspectival forms of visual perceiving are earthed by an imaginative generation of their real shape. The oval perceptual imaging which we call a plate is grounded by circular imaginative imaging of the plate. What makes our being in a world real is a pure imagination of its geometric form as a base for its perceptual perspectives. It is such imagination which provides the shape, size and distance constancies, without which we would not find our world a reality. In this interplay between perceptual perspectives and imagined reality there is a rich arena of primary meaning.

Similarly with the ongoing processes and movements in our world. We hear a series of sounds; with our imagination we construe the tune. We see a series of movements; with our imagination we realize the form of a dance or a dive or of the swoop of a bird. Our own movements become manifest through being grounded in their pre-existent imaging, as if the series of movements pours into the image of their whole sequential temporal form.

Centre and circumference

The perceptual world has a centre of reference and a defining boundary relative to it. I never just perceive a world, I always perceive my being in a world: a bounded field around my centre of reference. The given cosmos participates in, and transcends, the boundary. I participate in, and transcend, the centre of reference.

Every boundary, every finite limit to the seeing and hearing of my perceptual field, declares its latent infinity. Each limit in containing the known declares there is an unknown beyond it. It announces a series of limits that is unlimited, boundless. In one horizon we have tacit acquaint-ance with infinite horizons. The circumscription of our perceiving is fraught with the boundlessness of the given. For imaginal, primary meaning, unlimited knowing and extension beckon at the edge of every perceptual field; and the knowing is not separate from the extension.

Likewise, my finite centre of reference has no ultimate centre, hence people like Hume who said whenever he looked for a self he couldn't find it, and the Buddhists with their doctrine of *anatta*, the belief that there is no permanent centre of personal identity, only changing states of mind. If you attend to the centre of reference for touch, kinaesthetic sense, seeing and hearing, it is a delicious void, there is nothing there. It is an infinitude within. The fourfold modalities of imaging our being in a world coalesce at an apparent locus where they declare that within that there is full emptiness. It is full because it is like a cornucopia out of which our whole four-modal world pours. And it is empty because it is a womb of internal infinitude.

But the world does pour out, in and with the perceiver and perceiving process. Where the infinitude within, the void, first breaks into the manifest it appears as a finite locus, the centre of reference that is the distinct person. The presence-absence of the void within doesn't eliminate the person but gives rise to him or her. The perceiving process emerges out of the perceiver who emerges out of the void. Hume and the Buddhists, in attending too earnestly to the void, overlook the distinctness of the perceiver at the finite locus; whereas those who over-identify with the perceiver will aver there is no void.

We can, as beings who transcend the perceiving process, shift its finite centre of reference more and more towards the infinitude within, though we can never reach it. As we do so, we open our own identity towards its infinite source within. This is the transfiguration of immanence, the empty-ing out of personal identity, its increased porosity through its movement deeper into the void. In a complementary way, at the circumference and within its bounded field, we may participate in other entities through perceiving them and indwelling them in ways that reach more deeply into the womb of being out of which they emerge, but we will never plumb its ultimate depths.

Touching and the kinaesthetic sense create the continuous immediate finite locus of our centre of reference, reinforced by tasting and smelling, and by the elaborations of all four in terms of different kinds and degrees of pain and pleasure. Kinaesthetic imaging creates the felt shape of my local movement or being still. Touch is inseparable from it: to image anything tactually is also to image my felt shape in touching it. The reverse is not necessarily the case: in conditions of weightlessness you can kin-aesthetically image the shape of your movement without touching anything. Awareness of breathing combines kinaesthetic imaging of very local expansion and contraction with tactual imaging of air on inner surfaces: this combination generates perhaps the core of our centre of reference.

Seeing and hearing create boundary consciousness: they establish the periphery of our being in a world. And they also make plain the bearings of our centre of reference in relation to the boundary and what is within it. Seeing, when we look at our bodies, also yields visual form to our central locus of touching and moving; hearing gives it aural form, through the sounds of our touching and moving. So in the fourfold modes with which we image our being in a world, we generate within a bounded field a finite centre of imaging reference which we call, rather crudely, a body.

Figure and ground

Our perceptual world is present in a field of focal-expanded/figure–ground unities. We image the field with a bipolar unity of focal and expanded awareness. In imaging it we both attend to a focal sight or sound (or touch or movement) and at the same time with necessary complementarity we attend expansively to the rest of the field which becomes ground to that focal figure. The imaging process can incline to one pole more than the other or find the fulcrum of balance between them. You can disattend somewhat from any focal figure to be mainly expanded and image the field as a whole. Or you can disattend somewhat from imaging the ground and concentrate attention mainly on a focal figure. Or you can balance attention between the figure and its ground.

But whether you are focal or expanded you never lose awareness of the whole figure–ground field. Thus perceptual awareness is bipolar in another way: it is constituted by two forms of attention. There is grounded attention which provides the basic figure–ground pattern, and there is free-form attention, which, with its capacity for being selective and focal, or expansive and diffuse, is relatively independent of grounded attention and contracts or expands over it. Once grounded attention has chosen a particular figure and its ground, my free-form attention can light up the figure more than the ground, or vice versa, or light up the whole unified figure-in-its-ground.

There are figure–ground unities within each imaginal mode: a focal sound within a ground of other sounds; a focal shape within the visual field; a focal touch within the total tactual range; a focal movement within the whole kinaesthetic image. But also between the modes: to attend to a figure in one mode means that its immediate ground is in that mode, with all the other modes being extra grounds. Any figure we attend to is always fully grounded in our seamless fourfold way of perceiving our being in a world.

The point of this is that a figure derives some of its significance from the way it is related to its own immediate ground – the impact of a part is due to its relation with the whole interacting with the relatively autonomous nature of that part – and some of its significance from its setting in the context of the other three modal grounds. A tone has its imaginal meaning by virtue of its own nature interacting firstly with its ground of sound and secondly with its ground of vision and touch and sensed posture or movement.

Shifting figure–ground hierarchies constitute the play of imaginal meaning in our perceptual worlds. What I called above grounded attention – which elects a particular figure and its ground – is itself highly mobile. It can choose one bird song as figure to other simultaneous bird songs as ground; it can hold all the bird song as figure to a whole range of other simultaneous sounds; it can take all current sound as figure with the whole visual field as ground; and so on.

The ultimate shift in this play of hierarchies is to attend to everything that is going on in all four imaginal modalities – seeing, hearing, touching, and sensing movement or posture, with their enhancements – as figure to whatever is the ground of this whole fourfold perceptual imaging of being in a world with its bounded field and centre of reference. Such a ground is the infinitude without at the boundary and the infinitude within at this centre and all other centres. Taking all this together makes a boundlessly full void. For conceptual meaning this ground is a mathematical abstraction. For primary meaning it is the ground in relation to which the whole format of our being in a world has magical impact. It is, in short, a ground of extraordinary magic.

The body as imaginal artefact

Kinaesthetic sense of body posture and movement is a special case of the interdependence of primary imagination and reality. It is not perspectival: there is no view from one point of the total form of my posture or movement. I grasp the whole configuration in one go, imaging where everything is all at once. The imagination of three-dimensional form which grounds visual imaging and its perspectives in reality *constitutes* kinaesthetic imaging. I continually imagine the holistic shape of my ongoing gesture in space. This imagining is my body. To say it is produced by my body, or even that it is dependent on my body, is to put the cart before the horse and speak in the language of dissociated conceptual constructs. Bodies are bounded imagined forms in space. When dancers or Aikido experts or gymnasts intuitively grasp this, then their active imagination can articulate their bodily gestures in remarkable ways.

It is not that I imagine a body – as though first I imagine and then a body appears – but that imaging of a certain shape and set of processes is my body. This imaging at the conscious, waking level is normally limited to kinaesthetic imaging of posture and movement, pleasure and pain. At the subliminal level, both in sleeping and waking states, it includes the potent imaging that constitutes the internal parts and the total organism that is my body. This deep generative level of mind, this internal imaginal shaping of the organic form (that is, the shaping that *is* an organism) which I call my body, is one I can readily dissociate from, deny – and then reify its imaging as a body that is somehow other than me and I am in.

There is a continuity from the waking, ordinary, kinaesthetic level of imaging body posture to the deep level of imaging organic form and process. The kinaesthetic imaging that we call breathing is at the interface between ordinary and deep level mind; hence paying attention to the breath has been a classic route, for example in Tibetan Buddhism, for opening to our deep-level coming into being and to its ground.

The notion that the human body is a deep level of human imagination congealing in localized forms, in interaction with some cosmic given, is an outrage to a positivist cast of thought. This insists that bodies, like all other objects, are separate from subjects, or at least not very much to do with them; so they can be tinkered about with as if they are functionally autonomous. The greater part of modern medicine still rests on a repression of the deep levels of generative mind, hence the culture of medicine, quite apart from overt medical errors and the harm that follows from treatments based on research that uses inferential statistics and comparisons of means, is iatrogenic in the sense that it paralyses, inhibits and undermines intentional self-healing.

The subtle fear this repression generates in society, together with a pervasive disrespect of generative mind, may well be a major aetiological factor in much disease. Yet the evidence for imaginal regeneration of diseased tissue and process, garnered from among those who transcend the fear, lies around the fringes of 'objective' medical science, largely ignored. It is provided by hypnosis, auto-suggestion, bio-feedback, yogic physiological feats, the placebo effect, so-called spontaneous remission, healing consequent upon deep attitudinal restructuring and related forms of emotional, mental and spiritual self-help which evoke the generative power within.

Presences and objects

Our being in a world at the grounding level of empathic-imaginal meaning, which is extralinguistic, does not contain 'objects'. For language-users busy with conceptual meaning, the world is full of classified things – houses, trees, mountains, cups, sand and trains. For the purposes of this exposition, I use the word 'object' to refer exclusively to things that we perceive with these tacit linguistic-conceptual labels attached. In the extralinguistic, empathic-imaginal world there are no objects in this sense. It is a world free of all conceptual schema, all frameworks born of language mastery. Nothing is identified in terms of class-names.

Yet it is a world of distinct presences, which are perceptually identified and recognized and differentiated in terms of similarity and difference of form and process. And this perceiving process is grounded on attunement to, empathic communion with, their inner apprehension, their mode of awareness. This is clear from the experience of any sage, artist or phenomenologist who is open to extralinguistic perceiving. So I retain the term 'presence' or 'distinct presence' to refer, in the imaginal world, to what, in the conceptual world, I call an object.

Presences are very different from objects. A tree, as an object, is not the same as the unlabelled presence which we call a tree. The presence is a remarkable interfusion of my empathy, my imaging and the given. We participate in each other and we are distinct from each other. It has inwardness, a subtle discreet awareness, with which I can commune. It speaks to me through its total patterning, through its whole imaginal gesture within its context. It has a signature, a sound, it makes its own quiet statement. It has, in short, distinctive presence.

Language here gropes around what it cannot match. Yet language that is open can point to some of the magical immaterial qualities of this presence – its silence, dignity, lifted grace, hidden knowing – even though these qualities reach far beyond and are far more subtle than the propositions that point to them. But if language is used with closure, as soon as it attaches the class-name 'tree' to the presence, and we see a tree, the presence disappears behind the whole restricting conventional network of associations that come with 'tree'.

The world of presences is truly a magical world. It is the cosmic given appearing as myriad centres of inwardness within the communion of my empathy, a host of unique manifest signatures within the embrace of my perceiving. Each presence makes itself felt in a subtle, variegated, orchestrated intercommunion with all the other presences in my field of awareness. Intercommunion is a matter of mutual resonance, synchronous exchange of inward being, inseparable from the simultaneity of aesthetic dialogue between manifest form and process.

Any one presence is revealed through its pattern of form and process and through its gesture, that is, its posture and its motions. There is a web of connection between this revelation and that of every other presence. It is as if, in the world of presences, the manifestation of each is a precisely partial metaphor for that of every other according to some remarkably intricate analogical taxonomy.

The seamless realm of presences constitutes the participative otherness of the cosmos. In the empathic-imaginal world, we are not subjects separated from objects; we are presences in communion with other presences, in a great field of mutual participation. Other presences are not separate from us, nor are they totally available to us. Participation in presences is always partial, but it can be extended by deepening our communion with their inwardness, while paying heed to how we generate our perceiving of a world, how in the deeper levels of mind we reach out to give shape and form to them and engage in a transaction with their own reaching out. Yet however far we reach out, the other presence can never be fully accessible. It emerges from its own infinitude within, and has its own unplumbable depths. Participation is suspended between the magic of the manifest and the mystery of the unmanifest.

Consciousness is spatial

In the participative universe of imaginal meaning, there is no gap between space and consciousness. There is no separation between the conscious perceiver and the perceptual image, nor between the image and what is perceived. All images are spatial, have spatial properties: they are frames of space, forms of space. So when I image, my consciousness is adopting in and through that imaging a form of space: my mind becomes a temporary imaginal spaceframe. Perceiving my being in a world through fourfold imaging is to deploy a spatially extended consciousness. My perceived world is the form of my consciousness. Through articulating the spatial forms of perceptual imagery my consciousness participates in what is given. Consciousness is world-making and world-meeting through its imaginal power.

Kant thought that the cosmically given, which he called things-in-themselves, has no spatial properties, and that the interpretation of our experience as that of a spatially extended world is an act of the mind. It is, he wrote, an a priori scheme we impose on reality, nothing to do with reality itself. But Kant only laid hold here of the mind as world-making, not as world-meeting. He did not grasp that the mind not only makes its world, it also meets the given. Indeed it makes its world by meeting, by participating in, the given.

Each of the myriad of presences which manifests the cosmically given does so through its form and process, its gesture in space and time. Through perceiving we participate in and interfuse with that gesture and generate our own spacetime perspective of it. Space and time are not on this view a priori forms of the mind imposed on reality. They are a shared medium for the mutual participative apprehension of presences.

This view of consciousness, as spatially extended in perceptually imaging a world, constitutes a final break with the Cartesian paradigm that has held sway for the last three centuries. Descartes published his masterwork *Meditations* in 1641, following the *Discourse on Method* in 1637. His dualism of mind and matter – mind being nonspatial and having none of the properties of matter, and matter being spatial with none of the properties of mind – provided an instant warrant for the development of the natural sciences, the investigation of nature as a self-contained mechanistic system run by its own causal laws.

The problem of how a completely incorporeal mind can interact with an entirely mechanical corporeal body was never really faced by Descartes. He located the seat of the mind in the pineal gland. This did not in any way help him to explain how mind and body could interact, given his account of them as totally separate sorts of reality with no properties of any kind in common. He did, however, make two telling phenomenological admissions.

The first is on his route to that total, systematic doubt which leaves him doubting everything except the fact that he is doubting, that is, thinking, and therefore at the same time existing. He admits in the *First Meditation* that some sensory evidence is so clear that only a madman would doubt it: 'for example that I am here seated by the fire wearing a dressing gown'. He then dismisses this by indulging, without noting the anomaly, in the mad doubt that a demon could be deceiving him so that 'all external things are not more than the delusions of dreams'.

The second admission is in the *Sixth Meditation*, where he says 'Nature teaches us by the sensations of hunger, thirst, etc., that I am not merely present in my body as a sailor in a ship, but that I am very closely united and as it were intermingled with it'. From the point of view of primary, imaginal meaning, his first admission spotlights the world-making, world-meeting, spatially extensive power of perceptual imaging. The second admission highlights the inherent spatiality of the kinaesthetic imaging of bodily sensations.

Poised to launch the dualism of nonmental matter and nonspatial mind, Descartes notes *en passant*, without grasping its significance, the experience of the intermingling of consciousness and the body. For this kind of kinaesthetic imaging, there is no separation between consciousness, space and energy. Consciousness manifests as a dynamic, energetic imaginal form of space. It is not identical with this form, since consciousness is self-reflexive, self-transcending. In being conscious of any imaginal form of consciousness, there is an aspect of my consciousness that is always transcendental. Nor is there just one sort of space and energy which consciousness manifests *as*. For imaginal meaning there appear to be qualitatively different sorts of space and energy which may clothe consciousness.

The energetic forms of space which characterize consciousness in perceiving, dreaming, remembering, imagining, extrasensory perceiving are qualitatively different. They differ in terms of their subjective-objective transaction. How this transaction is organized, in terms of the role of, and the relation between, the subjective and objective poles, varies greatly among them. They also differ in terms of their spatial relation with each other. *Where* dreaming as a world-creating process is in relation to perceiving as a world-creating process, or to put it another way, *where* the space of dreams is in relation to the space of perception, is different from the spatial relation between the space of memory and the space of dreams, for example – although the differences cut every which way.

These differences are differences of interpenetration. The spatial relation between different sorts of spatial consciousness is itself a meta-space constituted by the several kinds and degrees of interpenetration between them. To say that one space interpenetrates another is to say that it is 'within' the other. This is not the kind of being-within that characterizes the way a gift is inside a parcel. It is Descartes's 'intermingling' sort of being-within. The space of primary or productive imagination that preserves the perceptual constancies is within perceptual space, in the intermingled sense. The imagined circularity of the plate is within, intermingles with, the perceived ellipticality of it. But the memory image, by virtue of which I recognize the plate, intermingles with both the perceptual image and the image of productive imagination.

Meta-space consists of at least five interpenetrating imaginal worlds: the worlds of perceiving, dreaming, remembering, imagining, extrasensory perceiving. By extrasensory perceiving I mean not only ESP in the wider sense of perceptions of other realities, but also those forms of subtle, extrasensory perceiving that are interwoven with sensory perceiving, such as perceiving the gaze of another person. The gaze is not the same as the eyes, nor is it projected onto the eyes: it is a phenomenal category *sui generis* (Heron, 1970). Perceiving it is a form of extrasensory perception.

The positivist separation of subject from object leads to the belief, in the realm of secondary, conceptual meaning, that reality is the objective world of sensory perceiving. This is the one reality and what goes on inside a person as dreaming, remembering, imagining and supposed extrasensory perceiving is purely subjective and is nothing to do with the real world. It is an evanescent chimera, it has no ontological status, it doesn't qualify as existing.

For primary meaning, our reality is the meta-reality generated by how we interweave the five imaginal worlds. Each is a world because of its inherent spatiality and its idiosyncratic kind of subjective-objective polarity: what is objective in a dream is organized in different ways to how what is objective is organized in memory or imagination or sensory perceiving. As worlds they are co-involved with each other in certain fundamental ways; and also are relatively independent of each other in certain respects.

The sensory world is inseparable from the two worlds of memory and imagination which deeply interpenetrate it and are in part constitutive of it. Perceiving involves *recognition* of sensory forms and the *imagined* grasp of their actual shape, colour, size, etc. Yet the worlds of memory and imagination have huge areas of independence of the immediate sensory field, and these can be brought to bear upon that field in radical ways.

The sensory world is interpenetrated by the extrasensory or subtle world in mutual gazing, in other forms of interpersonal perception, and in other ways – to all of which the culture of the day tends to turn a blind conceptual eye. And again the extrasensory worlds have a vast reach independent of the sensory.

One point that emerges from all this is that *what constitutes the sensory world is both ambiguous and variable*. It is ambiguous because there is so much memory, imagination and extrasensory perceiving interwoven with it; and it is variable because the kind and degree of this interweaving is alterable by creative human intention.

For imaginal meaning, all infinities are grounded in a shared infinity. The limitless horizons of the worlds of imagination, of dreaming, of memory, of sensory and extrasensory perceiving, are grounded in the limitlessness of meta-reality, of the meta-space of the five interwoven worlds. This is not the limitlessness of horizons as in the component worlds. It is the limitlessness of kinds and degrees of interpenetration, of constitutive interweaving and relative independence. It is a limitlessness of creativity, a potential infinity; whereas the limitlessness of horizons is an actual infinity. But the potential infinity within and the actual infinities without, point to their ground in an all-inclusive reality: the world-generative power within our own world-generative power, plus the infinite reach and givenness of each and every world we are involved in generating.

The spatial form of our own mind-energy is thus a finite locus within a vast multi-dimensional field of mind-energy. There is one experiential multispace with you and I as distinct loci within it. Each of us is not a limited nonspatial centre of conscious experience in a nonmental universal space as in the Cartesian universe, but a self-limiting mental space within a universal spatial experience. There are no longer many different nonspatial consciousnesses in one universal nonmental space, rather many mental spaces within one universal spatial mind. The Cartesian duality between space and mind is overcome: the individual mind is a local set within cosmic mind-energy-space. We are no longer beings mysteriously-in-here who are conscious of space-out-there, but experiential subjective-objective spaces within one trans-empirical consciousness.

Another way of saying all this is that if imaginal mind is inherently spatial, and there is intersubjective and interobjective congruence among our manifold of imaginal realities, then the spatiality of our minds together constitute one great multi-dimensional interconnected web disappearing into limitless horizons without all of us and the infinitude of a generative source within each of us.

Conclusion

This ends my fragile attempt to give a brief personal sketch of a post-conceptual world, to transform the primary meaning of my integral lived experience into the secondary meaning of a conceptual system that seeks to be open to its primary ground. What it needs, of course, is corrective elaboration by co-operative inquiry.

11
Arguments for Co-operative Inquiry

Here I present a range of arguments for the use of co-operative inquiry when researching persons. It is an extension, selection and update of views expressed in earlier papers (Heron, 1971, 1977a, 1981a). Several of the main points have been introduced in other chapters. I preface them with a digest of the limits of positivist inquiry, and with a more detailed account of these limits in a particularly telling case, that of conventional medical research.

The problems of positivism

The limits of positivist, quantitative research in the human sciences have been well reviewed for many years (Argyris, 1968; Harré and Secord, 1972; Israel and Tajfel, 1972; Gergen, 1973; Joynson, 1974; Shotter, 1975; Heather, 1976; Reason and Rowan, 1981a; Bernstein, 1983; Lincoln and Guba, 1985; Guba and Lincoln, 1994; Smith et al., 1995). I will give here a brief summary of some of the main criticisms.

The overarching criticism is that there are no objective facts against which to verify or falsify hypotheses:

- The findings of the observer are shaped by the observer in interaction with the phenomena. This is evident both in the physical sciences and the social sciences.
- So-called statements of fact are theory-laden. They can only be formulated within a pre-existing set of theoretical assumptions.
- So-called statements of fact are also value-laden. The underlying theoretical assumptions which shape them represent values preferred to the values implicit in other rejected assumptions.

More specific criticisms relate to quantitative approaches that use inferential statistics, the control of selected variables through randomized designs, and imported categories of understanding:

- Selecting and controlling variables means the exclusion of others that are influential. The resulting findings have little relevance to understanding how all the pertinent variables are at work in the real world.
- Inferential statistics bury individual differences under comparisons of means, and throw no light on the idiosyncratic nature of individual responses.

- People cannot be understood either in terms of externally measured variables, or in terms of researcher imported categories. A full understanding of people necessarily includes the meanings and purposes they invest in their actions, as these are interpreted through dialogue with them.
- The methodology presupposes strict causal determinism. A model of relative indeterminism and autonomous agency is better suited to the explanation of human behaviour.

Having swiftly despatched positivism in general terms, I now turn to a critique of a particular version of it.

Positivist research in trouble: the medical case

I consider here only conventional medical research in the form of clinical trial methodology (CTM), where there is a random allocation of subjects to an experimental treatment group and a matched control group (Heron, 1986). I chose medical research since it is a human science at a critical interface with physical science. The rigour which it seeks to import from the latter is at odds with what is needed for the former, and the issues about researching people stand out in clear relief.

Technically, CTM assumes the homogeneity of the research populations it studies. This is enshrined in its statistical method, which hides, through the comparison of means, what happens to individuals in the trial. The statistics on two treatment groups may show that one treatment is better than another, yet there may be some people in *both* groups who are worse after treatment. In general, CTM works to 'obscure rather than illuminate interactive effects between treatments and personal characteristics' (Weinstein, 1974). It can throw no light on the fact that individuals respond differently to the same treatment. Therefore it cannot help with the everyday clinical question 'What is the treatment of choice for this individual patient?'

There is thus a mismatch between research method and clinical reality. The former assumes that patients are the same and obscures their differences, while the latter repeatedly reveals the patient differences that defeat this assumption. The inevitable result is a therapeutic culture which has a significant iatrogenic effect. Treatment based on conventional inferential statistics is bound sooner or later to harm some patients in ways that medical research can neither predict nor understand. Any competent Department of Health in a modern government will have a figure, not usually made public, stating the percentage of hospital beds filled by patients with iatrogenic disease.

Another major technical limitation of CTM is its commitment to univariate analysis. It wants to separate the single treatment variable out from all other influences of a psychological or physical kind in order to consider its causal impact. Thus CTM is strangely wedded to the gross paradox of the extraneous variable. This is the variable which is controlled out of the results precisely because it is influential.

The placebo effect, the effect of mental expectation on physiological functioning, is for CTM such a variable. It is a highly influential one, which is why it has to be discounted in order to find out what the independent physical effect of a treatment is. This carries over into the therapeutic culture of clinical medicine, which crazily and systematically ignores the powerful and proven effect of mind on body, and the latent mental power in people for self-healing.

Another way of saying the same thing, is that CTM is exclusively researcher centred. It focuses only on observable disease categories, as chosen by the researchers. It takes no account of subjective illness categories as experienced and framed by the patient, and of the fact that the experience of illness may be functionally related to the observable disease. It misrepresents the illness-disease reality by considering only the outside of it and totally ignoring the inside. It thus suppresses a hidden variable, the tacit intentionality of illness, of unknown power. In other words, if there is intentionality at work in being ill, it can be raised into full consciousness and turned around into intentionality at work in becoming well.

CTM would indeed be in grave difficulty if it were to try to apply itself to test the effects of intentional self-healing in an experimental group. It is morally bound to seek the informed consent of people to participate in the trial. It would thus have to ask the subjects to agree to the possibility of being randomly allocated to a control group in which they are *not* to practise intentional self-healing. Apart from the dubious morality of this request, it is self-defeating, since the very making of it is a powerful suggestion which undermines it. So CTM is faced with a strong dilemma. If it tries to explore patient intentionality it disempowers itself; if it maintains its own authority, it ignores and disempowers patient intentionality.

CTM has a wider moral problem to do with informed consent, even when the patient is properly informed about the treatments being tested, about the reason for the trial, and about being randomized. For it is very shady to ask people to participate in research that: ignores individual differences and is therefore bound to produce results that harm some; treats patients' personality, intentionality and mental set as extraneous variables whose influence is to be discounted; and totally disregards the patients' right to participate in decisions about a research design that purports to generate knowledge about them.

The use of conventional statistical analysis, the restrictive split of variables between experimental and control groups, means that CTM can never address three important features of the real world:

- Individual differences among patients.
- The therapeutic effect as a dynamic pattern of interacting factors, physical and psychosocial.

- The potentially powerful effect of patients' mental states on their physiological processes.

All these things can only be addressed if:

- The variables are not split between an experimental and a control group, but all influential factors are studied together in the inquiry group.
- Control of variables is exercised internally, in the inquiry group, through discrimination within the total pattern of variables: the validity of the pattern is inherent in its organization, which can only be studied from within it.
- Patients become co-inquirers as well as subjects since their agency and their mental states are key variables and can only properly be used if the patients participate in deciding how and why they are to be used.
- Comparisons are made between the significant pattern of variables in autonomous inquiry groups with both a similar and a different kind of focus.

The outcome of all this is a form of participative medical research in which illness is seen as a way in which patients articulate their reality, and as a project which can be restructured to influence their disease, or to change the quality of their life, or both. For a valuable discussion of holistic method applied to medical research see Reason (1986).

Arguments for co-operative inquiry

I am closing this book with an account of some of the reasons for adopting co-operative inquiry as a way of doing research in the human sciences. This is a convenient way of reviewing what it is all about.

The human condition

You can't inquire into the human condition from outside it. You can't get outside it, except by committing suicide. You can only inquire into it from inside it. Even if you could get outside it, perhaps through out of the body experiences, you would have to get back into it in order to study it. The human condition is the condition you are in, I am in, he or she is in. It is an incarnate condition and is known only by insider knowledge. Above all, if we are to have communicable knowledge about it, the human condition is the condition *we* are in: it is face-to-face, interactive incarnation. It involves you and I in communion and dialogue with each other, each of us embodied in our shared world. To inquire into it is a matter of our insider knowledge. Our inquiry is a shared culture of dialogue mediated by language, agreement in the use of which presupposes and is grounded on a nonlinguistic context of shared experiential meaning.

The only way you can fully and properly discriminate the parameters of the human condition is from inside it; and the only way you can manage, manipulate, control, vary these parameters in order to learn more about them, their interactions and effects, is by your own intelligent personal action in co-operation with others with whom you choose to share the given condition. You can't do research on the human condition by controlling the parameters for other people and seeing what happens to the parameters and/or the people. This tells you nothing about their human condition – since only they can tell you that from within it, and on the basis of their own intelligent actions – and it tells you nothing about your own. It just tells you what happens when neither you nor they inquire properly into your respective conditions. It is a distraction from, and an avoidance of, true human condition inquiry.

I can certainly inquire about the human condition which you share with others, by asking you and them all about it in terms of categories of your and their devising, and by reporting it faithfully as you and they tell it. But I am not then inquiring into the human condition, which is the condition which I and other incarnate people share and within which we interact. I am trying to access your insider knowledge in terms of my outsider interests. I am neither fully in your condition, nor fully in my own, and so can do justice to neither. And the question is: why would I get myself in this anomalous position, rather than inquire into the human condition I share with others or join forces with you and inquire into our shared condition?

This is all a way of saying that to be in the human condition is to be embodied. It is only in and through your own total embodiment, in face-to-face relation with others similarly embodied, that you have insider access to the human condition. You cannot inquire into the human condition unless your incarnate manifold of sensibilities, in its full range, is a basic instrument of inquiry in interaction with others similarly engaged, the inquiry being about the condition you are all in.

Persons in relation

Persons are only persons in equal and reciprocal relation with other persons. Persons manifest as persons in the context of mutual communion and communication, in which those involved function as free, autonomous beings in loving, creative and intelligent dialogue and endeavour with each other. Does any aware, sensitive and intelligent researcher seriously doubt this? If you want to research persons who are functioning fully as persons, then as researcher you will need to be in a mutual relation with them, otherwise you are not researching them properly as persons. This means, of course, that they will need to be your equal, free, autonomous, loving and creative co-researchers, and you will need to be their equal co-subject. Hence the model of co-operative inquiry. If this argument seems too quick, try the next one.

Research behaviour and self-determination

The point about creative research behaviour – that is, the behaviour of someone who is doing innovative research – whether the researcher is busy with physical or social science, or, if the latter, with quantitative or qualitative methods, is that it is not predictable. Creative research generates a new idea and the new behaviour involved in stating, exploring and applying it. This behaviour, and the occurrence of the new idea that launches it, necessarily defy any sufficient explanation in terms of causal laws and antecedent conditions. They could not in any intelligible sense be new if they were in principle predictable on the basis of what is already known. We engage in research innovation precisely because we cannot know in advance what form it will take.

In the nature of the case, it constitutes creative advance, surmounting and transcending the predictable. It depends on the generation of fresh hypotheses and innovative theoretical formulations. There is no precise methodology for generating new ideas: they are not the logical product of empirical observation; rather they arise unpredictably to direct it into ever more fruitful channels. Popper (1959) was very clear about this.

Innovative research behaviour is necessarily, by virtue of what it is, self-determined, that is to say it is determined by autonomous creative thinking, by the person as an intelligent, self-directing, self-monitoring and self-critical agent. If this is the model of the human being necessarily pre-supposed by doing any kind of creative research, someone doing research on persons cannot with any consistency or integrity adopt a quite different model for the subjects of his or her research.

But if you do choose to regard your subjects as self-directing agents, whose creative thinking determines their actions, then you cannot do research *on* them or *about* them, but only *with* them. In other words, if their creative thinking is not as equally as involved as yours in devising and managing the research, then their behaviour within the research is not determined by them. They are not present within the research as self-directing agents, but only as other-directed, acquiescent, compliant or assenting subjects.

Unless you co-opt your human subjects as equal co-researchers, they are not fully present as persons and become subpersons suborned, or otherwise seduced or persuaded, to your will. This is still true of qualitative researchers who only want to research the self-determining lives of their subjects. As I said in an earlier chapter, if you relate to me to research my self-determination, but if I have no say in choosing the interpretative schema and method of our relating, and am simply assenting to your choice of format, how far am I present within our interaction as a self-determining being?

There is a rider to this argument about research behaviour. It is that it is impossible in principle, logically impossible, to research the antecedent conditions of any human behaviour. Suppose I try to record the prior conditions of my own behaviour, then this recording is also one of the prior conditions, so I have not only to record the conditions of my behaviour but also to record the conditions under which I am recording it. This launches me on an impossible regress of recording the conditions under which I record the conditions under which . . . *ad infinitum.*

The case is no better if you try to record the prior conditions of my behaviour, because these prior conditions now include their being recorded by you and the prior conditions of your recording, which you cannot record because of the same infinite regress. To research the antecedent conditions of any behaviour, whether your own or someone else's, always leaves you, as a necessary condition of making the inquiry, with a transcendent piece of research behaviour, which is itself an antecedent condition you have not accounted for and cannot account for. This is a more complicated way of saying that human beings cannot get out of the human condition in order to inquire into it, and takes us back to the opening argument.

Research behaviour and intentionality

The view that creative researchers are those who are the imaginative authors of their own behaviour in a way that transcends predictability and causal laws, includes the idea that they are also authors of their own way of giving meaning. In the light of their innovative idea and their chosen method, they make sense of their data and draw their research conclusions. Research behaviour presupposes a model of the person as characterized by this capacity for self-generated meaning.

Intentionality I redefine as the inherent and autonomous capacity of a person to articulate reality through finding meaning in it and giving meaning to it. The finding and giving are inseparable: I find meaning in by giving meaning to. There is no finding meaning other than by giving meaning. The meaning I find is always clothed in the meaning I give. Hence the reality I articulate is always a subjective-objective one.

Researchers will primarily think of giving and so finding meaning as construing reality in the conceptual terms that come with language, that is, in propositions. So let us take the autonomous capacity for construing reality in propositional form. Any innovative researcher, my argument goes, presupposes, by virtue of being an innovative researcher, a model of his or her personhood that necessarily includes this capacity.

Therefore he or she, when researching other persons, cannot without gross inconsistency and inconsideration deny them the same capacity. The researcher must invite the research subjects not only to help decide what aspects of their experience and behaviour are to be researched, but also ask them to be fully involved in making sense of these aspects, in devising conceptual constructs that give them meaning. If I, as a researcher, give meaning to your experience and behaviour, as a subject, in terms of my constructs without having regard for what your constructs about your own experience and behaviour might be, I have not researched you as a person, nor have I treated and respected you as a person. Hence the importance of human subjects being fully engaged as co-researchers in making sense of the data they provide and drawing conclusions from it.

Let me now widen out the argument. Any research methodology that is a vehicle for innovative research – that is, for a creative advance in the articulation of reality – presupposes a model of the person as a being with autonomous intentionality of a multiple kind. Intentionality I have defined as the inherent capacity of a person to articulate reality by finding meaning in it through the process of giving meaning to it. But this is not just a matter of conceptual construing, which is only part of it. For I give, and so find, meaning in four ways: by meeting reality through immediate encounter; by construing it in terms of imaginal patterns; by construing it in terms of the concepts that come with language; and by action in relation to it.

As a developed person, any creative researcher assumes, as a pre-condition of doing his or her inquiry, a model of his or her person as a being in whom these autonomous forms of intentionality are integrated. Hence the same integration needs to be honoured in persons when they are the subjects of research. Then they are empowered within the research, as full co-researchers and co-subjects, freely to choose to give meaning to reality by deciding what they meet, how they image it, how they conceptually make sense of it, how they act in relation to it, and how they put all this together and integrate it. This leads us over into the argument from an extended epistemology in the next section.

The potential person is to be defined, and the behaviour of the developed person is to be explained, without reduction to any other kind of explanation, in terms of mutliple intentionality, an autonomous capacity for a fourfold articulation of reality. This is not a sufficient explanation, but it is certainly a necessary one. It does not exclude other, subordinate accounts. Some of the behaviour may be explained as conventional, that is, as the result of socialization within the beliefs, values and norms of a culture. And the limits within which both autonomous and conventional behaviour is set may be explained in terms of causal laws within a model of relative determinism, or, which is the same thing, relative indeterminism (Heron, 1971, 1981a).

What is inalienable, and what every creative researcher bears witness to in his or her own behaviour, is that autonomous intentionality is a mark of developed personhood and, as an explanation of a creative person's behaviour, is *sui generis*.

An extended epistemology

The thesis here is very simple, and has already been stated above and in other chapters. It is that in any empirical inquiry the four forms of knowing necessarily go together and are grounded on each other, each later one being grounded on those below it in the pyramid of knowing. Experiential knowing, at the base of the pyramid, overlaps with and supports presentational or pattern knowing, which supports propositional or conceptual knowing, which upholds practical knowing, the exercise of skill.

Experiential knowing combines empathy and imaginal grasp. We feel, indwell, the presence of a being and its mode of awareness at the same time as, and as the ground of, penetrating it imaginally, enacting it through unrestricted perceiving on physical and subtle levels. This is the twin form of participative knowing which I discussed in Chapters 7, 9 and 10.

Experiential knowing, when fully opened up, is not just a spare, bare, functional noticing and identification of things. When in this minimal form, it is suborned to linguistic dominance, harnessed to conform only to the linguistic, conceptual world. When opened up, it is active, intentional, capable of increasing degrees of participative articulation and engagement. It finds more and more meaning, in its own empathic and imaginal terms, by giving more and more. It involves generosity of heart, active congeniality of resonance, dissolving restrictive boundaries of emotion to feel the inner being of, and to shape more richly, more fully, more obviously, more subtly, what there is.

It is therefore the grounding instrument of empirical inquiry. But this is a radical empiricism, one that articulates the postlinguistic, postconceptual world, a world liberated from the stranglehold of language. A world of participative knowing, of deeply felt inward presences and penetrated outward patterns. A world enhanced and celebrated through language and its conceptual constructs. Such radical empiricism involves full personal engagement, the whole transparent body-mind active in integral and unrestricted lived experience. Participative knowing, through empathic and imaginal interpenetration, cannot be done for me as researcher by you as subjects.

I cannot ground *my* propositions on *your* participative knowing. If I try to do that they will hang in a non-empirical limbo, in a no person's land, grounded neither in my experience nor in yours. The grounding is necessarily internal to the participative knower. The researcher can only build his or her propositional knowledge on his or her own experiential knowledge, in relation with co-researchers similarly engaged. The human condition is incarnate and shared, open to inquiry only through insider knowledge and dialogue, using the whole range of articulating sensibilities involved in living, fully felt embodiment.

The use of language

The generation and use of language is the original, paradigm case of human inquiry, and provides a model and a template for any subsequent form of human inquiry. It is a classic form of insider inquiry into the human condition.

Language enables us to symbolize our personal experiences – whether one particular one or many – and communicate them to each other by the use of its general terms and concepts. This presupposes agreement in use about the sense and reference of its terms and about the rules of its syntax. How is such agreement in use established? It cannot, at the dawn of the first language, be mediated by the use of language, since this is the use that needs to be agreed upon.

As I wrote in Chapter 10, it can only be mediated, for the first language-users, by nonlinguistic expressive signs, the inner meaning of which is grasped intersubjectively by direct harmonic resonance of lived experience, immediate empathic communion, between the signmakers, at the level of tacit and oceanic primary meaning. Thereafter, all linguistic discourse continuously presupposes this substrate of shared pre-understanding.

This is an intersubjective, subliminal, participative Tao of knowing a shared world of incarnation, a knowing that is the ground of agreement for the generation and use of language, which can then articulate in more explicit form the tacit knowing on which it is founded. This is the profound infralinguistic context of primary meaning within which all language use occurs, and of which it gives a continuous conceptual transformation.

What this account means is that language, which as a medium of communication is necessarily public and shared, is ultimately validated by interpersonal experiential participative knowing. It is a collective product whose primary locutions are collegial: 'we', 'our signs', 'our language', 'our world', 'our reality'. At the same time it allows us huge latitude in framing idiosyncratic statements about our world.

The generation of language, on this view of it, contains within it the paradigm of co-operative inquiry and is the prototype of it. It presents an archetypal insider model of inquiry into what, for the first language-users, was a prelinguistic, preconceptual world. It is model which we cannot disown, inquiring into what for us is a postconceptual world. Post-conceptual research into the human condition entails the revisionary use of language. Co-operative inquirers in deep relations of participative knowing recreate and regenerate language, revise and extend its protocols, to symbolize the ways in which they have both deepened and extended their shared communion with and visioning of their reality.

The rights and duties of subjects and researchers

Doctrines of human rights seek to spell out the basic kinds of freedom which justice requires for the fulfilment of human well-being: the right to freedom of speech and expression; the right to freedom of association and contract; the right to political membership of the community, to participate in the framing and working of political institutions. Such doctrines have been on the march throughout the modern world since their formulation by John Locke in the seventeenth century. And this forward march, or the repression of it, is found in a variety of forms in all contemporary societies.

The right to political membership of the community is a special case of an all-pervasive general right of persons to participate, directly or through appropriate representation, in decision-making that affects their concerns and the fulfilment of their human needs and interests. While acknowledging this right in the restricted political sense, in the arena of local and national government, our society has been slow or unable to acknowledge its relevance in the extended political sense to industry and commerce, to organizational structures generally, to the family, to education (especially higher education), and, of course, to research.

But the same participative right extends into the politics of research on persons. For persons as autonomous beings have a moral right to participate in the research decision-making that claims to generate knowledge about them. This includes the design of the research, its management and the conclusions drawn from it. If this right is not respected, then the autonomous intentionality of the research subjects is dishonoured:

- They have no opportunity to identify and express their own preferences and values in the design that determines their behaviour within the research.
- They are therefore disempowered and oppressed. They are not present in the research as fully functioning, self-directed persons. And they are subjected to preferences and values not of their own choosing.
- They are also misrepresented by a design based only on the researchers' preferences and values. Their intentionality has not been party to planning how the findings will be generated and stated.
- They become accessories to knowledge-claims about them that are invalid, and that are therefore inappropriate and harmful when applied to others.
- They are manipulated, both in the acquisition and in the application of knowledge about them, in ways of which they are not informed and so can neither assent to nor dissent from.
- They are denied an opportunity for increased self and peer generated knowledge of their human condition. Their ignorance of their rights is abused.
- They are subtly oppressed and exploited by researchers for ulterior motives of career advancement, and by the researchers' paymasters for ulterior purposes of social control.

Politics is about power, and power is about who effectively makes decisions in what manner about what and about whom. In this sense, political issues are about the who, the how and the what of decision-making, and pervade every arena of social life, including social science and research relating to persons. Knowledge fuels power: it increases the efficacy of human decision-making.

Manipulatively acquired knowledge about people as other-directed subpersons can fuel power over people and be used for political ends to sustain their status as subpersons. Such research becomes another agent of authoritarian social control. Knowledge and power are all on the side of the researchers and their political masters, and none is on the side of those who generate the data and/or who are subject to the application of conclusions drawn from it.

The value principle of respect for human autonomy requires that power is shared both in the generation and in the application of knowledge about persons. Only then can the research claim to have any human validity and human relevance. On this view, social scientists have an obligation, a duty *qua* researchers, to initiate their subjects into the entire rationale of the inquiry and empower them to become equal and autonomous co-researchers. Put in other words, doing people research involves an inescapable educational commitment: to facilitate in research subjects the development of their self-determination in acquiring knowledge of the human condition.

References

Anderson, E. (1989) 'Critical ethnography in education: origins, current status, and new directions', *Review of Educational Research*, 59: 249–70.

Archer, L. and Whitaker, D. (1994) 'Developing a culture of learning through research partnerships', in P. Reason (ed.) *Participation in Human Inquiry*. London: Sage.

Argyris, C. (1968) 'Some unintended consequences of rigorous research', *Psychological Bulletin*, 70: 185–97.

Argyris, C. (1970) *Intervention Theory and Method: A Behavioural Science View*. Reading, MA: Addison Wesley.

Argyris, C. and Schön, D. (1974) *Theory in Practice: Increasing Professional Effectiveness*. San Francisco: Jossey-Bass.

Argyris, C., Putnam, R. and Smith, M.C. (1985) *Action Science: Concepts, Methods and Skills for Research and Intervention*. San Francisco: Jossey-Bass.

Barfield, O. (1957) *Saving the Appearances: A Study in Idolatry*. London: Faber & Faber.

Bateson, G. (1972) *Steps to an Ecology of Mind*. San Francisco: Chandler.

Bateson, G. (1979) *Mind and Nature: A Necessary Unity*. New York: Dutton.

Belenky, M., Clinchy, B., Goldberger, N. and Tarule, J. (1986) *Women's Way of Knowing: The Development of Self, Voice, and Mind*. New York: Basic Books.

Berne, E. (1961) *Transactional Analysis in Psychotherapy*. London: Evergreen Books.

Bernstein, R.J. (1983) *Beyond Objectivism and Relativism*. Oxford: Basil Blackwell.

Bertalanffy, L. von (1968) *General System Theory*. New York: Braziller.

Bohm, D. (1980) *Wholeness and the Implicate Order*. London: Routledge & Kegan Paul.

Bookchin, M. (1991) *The Ecology of Freedom: The Emergence and Dissolution of Hierarchy*. Montreal and New York: Black Rose Books.

Bortoft, H. (1986) *Goethe's Scientific Consciousness*. Tunbridge Wells: Institute for Cultural Research.

Bradford, L.P. et al. (eds) (1964) *T-group Theory and Laboratory Method*. New York: Wiley.

Brown, L.D. and Kaplan, R.E. (1981) 'Participative research in a factory', in P. Reason and J. Rowan (eds) *Human Inquiry: A Sourcebook of New Paradigm Research*. Chichester: Wiley.

Buber, M. (1937) *I and Thou*. Edinburgh: Clark.

Cancian, F. (1992) 'Participatory research', in E.F. Borgatta and M. Borgatta (eds) *Encyclopedia of Sociology*. New York: Macmillan.

Carr, W. and Kemmis, S. (1986) *Becoming Critical: Education, Knowledge and Action Research*. Basingstoke: Falmer Press.

Cooperrider, D. L. and Srivastva, S. (1987) 'Appreciative inquiry in organizational life', in R. Woodman and W. Pasmore (eds) *Research in Organizational Change and Development, Vol 1*. Greenwich: JAI Press.

Cosier, J. and Glennie, S. (1994) 'Supervising the child protection process: a multidisciplinary inquiry', in P. Reason (ed.) *Participation in Human Inquiry*. London: Sage.

Craddock, E. and Reid, M. (1993) 'Structure and struggle: implementing a social model of a well woman clinic in Glasgow', *Social Science and Medicine*, 19: 35–45.

Creswell, J.W. (1994) *Research Design: Qualitative and Quantitative Approaches*. Thousand Oaks, CA: Sage.

Culler, J. (1982) *On Deconstruction*. Ithaca, NY: Cornell University Press.

Cunningham, I. (1988) 'Interactive holistic research: researching self managed learning', in P. Reason (ed.) *Human Inquiry in Action*. London: Sage.

Damasio, A. (1995) *Descartes' Error: Emotion, Reason and the Human Brain*. London: Picador.

De Venney-Tiernan, M., Goldband, A., Rackham, L. and Reilly, N. (1994) 'Creating collaborative relationships in a co-operative inquiry group', in P. Reason (ed.) *Participation in Human Inquiry*. London: Sage.

Denzin, N.K. (1989) *Interpretive Interactionism*. Newbury Park, CA: Sage.

Denzin, N.K. (1994) 'The art and politics of interpretation', in N.K. Denzin and Y.S. Lincoln (eds) *Handbook of Qualitative Research*. Thousand Oaks, CA: Sage.

Denzin, N.K. and Lincoln, Y.S. (1994) 'Introduction: entering the field of qualitative research', in N.K. Denzin and Y.S. Lincoln (eds) *Handbook of Qualitative Research*. Thousand Oaks, CA: Sage.

Derrida, J. (1976) *Of Grammatology*. Baltimore: Johns Hopkins.

Derrida, J. (1981) *Positions*. Chicago: University of Chicago Press.

Devereaux, G. (1967) *From Anxiety to Method in the Behavioral Sciences*. The Hague: Mouton.

Dewey, J. (1929) *The Quest for Certainty*.

Dewey, J. (1938) *Experience and Education*. Kappa Delta Pi.

Eagley, A.H. (1987) *Sex Differences in Social Behaviour: A Social Role Interpretation*. Hillsdale, NJ: Erlbaum.

Erlandson, D.A., Harris, E.L., Skipper, B.L. and Allen, S.D. (1993) *Doing Naturalistic Inquiry: A Guide to Methods*. Newbury Park, CA: Sage.

Fals-Borda, O. and Rahman, M.A. (eds) (1991) *Action and Knowledge: Breaking the Monopoly with Participatory Action Research*. New York: Intermediate Technology/Apex.

Fetterman, D.M. (1993) *Speaking the Language of Power: Communication, Collaboration and Advocacy*. London: Falmer Press.

Feuerstein, G. (1987) *Structures of Consciousness*. Lower Lake, CA: Integral.

Fine, M. (1992) 'Passions, politics and power: feminist research possibilities', in M. Fine (ed.) *Disruptive Voices*. Ann Arbor: University of Michigan Press.

Friedan, B. (1963) *The Feminine Mystique*. New York: Norton (London: Penguin, 1965).

Fryer, D. and Feather, N.T. (1994) 'Intervention techniques', in C. Cassell and G. Symon (eds) *Qualitative Methods in Organizational Research*. London: Sage.

Gadamer, H.G. (1976) *Philosophic Hermeneutics*. Berkeley: University of California Press.

Gebser, J. (1985) *The Ever-present Origin*. Athens: Ohio University Press.

Gergen, K.J. (1973) 'Social psychology as history', *Journal of Personality and Social Psychology*, 26: 309–20.

Gilligan, C. (1982) *In a Different Voice: Psychological Theory and Women's Identity*. Cambridge, MA: Harvard University Press.

Glasersfeld, E. von (1991) 'Knowing without metaphysics: aspects of the radical constructivist position', in F. Steier (ed.) *Research and Reflexivity*. Newbury Park, CA: Sage.

Goetz, J.P. and LeCompte, M.D. (1984) *Ethnography and Qualitative Design in Educational Research*. New York: Academic Press.

Goldberger, N.R., Clinchy, B.M., Belenky, M. and Tarule, J.M. (1987) 'Women's way of knowing: on gaining a voice', in P. Shaver and C. Hendrick (eds) *Sex and Gender*. Newbury Park, CA: Sage.

Goleman, D. (1995) *Emotional Intelligence*. New York: Bantam.

Goodman, N. (1984) *Of Mind and Other Matters*. Cambridge, MA: Harvard University Press.

Govinda, L.A. (1960) *The Foundations of Tibetan Mysticism*. London: Rider.

Greer, G. (1970) *The Female Eunuch*. London: McGibbon & Kee.

Griffin, S. (1984) *Woman and Nature: the roaring inside her*. London: The Women's Press.

Grundy, S. and Kemmis, S. (1982) 'Educational action research in Australia', in S. Kemmis (ed.) *The Action Research Reader*. Victoria: Deakin University Press.

Guba, E.G. and Lincoln, Y.S. (1989) *Fourth Generation Evaluation*. Newbury Park, CA: Sage.

Guba, E.G. and Lincoln, Y.S. (1994) 'Competing paradigms in qualitative research', in N.K. Denzin and Y.S. Lincoln (eds) *Handbook of Qualitative Research*. Thousand Oaks, CA: Sage.

Habermas, J. (1978) *Knowledge and Human Interest*. London: Heinemann.

Hammond, M., Howarth, J. and Keat, R. (1991) *Understanding Phenomenology*. Oxford: Basil Blackwell.

Haney, C., Banks, C. and Zimbardo, P.G. (1973) 'Interpersonal dynamics in a simulated prison', *International Journal of Criminology and Penology*, 1: 69–97.

Harré, R. and Secord, P.F. (1972) *The Explanation of Social Behaviour*. Oxford: Basil Blackwell.

Hawkins, P. (1986) 'Living the learning: an exploration of learning processes in primary learning communities and the development of a learning perspective to inform team development'. Ph.D. dissertation, University of Bath.

Hawkins, P.J. (1986) 'Catharsis in psychotherapy'. Ph.D. dissertation, University of Durham.

Heather, N. (1976) *Radical Perspectives in Psychology*. London: Methuen.

Heidegger, M. (1962) *Being and Time*. New York: Harper and Row.

Heron, J. (1970) 'The phenomenology of social encounter: the gaze', *Philosophy and Phenomenological Research*, 31(2): 243–64.

Heron, J. (1971) *Experience and Method*. Guildford: University of Surrey.

Heron, J. (1972) 'Re-evaluation counselling', *British Journal of Guidance and Counselling*, 1.

Heron, J. (1973a) *Experiential Training Techniques*. Guildford: University of Surrey.

Heron, J. (1973b) *Re-evaluation Counselling: A Theoretical Review*. Guildford: University of Surrey.

Heron, J. (1974a) *Reciprocal Counselling Manual*. Guildford: University of Surrey.

Heron, J. (1974b) *The Concept of a Peer Learning Community*. Guildford: University of Surrey.

Heron, J. (1974c) *Course for New Teachers in General Practice*. Guildford: University of Surrey.

Heron, J. (1974d) *South West London College: Inauguration of a Peer Learning Community*. Guildford: University of Surrey.

Heron, J. (1974e) *Life-style Analysis: The Sexual Domain*. Guildford: University of Surrey.

Heron, J. (1975a) *Six Category Intervention Analysis*. Guildford: University of Surrey.

Heron, J. (1975b) *Practical Methods of Transpersonal Psychology*. Guildford: University of Surrey.

Heron, J. (1975c) *Criteria for Evaluating Growth Movements*. Guildford: University of Surrey.

Heron, J. (1977a) *Dimensions of Facilitator Style*. Guildford: University of Surrey.

Heron, J. (1977b) *Behaviour Analysis in Education and Training*. Guildford: University of Surrey.

Heron, J. (1977c) *Catharsis in Human Development*. Guildford: University of Surrey.

Heron, J. (1977d) *Co-counselling Teachers' Manual*. Guildford: University of Surrey.

Heron, J. (1978a) *An ASC Peer Research Group*. Guildford: University of Surrey.

Heron, J. (1978b) *Facilitator Styles Course Prospectus*. Guildford: University of Surrey.

Heron, J. (1978c) *Project for a Self-generating Culture*. Guildford: University of Surrey.

Heron, J. (1979) *Peer Review Audit*. Guildford: University of Surrey.

Heron, J. (1981a) 'Philosophical basis for a new paradigm', in P. Reason and J. Rowan (eds) *Human Inquiry: A Sourcebook of New Paradigm Research*. Chichester: Wiley.

Heron, J. (1981b) 'Experiential research methodology', in P. Reason and J. Rowan (eds) *Human Inquiry: A Sourcebook of New Paradigm Research*. Chichester: Wiley.

Heron, J. (1982a) *Education of the Affect*. Guildford: University of Surrey.

Heron, J. (1982b) *Empirical Validity in Experiential Research*. Guildford: University of Surrey.

Heron, J. (1985) 'The role of reflection in co-operative inquiry', in D. Boud, R. Keogh and D. Walker (eds) *Reflection: Turning Experience into Learning*. London: Kogan Page.

Heron, J. (1986) 'Critique of conventional research methodology', *Complementary Medical Research*, 1(1): 12–22.

Heron, J. (1988a) 'Assessment revisited', in D. Boud (ed.) *Developing Student Autonomy in Learning*. London: Kogan Page.

Heron, J. (1988b) 'Validity in co-operative inquiry', in P. Reason (ed.) *Human Inquiry in Action*. London: Sage.

Heron, J. (1988c) 'Impressions of the other reality: a co-operative inquiry into altered states of consciousness', in P. Reason (ed.) *Human Inquiry in Action*. London: Sage.

Heron, J. (1989) *The Facilitators' Handbook*. London: Kogan Page.

Heron, J. (1990) *Helping the Client: A Creative, Practical Guide*. London: Sage.

Heron, J. (1992) *Feeling and Personhood: Psychology in Another Key*. London: Sage.

Heron, J. (1993a) *Group Facilitation: Theories and Models for Practice*. London: Kogan Page.

Heron, J. (1993b) 'Co-operative inquiry and the transpersonal', unpublished manuscript.

Heron, J. (1995) 'Transpersonal inquiry within a self-generating culture', unpublished manuscript.

Heron, J. and Reason, P. (1981) *Co-counselling: An Experiential Inquiry*. Guildford: University of Surrey.

Heron, J. and Reason, P. (1982) *Co-counselling: An Experiential Inquiry 2*. Guildford: University of Surrey.

Heron, J. and Reason, P. (1984) 'New paradigm research and whole person medicine', *The British Journal of Holistic Medicine*, 1(1): 86–91.

Heron, J. and Reason, P. (1985) *Whole Person Medicine: A Co-operative Inquiry*. London: British Postgraduate Medical Federation.

Heron, J. and Reason, P. (1986a) 'Research with people', *Person-centered Review*, 4(1): 456–76.

Heron, J. and Reason, P. (1986b) 'The human capacity for intentional self-healing and enhanced wellness', *The British Journal of Holistic Medicine*, 1(2): 123–34.

Hess, B. (1990) 'Beyond dichotomy: drawing distinctions and embracing differences', *Sociological Forum*, 5: 75–94.

Hillman, J. (1975) *Revisioning Psychology*. New York: Harper Colophon.

Husserl, E. (1964) *The Idea of Phenomenology*. The Hague: Martinus Nijhoff.

Ihde, D. (1971) *Hermeneutic Phenomenology*. Evanston: Northwestern University Press.

Israel, J. and Tajfel, H. (eds) (1972) *The Context of Social Psychology: A Critical Assessment*. New York: Academic Press.

Jackins, H. (1965) *The Human Side of Human Beings*. Seattle: Rational Island Publishers.

Janesick, V.J. (1994) 'The dance of qualitative research design: metaphor, methodolatry and meaning', in N.K. Denzin and Y.S. Lincoln (eds) *Handbook of Qualitative Research*. Thousand Oaks, CA: Sage.

Jourard, S. (1967) 'Experimenter–subject dialogue: a paradigm for a humanistic science of psychology', in E.F.T. Bugental (ed.) *Challenges of Humanistic Psychology*. New York: McGraw-Hill.

Joynson, R.B. (1974) *Psychology and Common Sense*. London: Routledge & Kegan Paul.

Keeton, M. and Tate, P. (eds) (1978) *Learning by Experience – What, Why, How*. San Francisco: Jossey-Bass.

Kelly, G.B. (1993) *Karl Rahner: Theologian of the Graced Search for Meaning*. Edinburgh: Clark.

Kemmis, S. and McTaggart, R. (eds) (1988) *The Action Research Planner*. Victoria: Deakin University Press.

Kenny, A. (1963) *Action, Emotion and Will*. London: Routledge & Kegan Paul.

Kincheloe, J.L. and McLaren, P.L. (1994) 'Rethinking critical theory and qualitative research', in N.K. Denzin and Y.S. Lincoln (eds) *Handbook of Qualitative Research*. Thousand Oaks, CA: Sage.

Koestler, A. (1964) *The Act of Creation*. London: Hutchinson.

Kolb, D.A. (1984) *Experiential Learning*. Englewood Cliffs, NJ: Prentice-Hall.

Kremer, J. (1992) 'The dark night of the scholar: reflections on culture and ways of knowing', *ReVision*, 14(4): 169–78.

Krim, R. (1988) 'Managing to learn: action inquiry in City Hall', in P. Reason (ed.) *Human Inquiry in Action*. London: Sage.

Langer, S.K. (1951) *Philosophy in a New Key*. London: Oxford University Press.

Leininger, M. (1994) 'Evaluation criteria and critique of qualitative research studies', in J.M. Morse (ed.) *Critical Issues in Qualitative Research Methods*. Thousand Oaks, CA: Sage.

Leonard, P. (1984) *Personality and Ideology*. Basingstoke: Macmillan.

Lewin, K. (1952) *Field Theory in Social Science*. London: Tavistock.

Lewin, R. (1993) *Complexity: Life at the Edge of Chaos*. London: Phoenix.

Light, L. and Kleiber, N. (1981) 'Interactive research in a feminist setting', in D.A. Messerschmidt (ed.) *Anthropologists at Home in North America: Methods and Issues in the Study of One's Own Society*. Cambridge: Cambridge University Press.

Lincoln, Y.S. and Denzin, N.K. (1994) 'The fifth moment', in N.K. Denzin and Y.S. Lincoln (eds) *Handbook of Qualitative Research*. Thousand Oaks, CA: Sage.

Lincoln, Y.S. and Guba, E.G. (1985) *Naturalistic Inquiry*. Beverly Hills, CA: Sage.

Long, A. (1992) *In a Chariot Drawn by Lions: The Search for the Female in Deity*. London: The Women's Press.

Lopez-Pedraza, R. (1995) 'Dionysus', paper presented at a Jungian conference in Sicily.

Lowen, A. (1970) *Pleasure: A Creative Approach to Life*. New York: Lancer Books.

Macmurray, J. (1957) *The Self as Agent*. London: Faber & Faber.

Marcuse, H. (1964) *One Dimensional Man*. Boston: South End.

Marshall, C. and Rossman, G.B. (1995) *Designing Qualitative Research*. Thousand Oaks, CA: Sage.

Marshall, J. (1993) 'Viewing organizational communication from a feminist perspective: a critique and some offerings', in *Communication Yearbook*, 16. Thousand Oaks, CA: Sage.

Marshall, J. and McLean, A. (1988) 'Reflection in action: exploring organizational behaviour', in P. Reason (ed.) *Human Inquiry in Action*. London: Sage.

Maslow, A. (1962) *Toward a Psychology of Being*. Princeton, NJ: Van Nostrand.

Maslow, A. (1966) *The Psychology of Science*. New York: Harper and Row.

Merleau-Ponty, M. (1962) *Phenomenology of Perception*. London: Routledge & Kegan Paul.

Miller, G.A. (1969) 'Psychology as a mean of promoting human welfare', *American Psychologist*, 24: 1063–75.

Miller, J.B. (1976) *Toward a New Psychology of Women*. London: Penguin.

Miller, W.L and Crabtree, B.F. (1994) 'Clinical research', in N.K. Denzin and Y.S. Lincoln (eds) *Handbook of Qualitative Research*. Thousand Oaks, CA: Sage.

Millett, K. (1977) *Sexual Politics*. London: Virago.

Moustakas, C. (1994) *Phenomenological Research Methods*. Thousand Oaks, CA: Sage.

Olesen, V. (1994) 'Feminisms and models of qualitative research', in N.K. Denzin and Y.S. Lincoln (eds) *Handbook of Qualitative Research*. Thousand Oaks, CA: Sage.

Parsons, T. (1957) *The Structure of Social Action*. New York.

Peters, R.S. (1958) *The Concept of Motivation*. London: Routledge & Kegan Paul.

Plant, J. (ed.) (1989) *Healing the Wounds: The Promise of Eco-feminism*. London: Greenprint.

Popper, K. (1959) *The Logic of Scientific Discovery*. London: Hutchinson.

Prigogine, I. (1980) *From Being to Becoming*. San Francisco: Freeman.

Reason, P. (1976) 'Explorations in the dialectics of two-person relations'. Ph.D. dissertation, Case Western Reserve University.

Reason, P. (1986) 'Innovative research techniques', *Complementary Medical Research*, 1(1): 23–39.

Reason, P. (1988a) (ed.) *Human Inquiry in Action*. London: Sage.

Reason, P. (1988b) 'The co-operative inquiry group', in P. Reason (ed.) *Human Inquiry in Action*. London: Sage.

Reason, P. (1988c) 'Whole person medical practice', in P. Reason (ed.) *Human Inquiry in Action*. London: Sage.

Reason, P. (1988d) 'Experience, action and metaphor as dimensions of post-positivist inquiry', *Research in Organizational Change and Development*, 2: 195–233.

Reason, P. (1991) 'Power and conflict in multi-disciplinary collaboration', *Complementary Medical Research*, 5(3): 144–50.

Reason, P. (1993) 'Reflections on sacred experience and sacred science', *Journal of Management Inquiry*, 2(3): 273–83.

Reason, P. (1994a) (ed.) *Participation in Human Inquiry*. London: Sage.

Reason, P. (1994b) 'Three approaches to participative inquiry', in N.K. Denzin and Y.S. Lincoln (eds) *Handbook of Qualitative Research*. Thousand Oaks, CA: Sage.

Reason, P. and Hawkins, P. (1988) 'Storytelling as inquiry', in P. Reason (ed.) *Human Inquiry in Action*. London: Sage.

Reason, P. and Heron, J. (1995) 'Co-operative inquiry', in J.A. Smith, R. Harré and L. Van Langenhove (eds) *Rethinking Methods in Psychology*. London: Sage.

Reason, P. and Rowan, J. (1981a) (eds) *Human Inquiry: A Sourcebook of New Paradigm Research*. Chichester: Wiley.

Reason, P. and Rowan, J. (1981b) 'On making sense', in P. Reason and J. Rowan (eds) *Human Inquiry: A Sourcebook of New Paradigm Research*. Chichester: Wiley.

Reason, P. and Rowan, J. (1981c) 'Issues of validity in new paradigm research', in P. Reason and J. Rowan (eds) *Human Inquiry: A Sourcebook of New Paradigm Research*. Chichester: Wiley.

Rinpoche, S. (1992) *The Tibetan Book of Living and Dying*. San Francisco: Harper.

Rogers, C.R. (1961) *On Becoming a Person*. London: Constable.

Rogers, C.R. (1969) *Freedom to Learn*. Columbus, OH: Merrill.

Rowan, J. (1974) 'Research as intervention', in N. Armistead (ed.) *Reconstructing Social Psychology*. Harmondsworth: Penguin.

Rowan, J. (1981) 'A dialectical paradigm for research', in P. Reason and J. Rowan (eds) *Human Inquiry: A Sourcebook of New Paradigm Research*. Chichester: Wiley.

Ryle, G. (1949) *The Concept of Mind*. London: Hutchinson.

Scheff, T. (1971) 'The theory of re-evaluation counselling: hypotheses'. Unpublished paper, University of California: Santa Barbara.

Schön, D. (1983) *The Reflective Practitioner: How Professionals Think in Action*. New York: Basic Books.

Schroedinger, E. (1964) *My View of the World*. London: Cambridge University Press.

Schroedinger, E. (1969) *What is Life? and Mind and Matter*. London: Cambridge University Press.

Schwandt, T.A. (1994) 'Constructivist, interpretivist approaches to human inquiry', in N.K. Denzin and Y.S. Lincoln (eds) *Handbook of Qualitative Research*. Thousand Oaks, CA: Sage.

Shotter, J. (1975) *Images of Man in Psychological Research*. London: Methuen.

Skolimowski, H. (1985) 'The co-creative mind as a partner of the creative evolution'. Paper read at the First International Conference on the Mind–Matter Interaction. Universidada Estadual de Campinas, Brazil.

Skolimowski, H. (1994) *The Participatory Mind*. London: Arkana.

Smith, J.A., Harré, R. and Van Langenhove, L. (1995) *Rethinking Psychology*. London: Sage.

Spiegelberg, H. (1960) *The Phenomenological Movement*. The Hague: Nijhoff.

Spretnak, C. (1991) *States of Grace: The Recovery of Meaning in the Postmodern Age*. New York: Harper Collins.

Stcherbatsky, T. (1962) *Buddhist Logic*. New York: Dover.

Tarnas, R. (1991) *The Passion of the Western Mind: Understanding the Ideas that have Shaped our World View*. New York: Ballantine.

Taylor, C. (1966) *The Explanation of Behaviour*. London: Routledge & Kegan Paul.

Teilhard de Chardin, P. (1961) *The Phenomenon of Man*. New York: Harper Torchbooks.

Torbert, W.R. (1983) 'Initiating collaborative inquiry', in G. Morgan (ed.) *Beyond Method*. Beverly Hills, CA: Sage.

Torbert, W.R. (1987) *Managing the Corporate Dream: Restructuring for Long-term Success*. Homewood, IL: Dow Jones/Irwin.

Torbert, W.R. (1991) *The Power of Balance: Transforming Self, Society and Scientific Inquiry*. Newbury Park, CA: Sage.

Traylen, H. (1994) 'Confronting hidden agendas: co-operative inquiry with health visitors', in P. Reason (ed.) *Participation in Human Inquiry*. London: Sage.

Treleaven, L. (1994) 'Making a space: a collaborative inquiry with women as staff development', in P. Reason (ed.) *Participation in Human Inquiry*. London: Sage.

Trungpa, C. (1986) *Shambhala: The Sacred Path of the Warrior*. New York: Bantam Books.

Varela, F., Thompson, E. and Rosch, E. (1993) *The Embodied Mind*. Cambridge, MA: MIT Press.

Wahl, J. (1953) *Traité de Métaphysique*. Paris: Payot.

Walker, R. (1983) 'The use of case studies in applied research and evaluation', in A. Hartnett (ed.) *The Social Sciences and Educational Studies*. London: Heinemann.

Warr, P. (1977) 'Aided experiments in social psychology', *Bulletin of the British Psychological Society*, 30: 2–8.

Weinstein, J. (1974) 'Allocation of subjects in medical experiments', *New England Journal of Medicine*, 291: 1278–85.

Whitmore, E. (1994) 'To tell the truth: working with oppressed groups in participatory approaches to inquiry', in P. Reason (ed.) *Participation in Human Inquiry*. London: Sage.

Wilber, K. (1983) *Up from Eden*. London: Routledge & Kegan Paul.

Wilber, K. (1995) *Sex, Ecology and Spirituality*. Boston: Shambhala.

Zener, K. (1958) 'The significance of experience of the individual for the science of psychology', in *Minnesota Studies in the Philosophy of Science*. University of Minnesota Press.

Zuber-Skerritt, O. (1992) *Action Research in Higher Education*. London: Kogan Page.

Zukav, G. (1979) *The Dancing Wu Li Masters*. New York: William Morrow.

Index

abreaction, 70–1, 151
absolute determinism, 3, 144, 198
academic status quo, 31
    four traditions of, 72
acceptable ambiguity, 175
action inquiry, 8–9, 82, 83, 118, 122
    supported, 24–5
action paradox, 109, 111, 113–14
action research, 1, 2, 7, 8, 16, 18, 45, 46
action science, 8
action, definition of, 16, 17, 118, 123
Aikido, 190
alaya-vijnana, 122
alien causes, 2
anatta, 188
anthropology, 45
anti-war student struggles, 2
anxious students, 31
aperspectival thinking, 143
Apollo, 45
appreciative inquiry, 8
Archer, L., 102
Argyris, C., 8, 18, 26, 197
Aristotle, 14, 17, 31
art as a mode of knowledge, 10, 89–90
articulation of reality, truth as, 163–4
Ash, M., 14
assessment
    of learning, 31, 63, 72
    of practice, 171
    of validity, 97–8, 103
association, free or directed, 144
asymmetry of thought and action, 16, 34,
    165, 166, 172
attitudinal restructuring, 191
audit trail, 160
authenticity criteria, 161–2
auto-suggestion, 191
autonomy and co-operation, 2, 3, 11, 16, 123,
    127, 172
axiology, 11, 16, 126, 161, 166, 172

Barfield, O., 14, 15, 184
Bateson, G., 11, 14, 121, 162, 183
Belenky, M., 15

belief, four kinds of, 52–6
    belief that and belief in, 53–4
Benedict, R., 45
Bergson, H., 14
Berman, M., 14
Berne, E., 3
Bernstein, R.J., 197
Bertalanffy, L. von, 2, 14
bio-energetic analysis, 3
bio-feedback, 191
bipolar attention, 189
bipolar thinking, 143
body as imaginal artefact, 190–1
body-mind
    therapies, 2
    transparent, 1, 20, 36, 85, 91, 122, 183,
    205
bodywork, 70
Bohm, D., 14
Bookchin, M., 14, 182
bootstrap group, 40, 62,
Bortoft, H., 91, 174
bracketing, 54, 58, 73, 82, 84, 118, 120–1,
    125, 142
Bradford, L.P., 2
breathing, 70
British Journal of Guidance and Counselling, 3
British Postgraduate Medical Federation, 5, 6
British Psychological Society, 2
Brown, L.D., 175
Buber, M., 11, 14
Buddhism, 14, 122, 128, 130, 188, 191

Cancian, F., 8
Carr, W., 7
Cartesian universe, 100, 194, 196
categorial notions, 163
catharsis, 125, 152
celebration, 85–6
Centre for Action Research in Professional
    Practice, 6
centre of reference, 187–9
chaos, 46, 60, 71–2, 77, 88, 94, 97, 137,
    148–9
check for hidden projections, 71

Christian mystics, 14
circle dancing, 129
clinical research, qualitative, 9
clinical trial methodology, 198–9
co-counselling, 3, 71, 152
co-creation, 37, 91
co-operative inquiry
  agreement in, 63, 69, 87–8, 97, 101, 102,
    142, 153, 155, 157, 166, 174–5
  arguments for, 20–2, 197–208
  boundary issues in, 44–5, 83–4, 103, 156
  co-subjects, analogous and partial, 23–4,
    41
  co-researchers, 1, 7, 10, 19–24, 29, 36, 39,
    41, 42, 45, 50, 62, 64, 69, 73, 82, 86,
    87, 102, 110, 152, 154, 174–5, 201,
    202, 204, 205, 208
  collaboration in, 41, 62–9, 152–5
  consensus collusion in, 3, 70, 146, 151,
    152
  culture of, 11, 21, 45–7, 66, 74, 82, 89, 92,
    94, 95–7, 104, 153, 200
  data in
    generation of, 18, 80–1
    making sense of, 86–93, 98–103
    recording, 49, 50, 73, 74, 81, 82–4, 87,
      95, 103, 133, 141, 151
  definition of, 1, 11, 19–20, 36
  ending, 98–100
  extended epistemology and, 5, 11, 33, 52–7,
    104–5, 132, 163–8, 204–5
  facilitation in, 63–5, 153–5
  five domains and, 20
  history of, 1–6
  imagination in, 46, 54, 82, 94–5, 137–8,
    156, 173–4, 182, 184
  initiation, 62–72
    initiators' status, 23, 41, 65, 153
    three strands, 62–5
  launching, 38–40
    bootstrap group, 40, 62
    contracting, 39, 63
    induction meeting, 39, 63, 70
  meta-outcomes, 110
  outcomes of, 34–5, 36–7, 74, 103,
    104–10
  overlap with other methods, 7–9, 24
  participative paradigm and, *see*
    participation
  polarities of method, 138–9
  qualitative research and, 9–10
  range of topics in, 37–8
  report writing, 100–3
  snowperson diagram, 5, 51
  special skills in, 58–9, 82, 117–28

stages of inquiry cycle, 49–50, 73–4, 74–95
symbolic forms and, 180
time structure in, 39, 51–2, 73, 79–80, 95,
  102, 141–2
training for, 129–30
types of, 22–5, 40–8
  Apollonian and Dionysian, 45–7, 51,
    65–6, 73, 74, 77, 78, 79, 82, 87,
    95–6, 97, 98, 102, 103, 137, 139,
    142, 145
  informative and transformative, 7, 19,
    34, 36, 37, 38, 47–9, 50, 54, 55, 59,
    73, 74, 75, 81, 82, 85, 88, 92, 94, 98,
    101, 102, 104, 107, 109, 113,
    115–28, 138, 139, 142, 145, 157,
    171, 172, 180
validity in, 33–4, 52–55, 57–8, 158–9,
  163–75
  agreement about findings, 88, 174–5
  autonomous forms of, 169–70
  congruence of forms of knowing, 52–7,
    164–7
  practical outcomes, criteria for, 170–2
  propositional outcomes and, 172–4
  reporting on, 103
validity procedures, 59–61, 131–57
  challenging uncritical subjectivity, 60,
    145–8
  chaos and order, 60, 148–9
  divergence and convergence, 45, 50, 60,
    73, 74, 75, 76–8, 87, 88, 93–5, 97,
    103, 134–40, 144, 148–9, 153, 175
  managing unaware projections, 60–1,
    149–52
  research cycling, 50–6, 60, 131–4
  sustaining authentic collaboration, 61,
    67–9, 152–5
value premises, 63
co-operative inquiry citations
  altered states (1), 5, 43, 75, 86, 93, 99, 133,
    140, 141, 143, 145, 147, 149, 152,
    154
  altered states (2), 6, 114
  altered states (3), 6, 108
  child protection supervision, 65
  co-counselling (1), 5, 44, 75, 83, 88, 99,
    133, 140, 141, 144
  co-counselling (2), 5, 43, 44, 99, 137, 141
  dental practice, 78
  group energy, 40, 43, 44
  health care practitioners, 42
  health visitors, 43, 44, 75, 89, 97, 99–100,
    149, 152
  organizational culture, 41, 46–7, 99, 153
  participant evaluators, 151–2, 155

whole person medicine, 5, 41, 43, 44, 75, 77, 79, 80, 83, 94, 96–7, 99, 101, 109, 133, 136–7, 141, 145, 147, 149, 152, 154, 156
  womens' staff, 45, 46, 75, 96, 99, 108, 152, 155
  youth workers' learning, 40, 44, 64–5, 69, 75, 77, 80, 98–9, 101, 134, 147–8, 151, 154
Coleridge, S.T., 187
collusion with the system, 72
complementarities of being, 179
complexity theory, 94, 148
conceptual world, 182
concerns of the soul, 177
consciousness, *see also* participation
  altered states of, 38, *see also* co-operative inquiry citations
  boundary, 189
  expansion of, 7, 71
  extraordinary, 98, 128–9
  figure-ground form of, 189–90
  historical theory of, 15, 184
  newly emerging structure of, 122
  restructuring, 125
  second epoché and, 117
  spatiality of, 192–6
  threshold oscillation, 84–5
  transformation of, 174
  universal, 122, 195–6
  void and, 188
  world-making and world-meeting, 193
constructivism, 10, 160–3, 168, 177
consummation, 55, 57, 104, 157, 165–9
contextuality, 12, 92, 180, 181, 182, 183, 185
contribution rates, 67–8, 154–5
  sexist imbalance in, 154
conventional social scientist, 1
convergent thinking, 144
Cooperrider, D.L., 7, 8
Cosier, J., 65, 102
cosmic given, 10–11, 18, 37, 59, 91, 143, 158, 162–4, 168, 178, 182, 187, 191, 192, 193, 196
cosmic mirror, 129
cosmic philosophy, 16
Crabtree, W.L., 9
Craddock, E., 8
creativity, 67, 77, 85–6, 148, 195
  in research, 3, 202
credibility, 27, 160–2
Creswell, J.W., 27, 80
criteria of practice, 170–1
critical theory, 10
critical worker research, 9

critical/uncritical subjectivity, 59, 60, 97–8, 127–8, 131, 145–8, 150, 154
Culler, J., 12, 184
culture, 10, 14, 15, 20, 30, 38, 117, 120, 121, 122, 124, 128, 161, 168, 175–7, 179, 180, 204
Cunningham, I., 24, 44

Damasio, A., 124
database, small, 7
De Venney-Tiernan, M., 39, 40, 44, 65, 69, 75, 77, 80, 99, 101, 134, 148, 151, 154
decision-making methods, 68–9
deconstruction, 12, 185
defensiveness, 130, 149–51
  research distortion by, 150–1
demonstration of skill, 34–5, 92–3, 106, 107
Denzin, N.K., 9, 12, 29, 90
Derrida, J., 12
Descartes, R., 193, 194
deterministic thinking, 144
Devereaux, G., 150
devil's advocate procedure, 60, 140, 145, 146–8, 149, 151, 152, 154
Dewey, J., 14, 16, 168, 169
Dionysus, 45
discharge of distress, 71, 152
dissipative structure, 148
dissociated intellectual command, 31
divergent thinking, 144
dogmatic common sense, 178
duty of researchers, 21, 26, 208
dynamic congruence, 54, 59, 82, 122–4, 126

Eagley, A.H., 18
Eckhart, 14
eco-feminists, 15
embodiment, 21, 37, 129, 200, 201, 205
emotional arousal, 51, 94, 138
emotional climate, 69–70
emotional competence/intelligence, 17, 31, 59, 63, 66, 69–71, 82, 103, 121, 124–5, 128, 149–52
emotional processes, 70–2
empathic communion, 11, 14, 20, 21, 52, 54, 58, 91, 92, 116, 117, 119, 120, 132, 164, 173, 174, 176, 178, 181, 186, 191, 192, 205, 206
empowering evaluation, 9
empowerment, 7, 8, 9, 13, 21, 22, 28–9, 30, 31, 42, 63–72, 101, 102, 106, 108, 129, 132, 153, 161, 204, 208
  two levels of, 28

epistemology, extended, *see* co-operative inquiry
Erlandson, D.A., 27, 106, 159, 160
ethos, 112, 113
European Convention on Human Rights, 17
Evans-Pritchard, E.E., 45
existentialism, 2
experiential knowledge, 5, 14, 33, 52, 54, 55, 104, 132, 158, 163–70 *passim*, 173–4, 176, 178–80, 205, *see also* participative knowing
  bipolarity of, 14, 178
  immersion in, 49, 73–4, 84–6
experiential learning, 1, 2, 16
experiential research, 2–3
experimenter–subject dialogue, 2
explanation, 41, 90, 91–2, 103, 106, 108, 109, 143–4, 147, 198, 202, 204
extraordinary heed
  perceptual, 116–17
  practical, 118

facilitation sequence, 63–4, 65, 67
facts, objective, 159–60, 197
Fals-Borda, O., 8
Feather, N.T., 9
feminine wisdom principle, 15
feminine, repression of the, 15
feminism, 2, 12, 15
feminist research, 7–8, 18, 46, 108, 155
Fetterman, D.M., 9
Feuerstein, G., 122
figure-ground hierarchy/unities, 179, 183, 189–90
Fine, M., 8
firm construing, 144
fourth generation evaluation, 28
freedom, 2, 17, 32, 147, 182, 206
  leading people into, 67, 153
Freire, P., 14
Freudian, 128
Friedan, B., 2
Fryer, D., 9

Gadamer, H.G., 185
gaze
  mutual, 176, 186, 195
  properties of, 1
  research on, 1
Gebser, J., 14, 121, 122, 183
generative mind, 190–1
Gergen, K.J., 197
German idealism, 15
Gestalt psychology, 183
Gifford Lectures, 105

Gilligan, C., 15
Glasersfeld, E. von, 168
Glennie, S., 65, 102
Goethe, J.W., 91, 167, 174
  Goethian science, 91, 174
Goetz, J.P., 160
Goldberger, N.R., 15
Goleman, D., 7, 70, 124
Gombrich, E., 185
Goodman, N., 163
Govinda, L.A., 14, 122
Greek drama, 45
Greer, G., 2
Griffin, S., 150
ground of grounds, 190
grounding, 11, 33, 51, 52–7, 165, 166, 169, 170, 172–4
group dynamics, 2
group stages, three, 69–70
Grundy, S., 7
Guba, E.G., 9, 10, 27, 28, 106, 159, 160, 161, 162, 197
Guntrip, H., 150

Habermas, J., 14
Hammond, M., 178
Haney, C., 18
Harré, R., 197
Hawkins, P., 86, 89, 90, 106, 108
Hawkins, P.J., 87
Heather, N., 197
Hegel, G., 15
Heidegger, M., 185
hermeneutic situation, 185
hermeneutic thinking, 143
Heron, J., 1, 3, 4, 5, 6, 11, 15, 21, 33, 41, 43, 44, 46, 52, 55, 64, 75, 77, 78, 79, 80, 83, 86, 88, 93, 94, 97, 99, 101, 102, 105, 108, 109, 124, 125, 133, 136, 137, 140, 141, 143, 144, 145, 147, 148, 149, 150, 152, 153, 154, 156, 162, 167, 171, 173, 195, 197, 198, 204
Hess, B., 8
hierarchy, 11, 15, 16, 63, 79, 127, 172
  down-hierarchy, 34
  of grounds/contexts, 179, 183
  up-hierarchy, 33, 52–3, 165–7
higher education, 7, 16, 31, 207
Hillman, J., 185
holistic education, 2, 16, 63
holistic knowledge, 16, 33–4, 52–7, 104–5, 132, 163–7, 168, 204–5
holistic thinking, 143
holographic logic, 14
holonomic principle, 14

holons, 183
Human Potential Research Project, 2, 3
human condition, 1, 2, 4, 7, 8, 10, 14, 16, 20,
    21, 36, 37, 61, 65, 85, 126–30 *passim*,
    149, 200–2, 205–8 *passim*
human flourishing, 11, 12, 16, 34, 55, 127,
    165, 166, 172, 173
human project, 179
human rights, 16–17, 32, 171
    civil rights, 2
    extension of, 32
    of research subjects, 17–18, 21–2, 26, 29,
        206–8
    universal participative rights, 16–17, 32
Hume, D., 188
Husserl, E., 117
hypnosis, 191

idiosyncratic behaviour, 77
Ihde, D., 106
illness-disease reality, 199
imagery
    autonomy of, 185
    fourfold perceptual, 186–7
    meaning of, *see* meaning, primary
    spatiality of, 193
imaginal, *see also* presentational
    mind/knowing, 11, 91, 92, 100, 124, 173,
        179, 181, 196
    openness, 54, 58, 82, 118–20, 121
    patterns/symbols, 33, 37, 52, 55, 81, 104,
        105, 106, 164, 185, 191, 192, 194,
        204
    reality/world, 100, 182, 191, 192, 195
imagination, *see also* co-operative inquiry
    Goethe and, 91, 173–4
    primary 187, 190, 194
    reality and, 187
inferential statistics, 197, 198
infinity, potential and actual, 195
informed consent, 28, 199
inherent openness, 14
intentional self-healing, 10, 199–200
intentionality
    multiple, 203–4
    self-transcending, 59, 126
    tacit, 199
interpenetration of spaces/worlds, 194–5
interpersonal competence, 31
interpersonal conflict/tension, 44, 70–1, 97,
    151, 152
interpretive studies, 29
intersubjectivity, 11, 14, 20, 21, 61, 88, 92,
    105, 112, 117, 120, 146, 164, 166, 168,
    174–6, 178, 180–1, 196, 206

intervention research, 9
irrealism, 163
Israel, J., 197

Jackins, H., 3, 150
James, W., 14, 15
Janesick, V.J., 27
Janov, A., 150
Jourard, S., 2, 18
Joynson, R.B., 197
justification, beyond, 13, 34, 58, 158, 165–9

Kant, I., 2, 17, 187, 193
Kaplan, R.E., 175
Keeton, M., 16
Kelly, G.B., 14
Kemmis, S., 7, 45
Kenny, A., 2
Kincheloe, J.L., 9, 12
Kleiber, N., 8
knack, 58, 59, 92, 106, 114, 126
    ineffability of, 111–12
    self-validating, 170
knowledge as power, 8, 12–13, 17–18, 20–2,
    207–8
Koestler, A., 2
Kolb, D.A., 16
Kremer, J., 15
Krim, R., 4
Kwakiutl Indians, 45

Langer, S., 14
language
    agreement about use of/ground of, 11, 20,
        91, 117, 176, 180–1, 200, 206
    ambiguities of, 116
    subject–object split and, 116, 181
    transformation of primary meaning, 20,
        91–2, 117, 119, 120, 169, 174, 179,
        180–5
    scientific/conceptual, 183
Learning III, 121, 183
LeCompte, M.D., 160
Leicester–Tavistock conferences, 2
Leininger, M., 160
Leonard, P., 18
Lewin, K., 1, 2, 7, 16
Lewin, R., 94, 148
liberatory praxis, 12, 34, 38, 67
Light, L., 8
limitlessness of horizons, 195
Lincoln, Y.S., 9, 10, 12, 27, 28, 106, 159, 160,
    161, 162, 197
lived experience, 20, 21, 85, 91, 92, 158, 164,
    166, 174, 178–85, 196, 205, 206

Locke, J., 17, 206
Long, A., 15
loose construing, 144
Lopez-Pedraza, R., 45
Lowen, A., 150

Macmurray, J., 2, 16, 17, 105, 165, 169
Mahayana Buddhism, 14
manas, 122
mano-vijnana, 122
Marcuse, H., 2
Marshall, C., 27
Marshall, J., 15, 41, 46, 47, 99, 102, 153
Maslow, A., 2, 14, 150
McLaren, P.L., 9, 12
McLean, A., 41, 46, 47, 99, 102, 153
McTaggart, R., 46
meaning
　primary/empathic-imaginal, 20, 58, 89,
　　91–2, 93, 117, 119, 120, 158, 169, 174,
　　178–96, 206
　secondary/conceptual, 20, 91, 117, 119,
　　120, 158, 178, 179–85, 195, 196
medical culture and research, 191, 198–200
meditation, 71, 84, 122, 129, 130
meeting, 11, 14, 33, 38, 52, 58, 105, 119, 162,
　164, 165, 176, 177, 186, 193–4, 204
member checking, 160–1
　impossibility of, 161
Merleau-Ponty, M., 11, 14, 120, 162, 178,
　185
meta-reality, 195
meta-space, 194–5
metaphor, 68, 82, 89, 90, 106, 107, 108, 112,
　153, 164, 170, 179, 184, 192
Miller, G.A., 18
Miller, J.B., 15
Miller, W.L., 9
Millett, K., 2
Mind I and II, 120, 180
mind
　everyday/ordinary, 117, 122
　integral-aperspectival, 121, 183
　intuitive, 122
　multi-level, 128–9
　reframing, 121, 183
　self-reflective mind, 121, 183
　spatial, 192–6
　universal, 122, 196
　world-meeting, 193
mind-energy-space, 196
mindfulness/awareness training, 117, 122,
　128–30
moral principles, 127
Moreno, J., 2

morphological leap, 177
Moustakas, C., 9
mutuality, human, 1, 11, 14, 48–9, 117, 127,
　129, 164, 176, 181, 186, 192, 193, 195,
　201
mystical thinking, 144
mysticism, 14, 144, 179

National Gallery, 185
Neoplatonism, 14
New Paradigm Research Group, 4–5
New Zealand, 6, 108, 114
Nicomachean Ethics, 14
Nietzsche, F., 45
nihilism, 12–13
non-attachment, 59, 82, 125–6
non-Cartesian account of mind, 192–6
nonlinguistic/extralinguistic, 11, 20, 21, 90,
　91, 92, 117, 119, 120, 158, 174, 182, 185,
　191, 200

Olesen, V., 7
ontology, 10, 11, 115–16, 159, 162–4, 177,
　179, 195
　epistemology, methodology and, 11, 159,
　162, 164
oppression, 4, 8, 15, 18, 21, 22, 28, 29, 38, 67,
　70, 150, 155, 163, 177, 207
organization of enlightenment, 14
orthodoxy, problem of, 6
out of the body experiences, 200

paradigm(s)
　assumptions of, 177
　Cartesian, 177, 193, 196
　enactive, 117
　four inquiry, 10
　new, of extraordinary living, 98, 129
　non-Cartesian, 1, 192–6
　old/positivist, 19, 25, 177, 197–8
　oriental, 128
　participative, *see* participation
　poststructural antiparadigm, 12–13
　prevalent Western, 128
Parsons, T., 17
part–whole polarity, 78–79, 138–9, 183
participant observer, 27
participation
　challenge of authentic, 23
　epistemic and political, 11–12, 20–2
　inchoate, 53
　participative decision-making, 11–12,
　　16–18, 20–4, 26, 28–30, 31, 32, 63,
　　67–9, 127, 153–5, 156, 199, 200,
　　206–8

participative knowing, 1, 6, 10–11, 14–16, 20, 21, 37–8, 52, 53, 54, 58, 59, 91–2, 100, 116–20, 130, 158, 162, 168, 170, 173–4, 178–96 *passim*, 205–6, *see also* experiential knowledge
  bipolarity of, 11, 178
  future nature of, 184
  range of, 37–8
participative paradigm, 10–12, 21, 33, 37, 158, 177, 206
  precursors of, 13–18
  three stage theory, 15, 184
participative action research, 8–9
participative medical research, 200
pathos, 17
pattern meaning, 33, 37, 52, 53–4, 55, 58, 81, 85, 87, 89, 90, 91, 93, 100, 104–9 *passim*, 116, 119, 120, 123–4, 125, 143, 164, 165, 173, 176, 178, 179, 184, 187, 189, 192, 199, 200, 204, 205
peer self-help groups, 2
Peirce, C.S., 174
perceptual constancies, 187
perceptual enactment/imaging, 11, 14, 52, 54, 58, 104, 116, 117, 119, 120, 132, 164, 173, 178, 185, 186–91, 193, 194, 205
Perls, F., 150
personalism, 2
persons
  intentionality and, 203–4
  in relation, 1, 2, 3, 11, 127, 166, 201
  self-direction/participative rights, 3, 16, 21–2, 26, 32, 127, 202–7
Peters, R.S., 2
phenomenology, 1, 4, 9, 26, 90, 114, 117, 119, 142, 183, 184–5, 191, 193
  second epoché, 117
Philosophy and Phenomenological Research, 1
placebo effect, 191, 199
planetary, 11, 15, 38, 122, 129, 172
Plant, J., 15
Plato, 16
Plotinus, 16
poiesis, 17
Polanyi, M., 14
Popper, K., 202
positivism, 6, 10, 13, 15, 25, 57, 96, 158, 159, 160, 163, 178, 191, 195, 197–8
postconceptual world, 91–2, 120, 182–4, 185–96, 205
postmodernism, 163, 184
postpositivism, 10
poststructuralism, 12–13, 163, 184
practical knowledge

account of, in holistic context, 33–4, 52–7, 104–5, 163–7, 168, 204–5
  outcomes of, 106
  primacy of the practical, 33–5, 37, 48, 104–5, 107, 111–14, 164–8, 172
    culture of competence, and, 38, 107, 111–13
  skills, range of, 35, 38, 92, 106, 111
  validation of, 58, 93, 109, 123, 158, 170–2
pragmatism, 16, 168–9
prajna, 14
pre-understanding, 20, 119, 181
preconceptual world, 181–2
preference and value, 17–18, 21, 69, 124, 207
prehension, 15, 21, 58, 143
premature closure, 60, 72, 140, 144, 148
prepersonal, 15, 120
presence and presences, 33, 52, 53, 54, 55, 58, 62, 85, 91, 104, 105, 106, 107, 108, 115, 116, 119, 120, 129, 144, 164, 165, 170, 173, 176, 178, 185, 188, 191–2, 193, 205
  being present, 58, 100, 118, 119
  presences and objects, 191–2
presentational
  belief, 52–7
  knowledge, 33, 52–7, 81, 104, 120, 131, 142, 157, 158, 163–70 *passim*, 172, 176, 182, 184, 205
    complementary to propositional, 88–90, 106
    criteria internal to, 170
  methods, 60, 68, 73, 74, 81, 82, 86, 87, 88–90, 103, 106, 113, 142, 144, 163
    emotional work and, 71
  outcomes, 36–7, 55, 74, 85–6, 101, 103, 106, 107, 110, 175, 180
Prigogine, I., 148
privileged setting, 8
propositional knowledge
  autonomous criteria of, 170, 172
  belief and, 52–7
  bias in favour of, 31–3, 34
  complementary to presentational, 88–90, 106
  ground of practical knowledge, 170–2
  holistic knowing and, 33–4, 52–7, 104–5, 132, 163–7, 168, 204–5
  outcomes of, 109–10
  pragmatism and, 168–9
  validation of, 172–4
pseudo-preference, 17–18
psychodrama, 70, 71, 130
pyramid of knowledge, 33, 52–3, 165–7, 170, 204–5

quantum logic, 14
quietism, 129

radical empiricism, 119, 205
radical memory, 73, 81, 82, 87, 115–18
  informative, 116–17
  transformative, 118
radical perception, 119–22
radical practice, 122–6
Rahman, M.N., 8
Rahner, K., 14
realism/idealism, 10, 162–3
reality
  all-inclusive, 195–6
  cosmos and, *see* cosmic given
  reality-making contracts, 175–7
  sacral, 100
  subjective–objective, 6, 11, 37, 88, 105,
      114, 116, 126, 140, 143, 156, 157, 158,
      162–8, 173, 174–7, 178, 180, 186, 194,
      195, 196
  truth and, 163–4
Reason, P., 4, 5, 6, 9, 11, 15, 21, 37, 39, 40,
      41, 42, 43, 44, 45, 46, 55, 65, 69, 70, 75,
      76, 77, 79, 80, 83, 87, 88, 89, 90, 94, 96,
      97, 98, 99, 100, 101, 102, 106, 108, 109,
      117, 119, 121, 122, 125, 128, 129, 133,
      136, 137, 140, 141, 144, 145, 147, 148,
      149, 150, 152, 153, 154, 156, 162, 183,
      184, 197, 200
reflection, aspects of, 142–5
reframing, 8, 59, 82, 87, 93, 96, 119, 121–2,
      126, 161, 177, 183, 184
Reich, W., 2, 150
Reid, M., 8
relative determinism/indeterminism, 144, 198
reliability, 159, 160
Renaissance, 17, 100
replication, 156–7
research, *see also* co-operative inquiry
  anxiety and, 150
  democratization of content and method in,
      9–10, 21, 24, 28
  old paradigm, 19, 25, *see also* positivism
  participative, 5, 6, 7–9, 19–25, 27–8, 129,
      175, 200
  qualitative, 9–10, 21, 22, 26–8, 33
    empowerment and, 28
    methods, 27
    problems for, 28–30
    validity in, 160–2
  quantitative, 21, 22, 25, 33
    methods, 25
    problems for, 26, 197–200
    validity in, 159–60

self-determination and, 26, 29
  subcultures, 176–7
  universities and, 31
    teaching/research collusion, 31–2
Rinpoche, S., 122
Rogers, C., 2
Rossman, G.B., 27
routinization of perception, 116
Rowan, J., 4, 5, 11, 18, 128, 162, 197
Ryle, G., 111

sacred science, 183
Scheff, T., 3
Scheler, M., 14
Schelling, F., 15
Schön, D., 8
Schroedinger, E., 14
Schwandt, T.A., 10, 160, 162
seamlessness, 186–7
second level collaboration, 28
Secord, P.F., 197
self
  as agent, 2, 16, 105
  directing, 3
  potential/true/real, 3, 150
  socially conditioned/alienated/false, 3, 150
  transformed, 3
self-actualization, 2
self-esteem, 2
self-generating culture, 4, 6, 8, 38
sensibilities, 1, 7, 11, 20, 21, 36, 37, 91, 158,
      173, 178, 179, 180, 201, 205
sensory world, ambiguity of, 195
shadows in European art, 185
Shotter, J., 197
situational responsiveness, 46, 47, 65, 78, 95,
      137–8
Skolimowski, H., 11, 14, 18, 100, 120, 130,
      162, 168, 174, 180
Smith, J.A., 197
spatiality of consciousness, 192–6
Spiegelberg, H., 119
Spretnak, C., 11, 162
Srivastva, S., 7, 8
Stcherbatsky, T., 14
stories, classification of, 89
subjective–objective canon of inquiry, 6, 36
subjective–objective, *see* reality
subtle thinking, 144
symbolic forms, four major, 180
synchronicity, 47, 78, 96
systematic doubt, Cartesian, 193
systemic logic, 33
systems theory, 183

T'ai Chi, 130
T-groups, 2
tacit concepts, 120, 142, 176, 191
tacit diffusion/transfer, 46, 47, 51, 78, 87, 95, 103, 145
tacit knowing, 14, 20, 91, 117, 119, 120, 128, 158, 174, 179, 181–2, 183, 188, 206
Tajfel, H., 197
Taoism, 14
Tarnas, R., 15
Tate, P., 16
Taylor, C., 2
Teilhard de Chardin, P., 14
theory-building, 7, 143–4
things-in-themselves, 193
Titans, 45
Torbert, W.R., 8, 24, 82, 83, 113, 117, 118, 121, 122, 183
trans-empirical consciousness, one, 196
transactional analysis, 3
transfiguring ritual, 71
transmutation of distress, 71, 151
transpersonal, 4, 6, 15, 16, 35, 38, 92, 97, 106, 108, 111, 179
Traylen, H., 39, 43, 44, 75, 89, 97, 100, 102, 149, 152
Treleaven, L., 41, 45, 46, 75, 89, 96, 99, 102, 108, 152, 155
Trungpa, C., 117, 120, 129
trust, 155–6
truth
    congruence theory of, 163–9
    correspondence theory of, 159, 160, 163
    meaning of, 13, 163–4, 168
    personal, 168
    relative-universal, 168
Tuscany, 6
Type I and Type II inquiries, 44

unanimity compulsion, 69
unaware projection, 60–1, 97, 146, 149–52, 154

undifferentiated consciousness, 15, 120, 184
United Nations' Universal Declaration of Human Rights, 17
univariate analysis, 198–9
University of Bath, 5, 129
unthematic experience, 14

valid, meaning of, 13, 163
validity, *see* co-operative inquiry, and *see* research
values, 2, 3, 11, 12, 13, 14, 16, 18, 22, 28–9, 34, 39, 47, 55, 58, 59, 63, 69, 86, 92, 100, 109, 112, 113, 118, 121, 123, 124, 126, 127, 143, 157, 158, 165–7, 171, 172, 176, 197, 204, 207
    intrinsic, 126–7
    research design and, 21–2, 28, 197
    truth-values and being-values, 11–12, 13, 34, 55, 58, 158, 166–8
Varela, F., 11, 117, 162, 164
variables, control of, 197, 198–9
Vedanta, 14
vijnana, 14
vision-logic, 122, 183
void, 188

Wahl, J., 14, 119
Weinstein, J., 198
Whitaker, D., 102
Whitehead, A.N., 14, 15
Whitmore, E., 102, 151, 152, 155
Wilber, K., 12, 14, 15, 16, 20, 122, 129, 183
Winnicott, D.W., 150
worlds, five imaginal, 195

yoga of participation, 130

Zen, 14
Zener, K., 92
Zuber-Skerritt, O., 7
Zukav, G., 14
Zuni Indians, 45

Learning Resources
Centre